From the library of

First published 1991 by
Merlion Publishing Ltd
2 Belinger Close
Greenways Business Park
Chippenham
Wiltshire SN15 1BN
UK

Design: Ann Samuel
Illustrations: Jeremy Gower and Matthew White (B.L. Kearley Ltd);
Annabel Milne; Jeremy Pyke; Oxford Illustrators Ltd
Cover illustration: Jeremy Gower (B.L. Kearley Ltd)

Printed in Spain by Cronion S.A.

Canadian Cataloguing in Publication Data

Main entry under title:

Science and technology

(The Illustrated dictionary of science)
Canadian ed.
Includes index.
ISBN 0-7172-2894-0

1. Science – Dictionaries, Juvenile. 2. Science –
Pictorial works – Juvenile literature. 3. Technology
– Dictionaries, Juvenile. 4. Technology –
Pictorial works – Juvenile literature. I. Series.

Q123.S35 1991 j503 C91-095811-4

The ILLUSTRATED DICTIONARY of SCIENCE and TECHNOLOGY

Contributors
Peter Mellett
Philip Morgan
Jane Walker

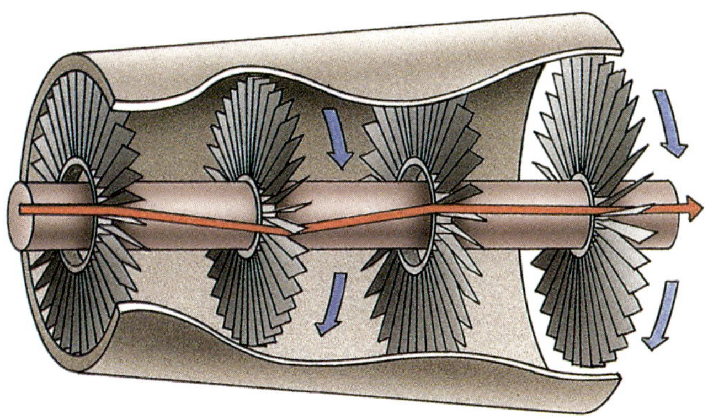

GROLIER LIMITED
CANADA

Reader's notes

The entries in this dictionary have several features to help you broaden your understanding of the word you are looking up.

- Each entry is introduced by its headword. All the headwords in the dictionary are arranged in alphabetical order.
- Each headword is followed by a part of speech to show whether the word is used as a noun, adjective, verb or prefix.
- Each entry begins with a sentence that uses the headword as its subject.
- Words that are bold in an entry are cross references. You can look them up in the dictionary to find out more information about the topic.
- The sentence in italics at the end of an entry helps you to see how the headword can be used.
- Many of the entries are supported by illustrations. The labels on the illustrations highlight the key points of information and will help you to understand some of the science behind the entries.
- Many of the labels on the illustrations have their own entries in the dictionary and can therefore be used as cross references.

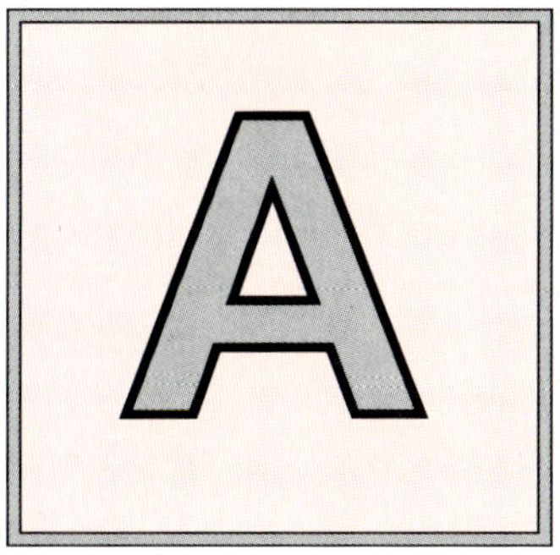

abacus *noun*
An abacus is a simple calculating **machine**. It is made from rows of beads which slide along straight wires. In some countries people work out counting problems on an abacus.
She added the numbers by moving the beads on the abacus.

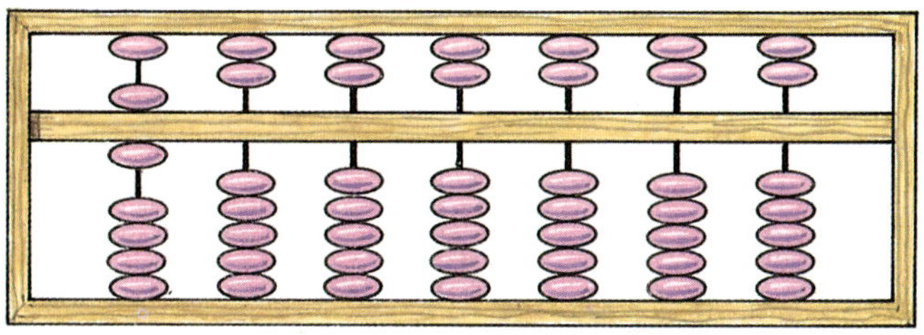

absolute zero *noun*
Absolute zero is the lowest measurement on a scale of **temperature**. On the **Celsius** scale, it is about 273 degrees below the temperature of melting ice.
Absolute zero is the lowest possible temperature.

absorb *verb*
Absorb is a word which describes how one substance takes in another **substance**. Some solids can absorb gases or liquids. Some liquids can absorb gases.
Plant roots absorb water from the soil.
absorption *noun*

accelerate *verb*
Accelerate is a word which describes an increase in **speed**. An object accelerates when a **force** makes it move faster.
The car accelerated to overtake the lorry.
acceleration *noun*

accumulator *noun*
An accumulator is a kind of electrical **battery**. It is sometimes called a storage battery. When an accumulator is exhausted or 'dead', it can be recharged by passing an **electric current** through it.
The accumulator in the car helps to start the engine.

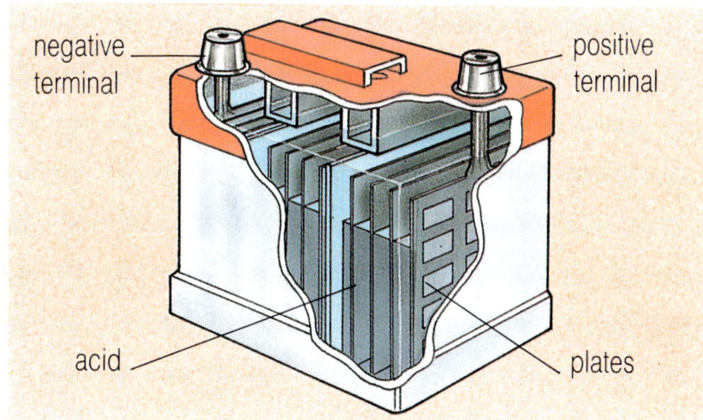

acetic acid *noun*
Acetic acid is a chemical **compound**. It is a weak acid with a strong smell. Vinegar contains a small amount of acetic acid. The modern name for acetic acid is ethanoic acid.
Special kinds of plastic and some medicines contain acetic acid.

acid *noun*
An acid is a kind of chemical **substance** which dissolves in water to make an acidic solution. Many acids can dissolve metals. Acids turn blue **litmus** paper red.
The chemist poured the acid into the beaker.
acidic *adjective*

acoustics *noun*
1. Acoustics is the study of **sound**. Acoustics helps us to understand how sound travels in different places.
Architects who design theatres must know about acoustics.
2. Acoustics is a word which describes the special features of a room or building. These features help us to hear sounds clearly and loudly.
The acoustics of the opera house were excellent.

acrylic *adjective*
Acrylic is a word which describes some kinds of plastic or man-made **fibre**. Perspex is one kind of tough acrylic plastic. Perspex can be used instead of glass. Acrilan is an acrylic fibre which is used to make cloth.
The coat is made from a mixture of wool and acrylic fibres.

addition *noun*
Addition is a kind of **arithmetic**. It is a way of working out problems with numbers. The sign for addition is +. Addition can work out that if there are five cars and six trucks, there are eleven vehicles all together. The **sum** is written 5 + 6 = 11.
At the supermarket we use addition to find out the cost of all our shopping.
add *verb*

aerate *verb*
Aerate is a word which describes what happens when **air** is blown or bubbled through a substance. Aeration forms froth or foam in soapy water.
He aerated the water in his aquarium so the fish had air to breathe.

aerial *adjective*
Aerial is a word which describes any part of a plant that grows upwards in the air and not downwards into the soil.
Mangrove trees have aerial roots.

aerial *noun*
An aerial is part of a **telecommunications** system. It can be a long piece of wire, a rod or a dish. An aerial transmits or receives radio signals.
The television aerial is fixed to the roof of the house.

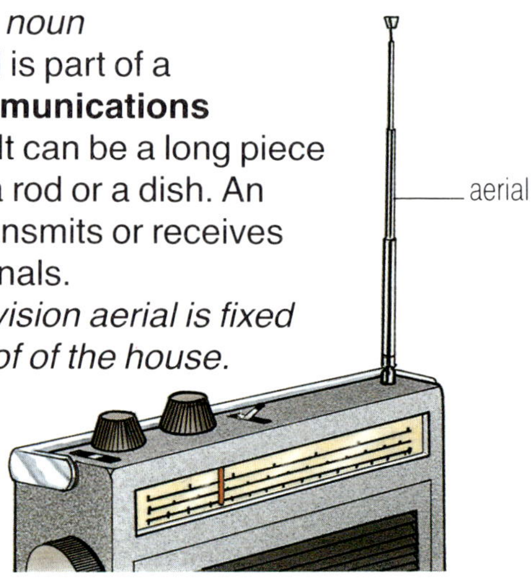

aero- *prefix*
Aero- describes anything which is to do with the air. An aeroplane flies through the air. Aerospace is the Earth's **atmosphere** and the space beyond it.
The team of skilful pilots performed aerobatics in the sky.

aerofoil *noun*
An aerofoil is a **surface** with a curved shape that is usually designed for flight. Aerofoils help aeroplanes to stay in the air or to change direction.
The wings of an aeroplane are aerofoils.

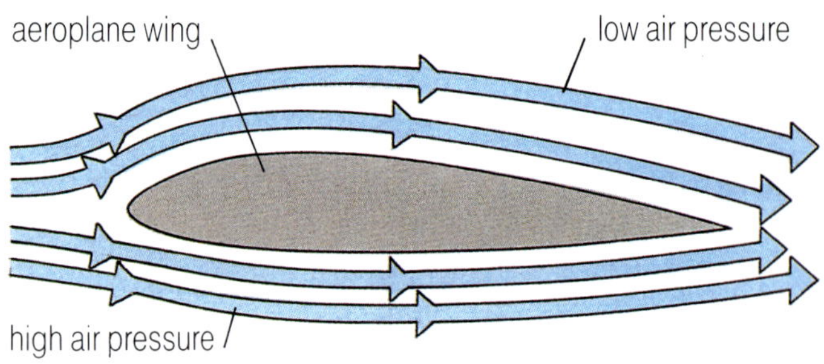

aerosol *noun*
Aerosol is the scientific name for a fine mist of liquid droplets or powder. The mist can be sprayed out of a can with a press-button. This kind of can is called an aerosol spray.
She used an aerosol to spray the plants with weedkiller.

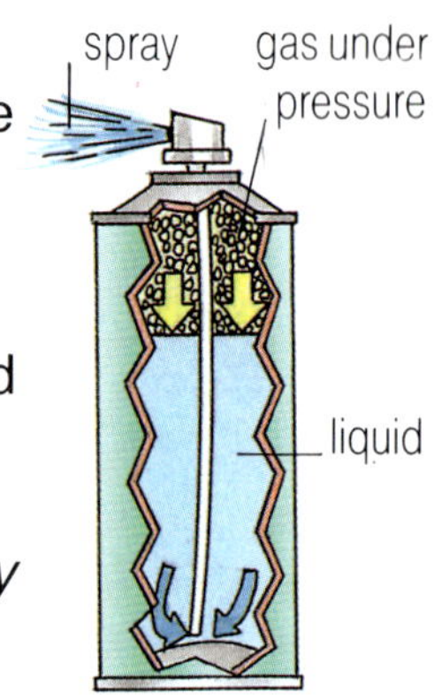

aileron *noun*
An aileron is part of an aeroplane. It is a flap which is attached to each wing by a hinge.
The pilot moves the ailerons up and down to help the aeroplane change direction.

air *noun*
Air is a mixture of **gases** which make up the **atmosphere** around the Earth. Air contains nitrogen, oxygen, argon and small amounts of carbon dioxide.
Oxygen in the air helps plants and animals to stay alive.

air pressure *noun*
Air pressure is caused by the **weight** of the air that surrounds the Earth. This weight is a **force** which pushes against the surfaces of all things on Earth.
The air pressure at the top of a mountain is less than the air pressure at sea level.

alcohol *noun*
An alcohol is a chemical **compound**. Alcohols are usually liquids with sweet smells. Alcohol is the common name for **ethanol**.
The chemist used an alcohol to dissolve the grease.

algebra *noun*
Algebra is a kind of **arithmetic**. It is a way of working out number problems which uses both letters and numbers. The letters can stand for any number.
He used algebra to work out where the rocket would land.

alkali *noun*
An alkali is a kind of chemical **compound** which can neutralize acids. Alkalis turn red **litmus** paper blue.
When an alkali dissolves in water it makes an alkaline solution.
alkaline *adjective*

alloy *noun*
An alloy is a kind of solid **substance**. An alloy is made by melting a metal and then mixing in smaller amounts of other metals or non-metals. The mixture is then cooled until it becomes solid.
Brass is an alloy which is made from copper and zinc.

alpha particle *noun*
An alpha particle is an invisible speck of **matter**. It is made up from two **protons** which are joined with two **neutrons**. A stream of alpha particles travels at very high speed and is called alpha **radiation**.
Some kinds of uranium give off alpha particles.

alternating current (AC) *noun*
An alternating current is an **electric current** which behaves in a special way. The current grows stronger and then weaker and then changes direction. This happens many times every second.
Alternating current flows through the electric wires in our homes.

alternator *noun*
An alternator is a **machine** which generates an **alternating current.** The current is generated when the alternator's shaft is spun at great speed by an engine or **turbine**.
Most power stations contain alternators which are driven by steam turbines.

aluminium *noun*
Aluminium is a chemical **element**. It is a soft silvery metal which is very light in weight. Aluminium does not **corrode** easily.
Saucepans and aeroplanes are often made from aluminium.

ammeter *noun*
An ammeter is an instrument. It measures the strength of an **electric current** in units called **amperes**.
The ammeter shows that the electric current measures 3 amperes.

ammonia *noun*
Ammonia is a colourless, poisonous **gas**. It is made up from nitrogen and hydrogen and has a very strong smell. Ammonia dissolves easily in water but it does not burn in air.
Ammonia is important in the manufacture of fertilizers and explosives.

ampere *noun*
The ampere, or A for short, is the **unit** for measuring **electric current**. The measuring scale on an **ammeter** is marked in amperes. Amperes are sometimes called amps.
A current of about half an ampere lights up an ordinary electric light bulb.

amplifier *noun*
An amplifier is a device which strengthens a weak electric **signal**. It is made up from **electronic** circuits.
The amplifier in the radio helps us to hear the music more clearly.
amplify *verb*

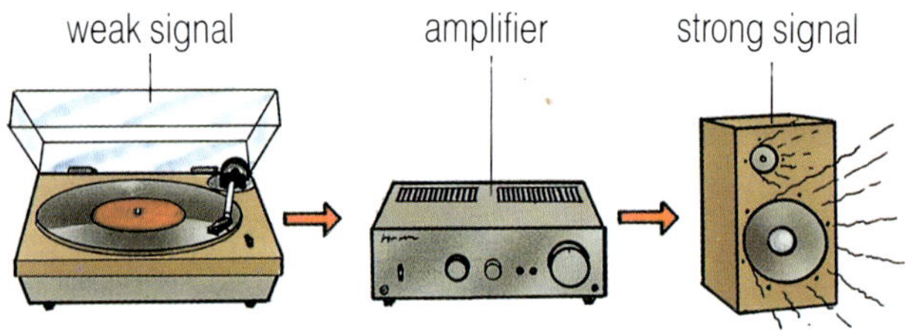

amplitude *noun*
Amplitude is a word which describes the size of a **wave**. The amplitude of a sound wave describes how loud the sound is. The amplitude of an **alternating current** describes the strength of the current.
The amplitude of a whisper is very small.

analogue *adjective*
Analogue is a word which means similar or like. It is used to describe the way some things work. For example, a watch with a dial and hands is an analogue model of the Earth. The movement of the watch's hands copies the **rotation** of the Earth. An alternative to analogue is **digital**.
An analogue clock has hands that move round steadily.

analyse *verb*
Analyse is a word which means to find out what something contains. Chemists analyse a **substance** to find out and name the **chemicals** in it.
A computer analyses information to find the answer to a problem.

angle *noun*
An angle is a kind of measurement. The angle between two lines measures how much one line turns away from the other line. Angles are measured in **degrees**.
He measured the angle between the two walls in the corner of the room.

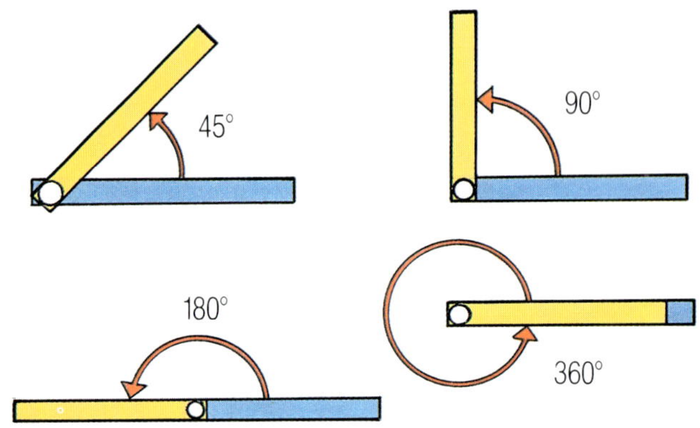

anhydrous *adjective*
Anhydrous is a word which describes a kind of chemical **substance**. An anhydrous substance contains no water. The opposite of anhydrous is **hydrated**.
She heated the crystals of washing soda to make them anhydrous.

animal *noun*
An animal is a kind of living thing. Almost all animals can move around. All animals eat other animals or plants for food.
Human beings, cats, spiders, worms and shellfish are different kinds of animal.

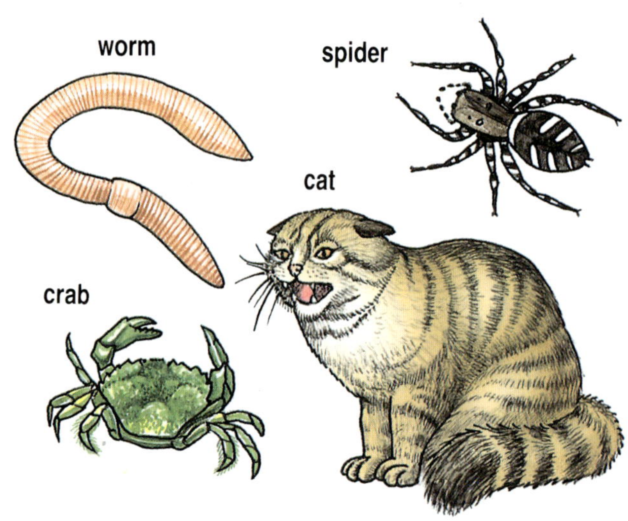

antenna (plural **antennae**) *noun*
1. Antenna is another word for **aerial**.
2. Antennae are long feelers on the heads of insects and some other animals. They are rod-shaped or feathery, and are attached in pairs to the animal's head.
Ants use their antennae to feel, taste and smell things.

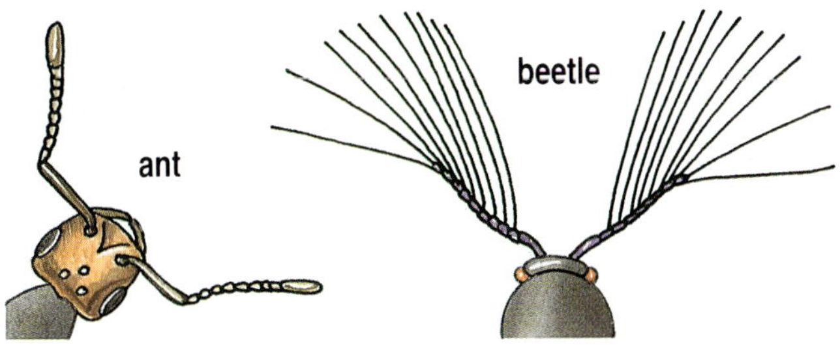

anterior *adjective*
Anterior is a word which describes the parts of an animal that face forwards.
A dog's anterior parts are its face and head.

aperture *noun*
An aperture is a kind of hole or opening. The **lens** of a camera has an aperture through which light can pass.
Photographers can make the aperture of their cameras become smaller or bigger.

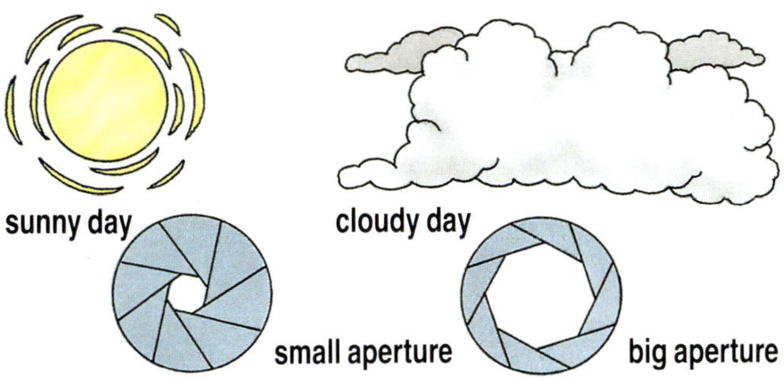

apparatus ► page 10

appliance *noun*
An appliance is a kind of object which is manufactured. Appliances do a special job or help something to happen. Refrigerators and fire extinguishers are appliances.
He plugged in the electric appliance before turning it on.

arc *noun*
1. An arc is a curved line which forms part of the **circumference** of a circle.
The archer bent his bow into the shape of an arc.

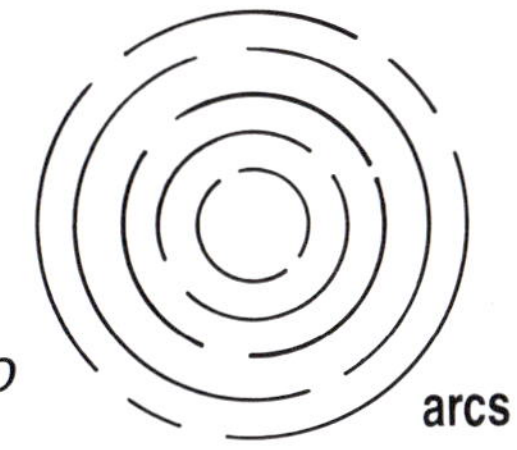

2. An arc is a kind of electric spark which is formed when an **electric current** jumps across a gap. An arc is very bright and has a **temperature** of over 3,000 degrees Celsius.
If you look directly at an electric arc, you may damage your eyes.

Archimedes' principle *noun*
Archimedes' principle is a scientific **law**. It explains why some objects can float. The weight of a ship is equal to the weight of the water which the ship has pushed out of the way, or displaced.
Archimedes' principle helps us to understand how huge steel ships can float in the water.

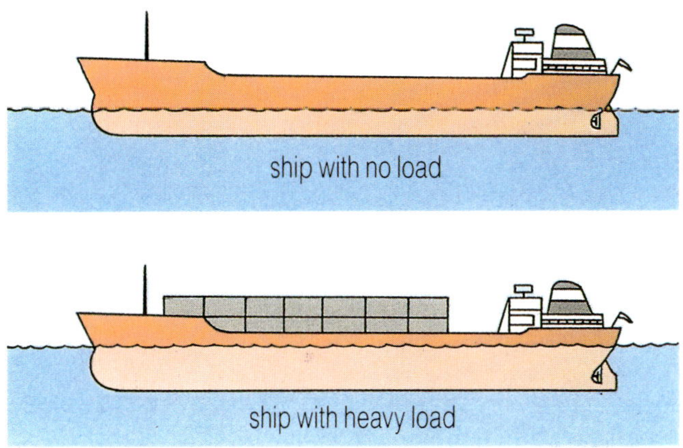

area *noun*
Area is a kind of measurement. It describes the amount of space on a particular **surface**. The main **unit** of area is the square metre, or m^2 for short.
The area of the garden was 400 square metres.

argon *noun*
Argon is a colourless **gas** which has no smell. The **atmosphere** contains about one per cent of argon. It does not dissolve in water and it does not burn. Things that normally burn in oxygen cannot burn in argon.
Argon is used to fill electric light bulbs.

apparatus *noun*
Apparatus is a word which describes the pieces of equipment used by scientists. Apparatus helps scientists to carry out **experiments** and to make measurements.
When he'd finished the experiment, the chemist carefully cleaned the apparatus he had used.

apparatus used for holding things

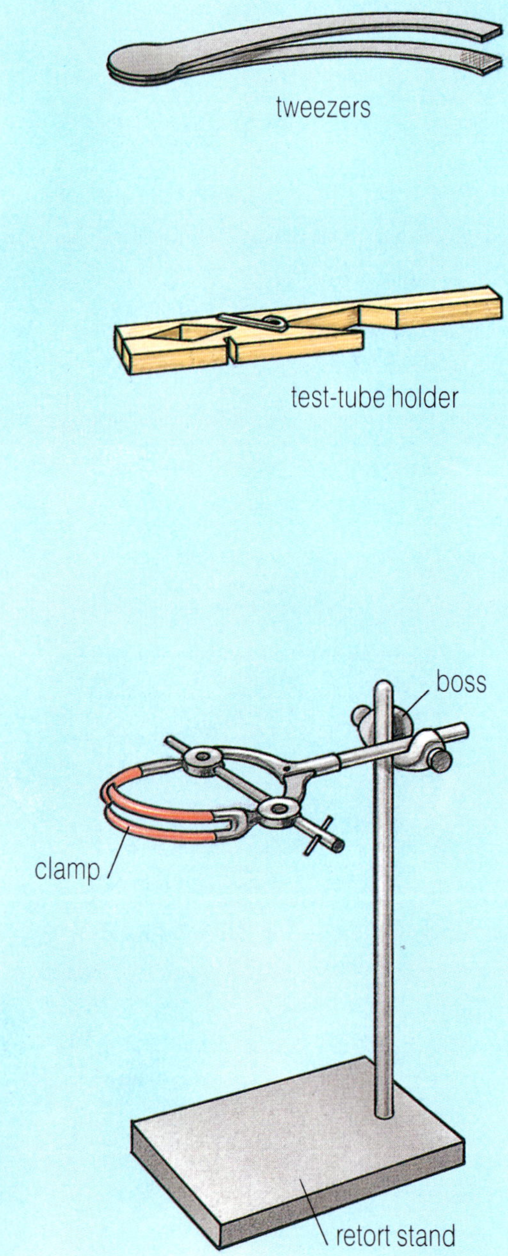

apparatus in which to put substances

apparatus for experiments with light

measuring apparatus

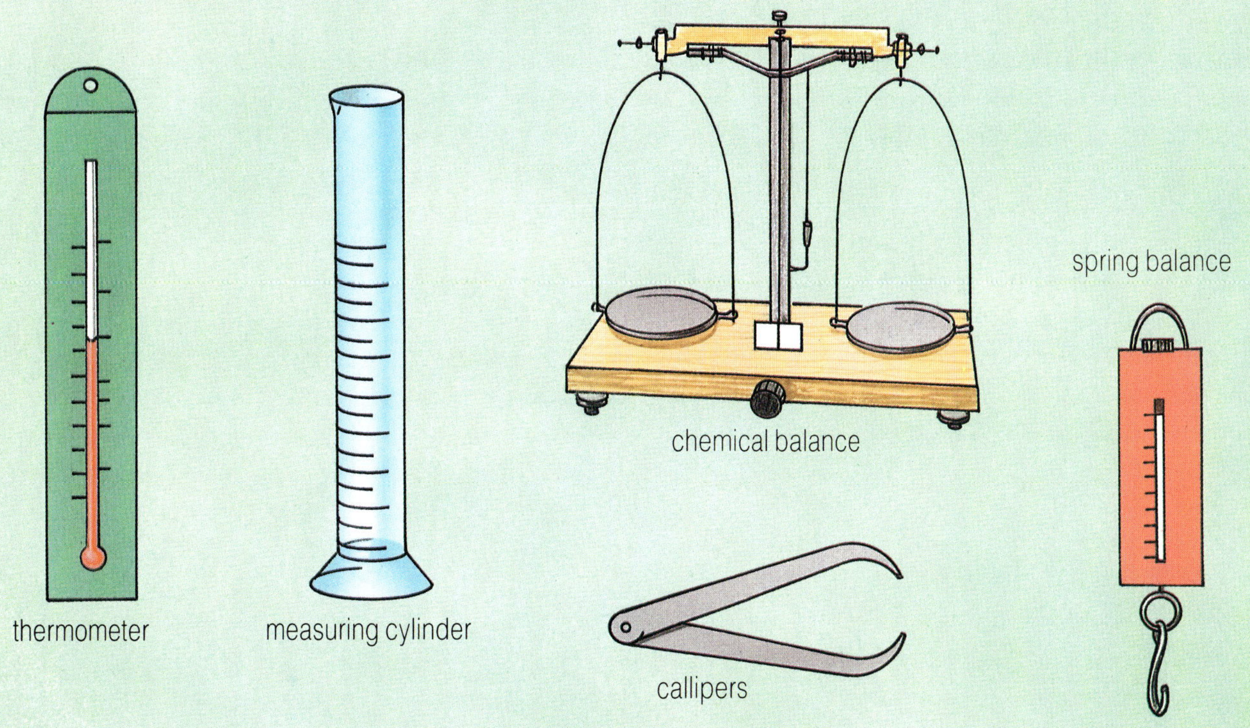

apparatus for electrical experiments

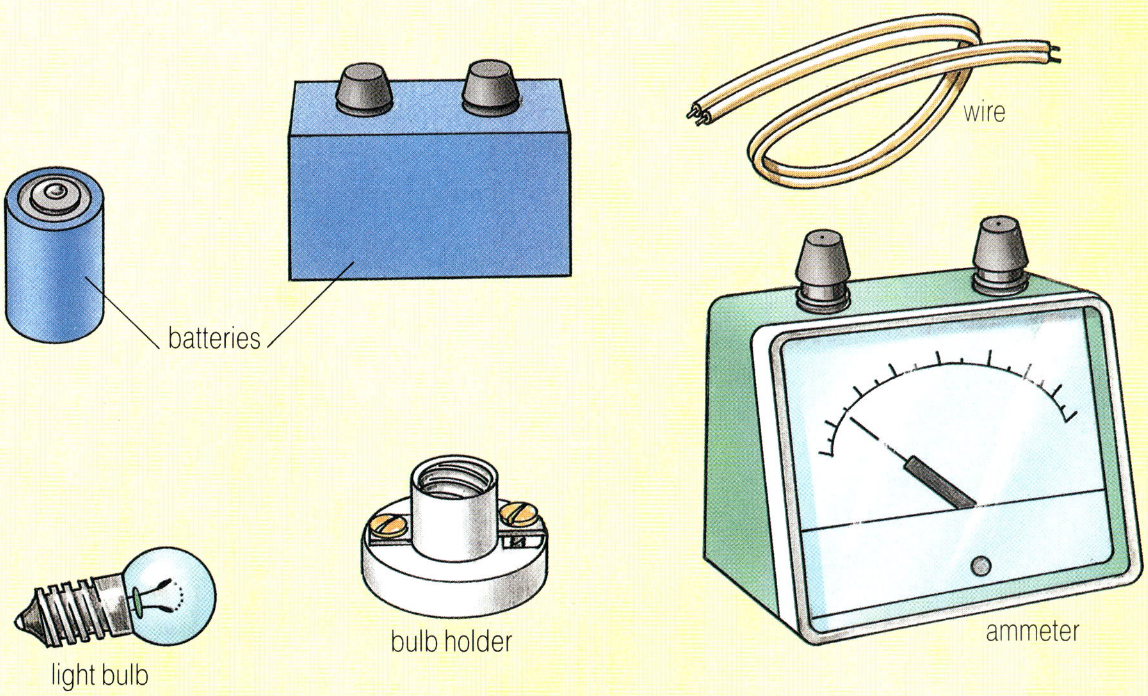

arithmetic *noun*
Arithmetic is a way of using numbers to work out **mathematical** problems using **addition**, **subtraction**, **multiplication** and **division**.
The baker uses arithmetic to work out how many kilograms of flour he needs.

armature *noun*
An armature is a part of some electric **machines**. The armature in electric motors and **dynamos** is made from a coil of wire. The **coil** spins between the opposite poles of a magnet.
An electric current flows through the wire in the armature.

arsenic *noun*
Arsenic is a chemical **element**. It is a solid **non-metal** which is poisonous. Arsenic is used to help make some kinds of **transistor** and some medicines.
The arsenic is kept in a jar marked with the label 'poisonous'.

asbestos *noun*
Asbestos is a **mineral**. It looks like bundles of thin threads. Asbestos does not change when it is heated or when chemicals are added to it. If you breathe in asbestos dust, you may suffer from a dangerous lung disease.
Some parts of motor car brakes are lined with asbestos.

asphalt *noun*
Asphalt is a mixture of **bitumen** and sand. The top surface of most roads is made from a layer of asphalt.
The asphalt is black, smooth and waterproof.

cross-section of a road

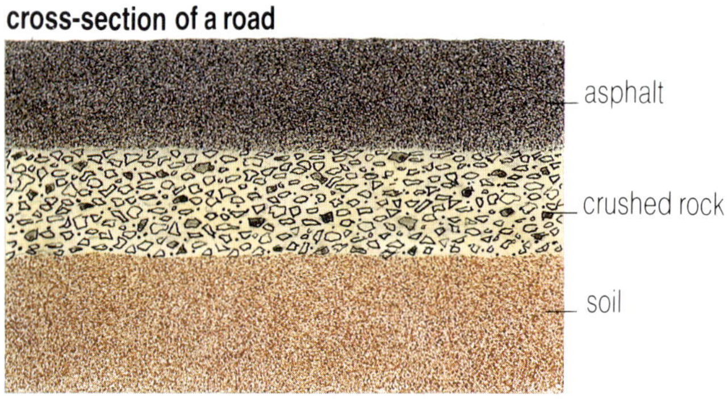

atmosphere *noun*
The atmosphere is the layer of **gases** which surrounds the Earth. It contains mostly **air** mixed with **water vapour**. The atmosphere around cities and factories can contain air pollution.
The atmosphere above the desert is usually clean and pure.

atom *noun*
An atom is a tiny part of an **element**. All the atoms in an element are the same. Each atom is made up of a number of **electrons** which move around a **nucleus**.
One grain of sand contains millions of atoms.

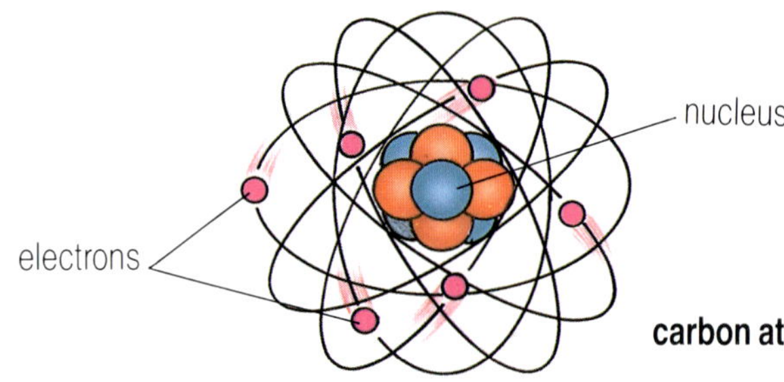

carbon atom

atomic energy ► **nuclear energy**

attract *verb*
Attract is a word which describes a kind of **force**. If two objects are attracted together, they move towards each other.
A magnet will attract a piece of steel.
attraction *noun*

auto- *prefix*
Auto- describes anything which affects or controls itself. An automobile is a vehicle which moves itself.
An automatic machine does not need a person to control it.

automation *noun*
Automation is a word which describes how the work inside some factories is done by **machines**. It means that some objects are made by machines instead of by people. **Computers** usually control these machines.
Only a few people work in this factory because automation does most of the work.

autopilot *noun*
An autopilot is a **device** inside an aeroplane. It controls automatically the flight of the aeroplane.
The autopilot flies the plane safely to the airport.

average *noun*
The average is a number which comes from a whole group of numbers. You find the average by adding together all the numbers in the group. Then you divide the total by the number of figures you have in the group.
The average of 10.5 metres, 12 metres and 15 metres is 12.5 metres.
average *adjective*

axis (plural **axes**) *noun*
1. An axis is an imaginary line which passes through a solid object. We imagine the axis to be in a position which allows the object to spin evenly around it.
The Earth spins round on its axis.
2. An axis is part of a **graph**. There are two axes and each one is marked with a **scale**. One axis is called the **vertical** axis, or y-axis. The other axis is the **horizontal** axis, or x-axis.
She started to draw the axis with a ruler and a pencil.

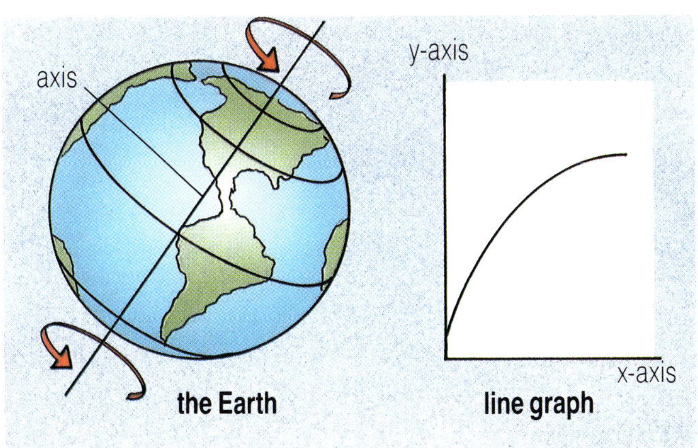

axle *noun*
An axle is a kind of rod. It is joined to the centre of a wheel so that the wheel can spin on it.
Most cars have four wheels and two axles.

B

bacteria (singular **bacterium**) *noun*
Bacteria are tiny living things. Each bacterium is a single **cell**. Most bacteria are harmless but some can cause diseases when they invade other **organisms**.
One drop of water in a lake contains thousands of bacteria.

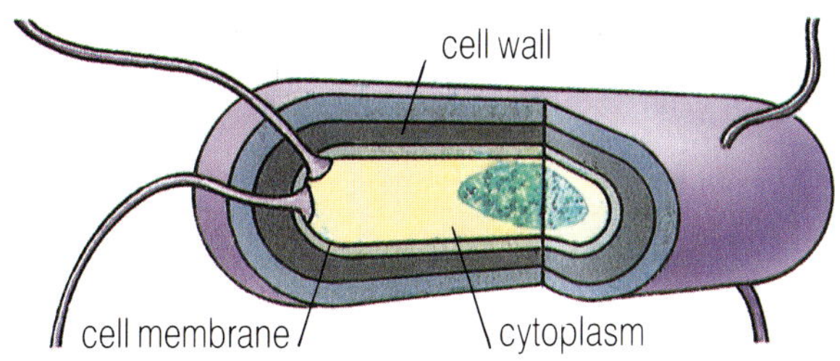

balance *noun*
A balance is a kind of weighing instrument. Scientists use balances to weigh things accurately.
The balance shows that one grain of sand weighs one-thousandth of a gram.

ball bearing *noun*
A ball bearing is a part of some **machines**. It is made from two steel rings which fit inside each other. The rings are kept apart by steel balls. The balls allow the rings to spin smoothly.
The ball bearing is fixed between the wheel and the axle.

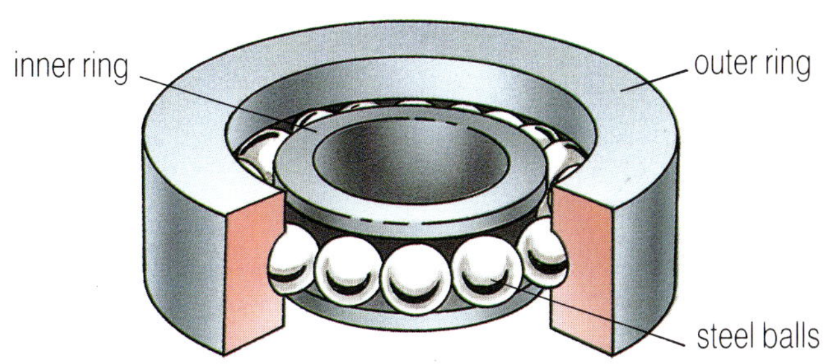

bar code *noun*
A bar code is a special pattern of thin and thick lines. The lines are parallel to each other. Bar codes are printed on the labels of goods in shops. Computers change the codes into numbers.
Computers in supermarkets read the bar codes on the packets of food.

barometer *noun*
A barometer is a kind of measuring instrument. It measures the **pressure** of the **atmosphere**. Barometers can help us to forecast the weather.
The barometer shows that the pressure is lower than normal.

base *noun*
1. Base is a word which describes a system of counting. It tells us how many different numbers or symbols are used. In **decimal** counting, the base is 10. In the **binary code**, the base is 2.
The binary code uses two symbols, 0 and 1, so the base is two.
2. A base is a kind of chemical **compound**. It is made when a **non-metal** joins with oxygen. Bases, like **alkalis**, can neutralize acids.
The chemist added the base to the mixture.

base metal *noun*
A base metal is a common kind of **metal**. Base metals include iron, lead and zinc. They are much cheaper than **precious metals** and they **corrode** more easily.
The knife was made from a base metal.

BASIC *noun*
BASIC is a language which is used by some kinds of **computer**. The name BASIC comes from the initial letters of Beginner's All-purpose Symbolic Instruction Code.
He used BASIC to write the computer program.

battery *noun*
A battery is a device which supplies an **electric current**. Batteries contain two different kinds of electrical **conductor**. These conductors are joined together by a chemical paste.
The new batteries make my flashlight shine brightly.

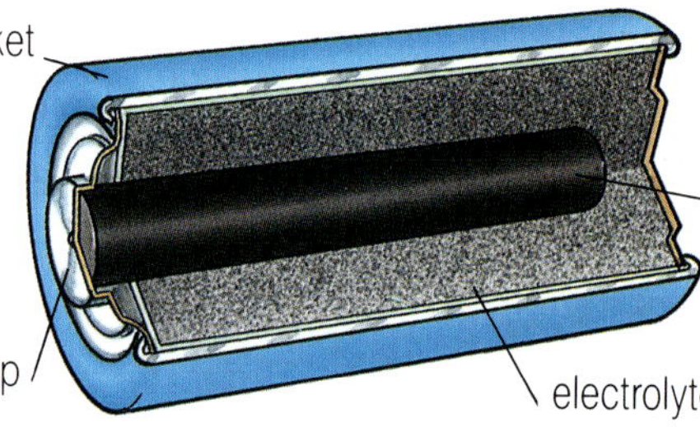

beaker *noun*
A beaker is a kind of **apparatus**. It is a container which is made of glass or metal. It has a flat bottom and no handle. A measuring **scale** is marked on the outside of some beakers. Chemists heat or store liquids in beakers.
The chemist carefully poured the liquid from the beaker.

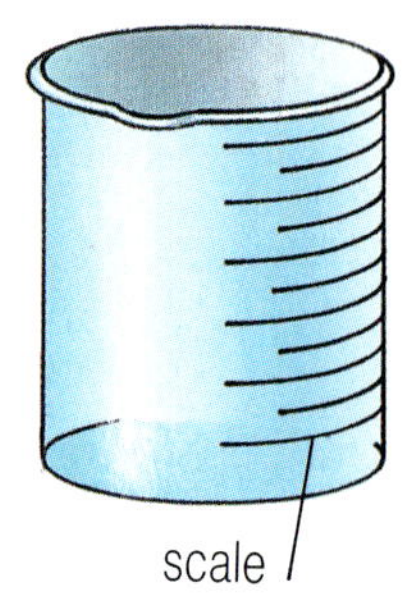

beam *noun*
1. A beam is a ray of **light** or some other kind of **radiation**.
You can see the beam of light which shines from a lighthouse.
2. A beam is a strong length of wood, metal, stone or concrete. It is placed in a **horizontal** position inside a building or other **structure** to provide support.
Bridges are often built from beams made of concrete or metal.

beam *verb*
Beam is a word which describes how **light** or some other kind of **radiation** is given off in rays. These rays usually travel in a particular direction.
Satellites beam television signals all over the world.

benzene *noun*
Benzene is a colourless liquid which burns easily. It is produced from **coal tar** or **petroleum**. Some plastics, detergents and dyes are made from benzene. Benzene **vapour** is poisonous if you breathe too much of it.
Benzene is important in the manufacture of synthetic rubber.

beta particle *noun*
A beta particle is an **electron** which is given off by a **radioactive** substance. A stream of beta particles travels at very fast speeds and is called beta **radiation**.
Beta particles move five metres through the air before they stop.

bicarbonate of soda *noun*
Bicarbonate of soda is a white, powdery **base**. It is used in cooking and making medicines. Bicarbonate of soda fizzes when it is mixed with acids. When heated, it gives off **carbon dioxide**.
Cooks use bicarbonate of soda to help make cakes and bread light and fluffy.

binary code *noun*
Binary code is a term which describes a way of counting. It is a kind of **code** which is made up from **binary digits.** Computers use the binary code.
In the binary code, the decimal numbers 5 and 6 are written as 101 and 110.

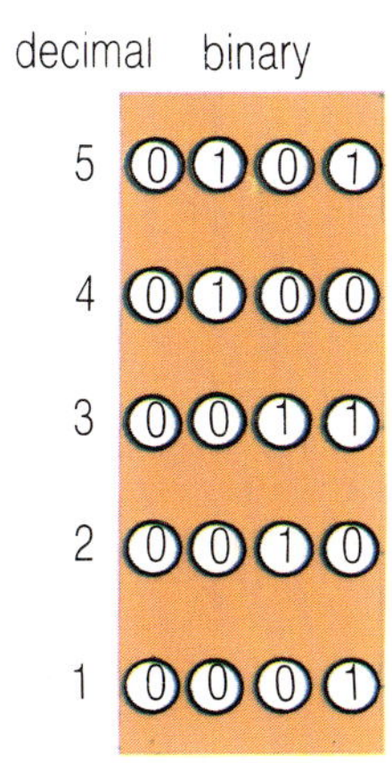

binary digit *noun*
A binary digit, or bit for short, is a number. It is either 1 or 0. Computers use these two binary digits for counting in the **binary code** and passing on information.
The ordinary decimal number 5 is written as 101 in binary digits.

bio- *prefix*
Bio- describes anything which is concerned with living things.
Biotechnology finds out how we can use living things to make medicine, food and fuels.

biofuel *noun*
A biofuel is a kind of fuel which is made from natural materials or waste. **Charcoal** and biogas are biofuels which can be burned to generate energy.
Motor cars which run on biofuel cause less pollution than motor cars which run on petrol.

biology *noun*
Biology is a scientific subject. It is the study of living things. Biology includes the subjects botany and **zoology**. A biologist is a person who studies biology.
She learned about plants and animals when studying biology.
biological *adjective*

biomass *noun*
1. Biomass is a kind of measurement. It measures the **mass** of the living things in a particular area.
There is a larger biomass of plants than animals in the world.
2. Biomass is any plant or animal material which is used as a source of **fuel**. Coal and oil are two different kinds of biomass.
Sugar cane is a kind of biomass which can be made into fuel for cars.

bit ► **binary digit**

bitumen *noun*
Bitumen is a black, sticky **solid**. It is left behind when useful substances are **distilled** from **crude oil**. Bitumen is used to make **asphalt**.
Bitumen melts when it is heated strongly.

blast furnace ► page 18

blood *noun*
Blood is a liquid which flows around the bodies of animals. It takes **oxygen** and food to all the **cells** in the body, and carries away **carbon dioxide** and other waste products.
The body of an adult human being contains more than 5 litres of blood.

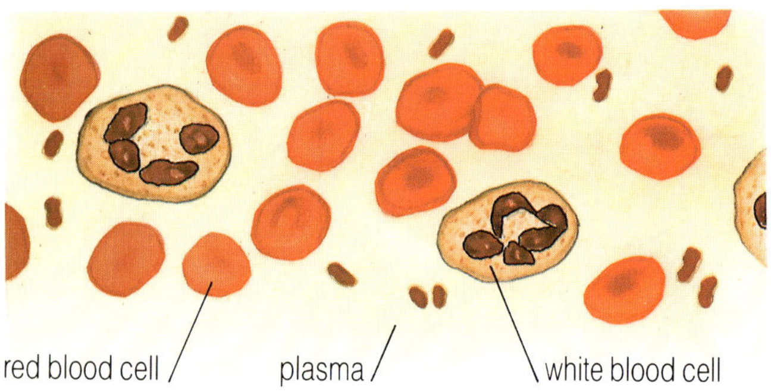

boil *verb*
Boil is a word which describes the change which takes place when a **liquid** is heated to **boiling point**. Bubbles of **vapour** appear in the liquid. They rise to the surface and then burst.
When a liquid boils, it turns into a gas.

boiler *noun*
1. A boiler is a device which is found inside a **power station** or a **steam engine**. It contains a **furnace** which heats water in metal pipes. The water boils and changes into steam.
The boiler makes the steam which drives the engine.
2. A boiler is a **device** which makes hot water for heating a house. It heats water in a metal tank. A pump makes the hot water flow through pipes around the house.
The temperature of the water in the boiler has reached 85 degrees Celsius.

boiling point *noun*
Boiling point is a term which describes the **temperature** of a boiling liquid. Different liquids have different boiling points. The boiling point changes if the liquid is not pure or if the **air pressure** around the liquid changes.
The boiling point of pure water is 100 degrees Celsius at sea-level.

bolt *noun*
A bolt is a rod which holds two things together. A spiral groove, called a thread, may run around the long part of the bolt. A **nut** twists onto this thread. The wide part of the bolt is called the head.
She pushed the bolt through the door handle and then tightened the nut.

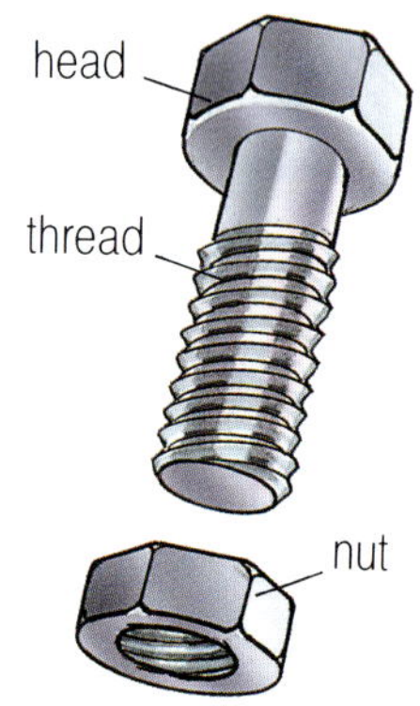

bond *noun*
A bond is a word which describes how **atoms** are held together in a chemical **compound**. For example, bonds can form between atoms of **sodium** and atoms of **chlorine**. When this happens, a compound called sodium chloride is made. Sodium chloride is known as common salt.
When a compound burns, the bonds between its atoms will break.

brake *noun*
A brake is a **device** which is found in a machine or a vehicle. Brakes slow down spinning wheels or **shafts** which spin. The two main kinds of brake are drum brakes and disc brakes.
When the driver put his foot on the pedals the brakes slowed down the motor car.

brass *noun*
Brass is a kind of **metal**. It is an **alloy** which contains copper and zinc. Brass is a silvery-yellow colour.
Bells and trumpets may be made from brass.

brine *noun*
Brine is a kind of **solution**. Brine is salt which has dissolved in water.
Many useful chemicals are made from brine.

brittle *adjective*
Brittle is a word which describes how **solids** behave. A solid which is brittle snaps easily when it is bent, and it shatters when it is struck. The opposite of brittle is **malleable**.
Some kinds of plastic are very brittle.

bromine *noun*
Bromine is a chemical **element**. It is a dark brownish-red liquid which gives off red poisonous fumes. Bromine is used to help make some medicines.
Bromine is stored in strong glass bottles because it is so poisonous.

bronze *noun*
Bronze is a kind of **metal**. It is an **alloy** which contains copper and tin. Bronze is a golden colour.
Parts of the car engine are made from bronze.

brush *noun*
A brush is a device which is found inside an electrical **machine**. It helps an **electric current** to flow from a fixed part to a moving part of the machine.
The brushes inside an electric motor are made of carbon.

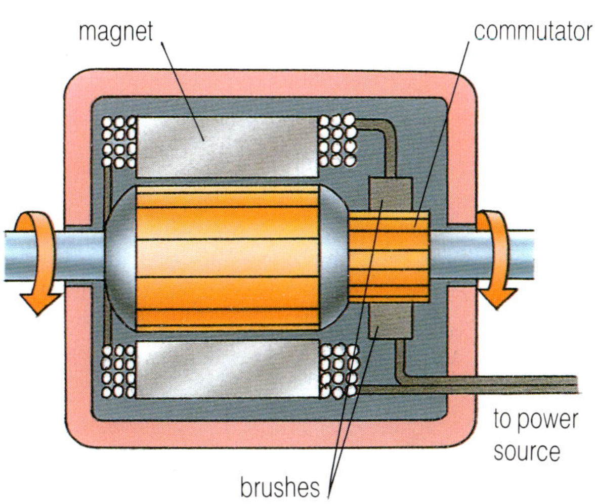

Bunsen burner *noun*
A Bunsen burner is a kind of **apparatus**. It is used to heat chemical **substances**. It has a tall, **vertical** pipe which is attached to a supply of gas. The gas mixes with air at the bottom of the burner and a hot flame burns at the top.
The Bunsen burner heated the beaker of cold water.

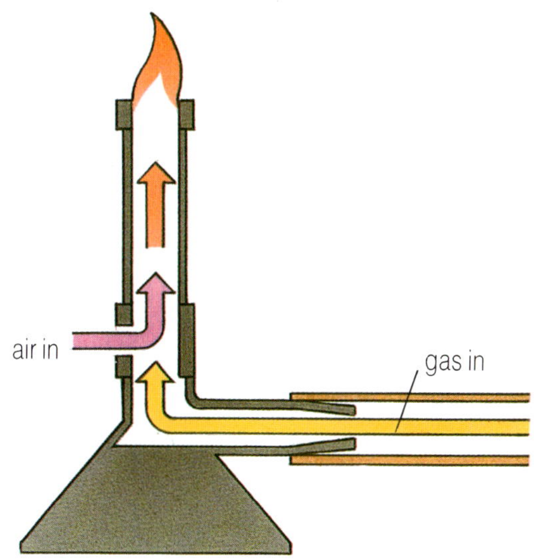

buoyancy *noun*
Buoyancy is a word which describes a kind of push or **force**. Liquids use this force to push against solid objects. The force makes some objects float in the liquid.
The buoyancy of the piece of wood makes it float on water.
buoyant *adjective*

burette *noun*
A burette is a kind of **apparatus**. It is a long, thin container which is made from glass or plastic. The burette has a small tap at the bottom, and a measuring **scale** is marked on the side. Burettes are used for measuring out accurate amounts of liquids.
She measured out 50 cubic centimetres of water from the burette.

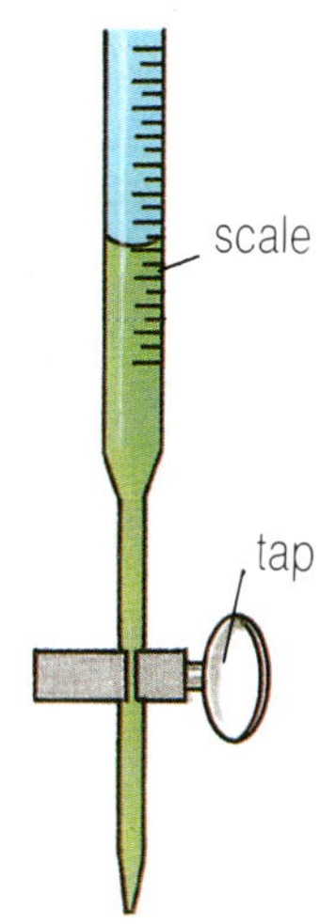

blast furnace *noun*

A blast furnace is a special kind of **furnace.** Iron is made inside a blast furnace. Iron **ore**, limestone and **coke** are tipped in at the top of the furnace. Hot air is blasted into the middle, heating the solids to a very high temperature. This heat turns the solids to a liquid called **pig iron**.

A glowing stream of liquid iron pours out of the bottom of the blast furnace.

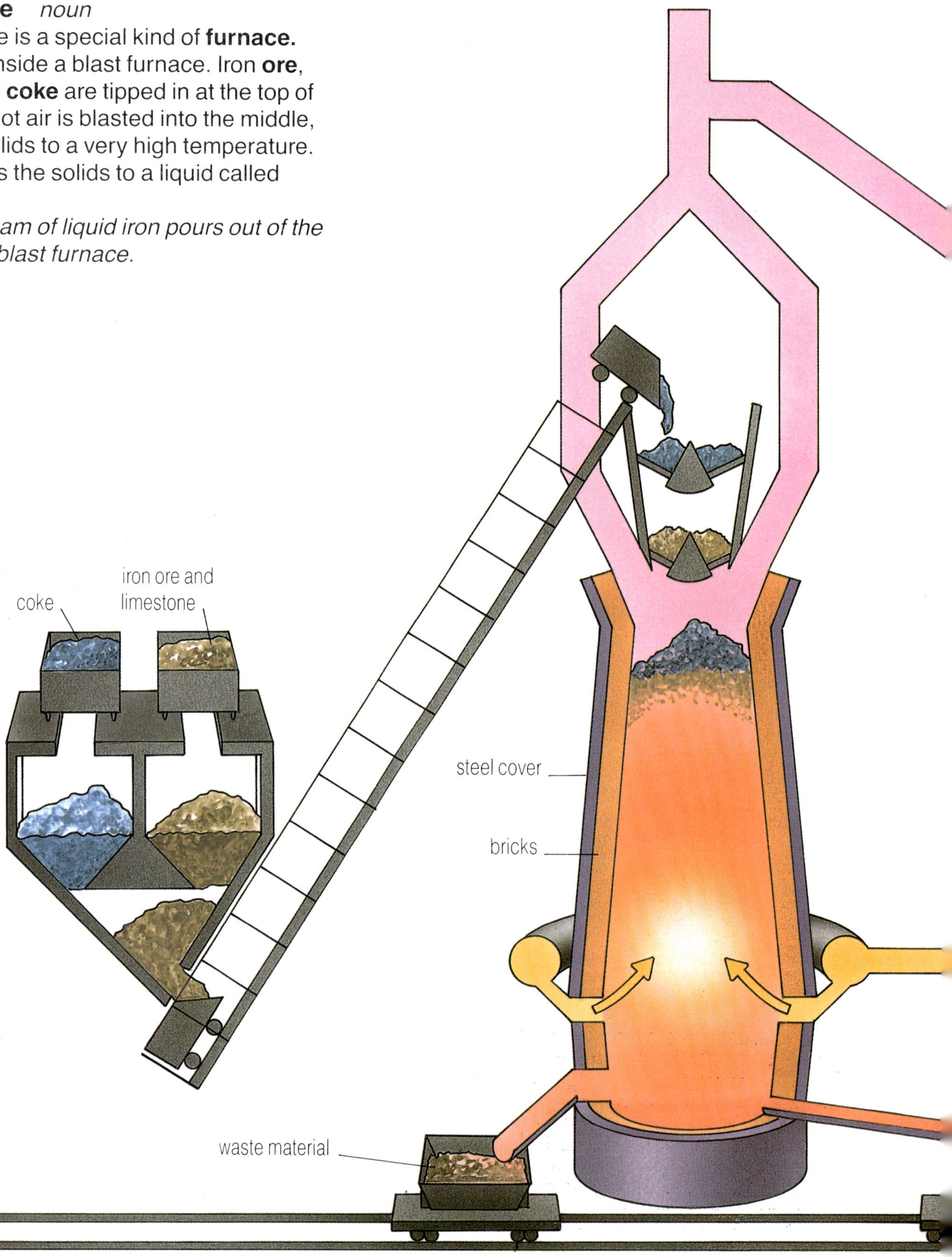

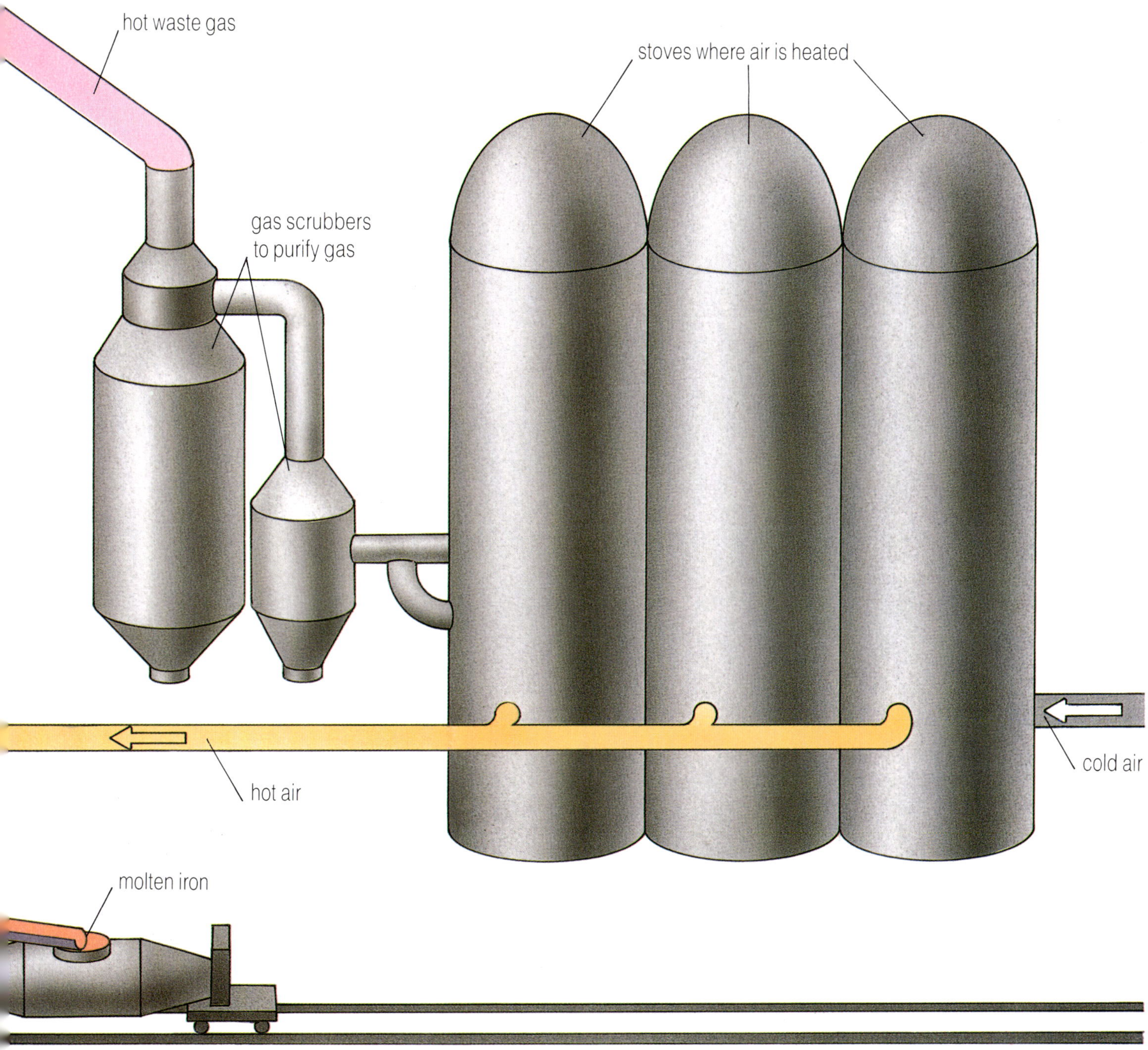
hot waste gas
stoves where air is heated
gas scrubbers
to purify gas
cold air
hot air
molten iron

burn *verb*
Burn is a word which describes a way of making heat by **combustion**. A fuel burns with the help of **oxygen**.
The gas burned with a bright flame.

butane *noun*
Butane is a chemical **compound**. It is a colourless gas and is a **hydrocarbon**. When butane is **compressed,** it changes easily into a liquid. The liquid can be changed back into a gas and used as a fuel.
Liquid butane is stored in steel cylinders.

by-product *noun*
A by-product is a kind of **substance** which is made during a **chemical reaction**. The main **product** of the reaction always contains a small amount of one or more by-products.
Butane is a by-product which is made at the oil refinery.

byte *noun*
A byte is a number. Bytes carry instructions or information inside computers. A byte is usually made up from eight **bits**. The size of the computer's **memory** is measured in bytes.
The small computer had a memory of 64,000 bytes.

C

cable *noun*
A cable is a kind of rope made from wires. Cables are usually made from steel or copper. Copper cables carry electricity and are often covered in plastic.
The cable is made up from 10 wires.

calcium *noun*
Calcium is a soft, silvery **metal**. It reacts quickly with water. Chemicals which contain calcium are found in some foods. They help to make strong teeth and bones.
Milk and other dairy products contain calcium.

calcium carbonate *noun*
Calcium carbonate is a chemical **compound**. It is a white **solid** which is found in rocks such as limestone, chalk and marble. Calcium carbonate is used to help make other chemicals and cement.
Calcium carbonate will dissolve in most acids.

calculator *noun*
A calculator is a kind of **machine**. It uses **arithmetic** to solve counting problems quickly. A calculator has number keys and control keys. When you press the number keys, information passes into the calculator. When you press the control keys, the answer appears on the display panel.
He used the calculator to find out the average of a group of numbers.

calculate *verb*

calibrate *verb*
Calibrate is a word which describes how a measuring **scale** is marked. Most rulers are calibrated in **centimetres**. Beakers are calibrated in **millilitres**.
She calibrated the container by marking a scale on its side.

calliper *noun*
A calliper is a kind of measuring **instrument**. It is used to measure the **diameter** or width of an object. It has two metal legs which grip the object. A **scale** is marked on some kinds of calliper.
The engineer used the calliper to measure the diameter of the rod.

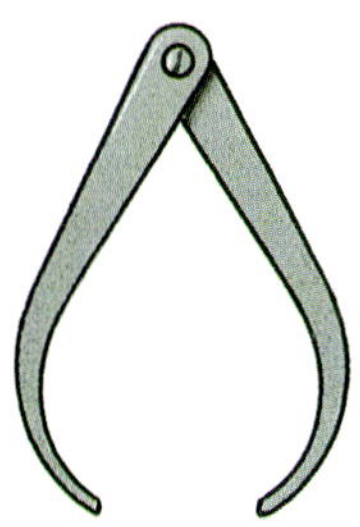

calorie *noun*
A calorie is a **unit** of measurement. It measures **energy**. One calorie is the amount of heat which is needed to raise the temperature of 1 gram of water by 1 degree Celsius.
She measured the amount of heat given off by the burning coal in calories.

cam *noun*
A cam is a kind of wheel. It is not a **circular** wheel. Cams spin around in **machines** and move rods which rest against their sides.
The cam controls the valve inside the engine.

camera ► page 22

camshaft *noun*
A camshaft is the spinning rod or **shaft** which turns a **cam**. Several cams are usually attached to a camshaft.
The camshaft turned four cams in the engine.

cantilever *noun*
A cantilever is a kind of **beam.** It is fixed at only one end.
The bridge had two cantilevers which stretched across the river.

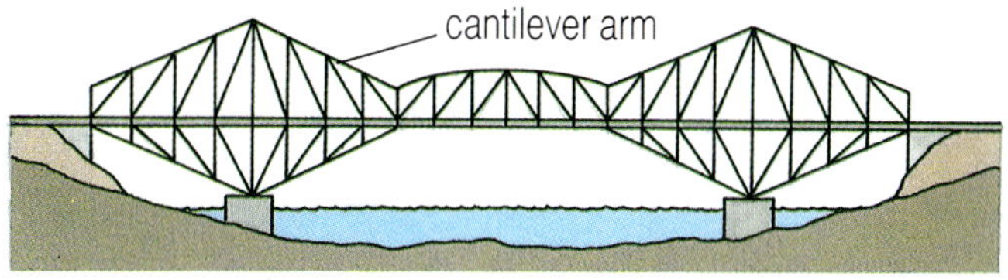

capacitor *noun*
A capacitor is a device which can store **electricity**. It is used in the **electric circuits** of radios, televisions and computers. Capacitors have two thin sheets of metal which are separated by an **insulator**.
Wires join the capacitor to the circuit.

capacity *noun*
Capacity describes the **volume** that a container can hold. Capacity is measured in **units**, such as cubic **centimetres**.
The capacity of the beaker was 500 cubic centimetres.

capillary action *noun*
Capillary action describes how a **liquid** rises up inside a narrow tube. If one end of the tube is placed in water, the water will rise up the tube above the level of the surrounding water.
Capillary action helped him to take a sample of water in the tube.

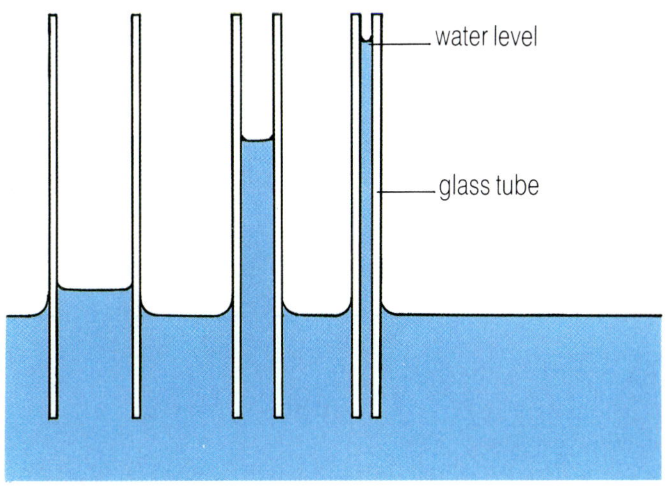

camera *noun*

1. A camera is a **device** which takes photographs. Light passes through **lenses** and a **shutter**. This forms an **image** which changes chemicals in a film inside the camera. The film is taken out and processed to make pictures that we can see.

A scratch on the lens of her camera spoiled the photographs she took.

2. A camera is a **device** which takes television pictures. Light passes through **lenses** and falls on a **screen**. An **electron gun** scans the screen and sends electric signals to television sets or **video cassette recorders**.

They needed four television cameras to make the television programme.

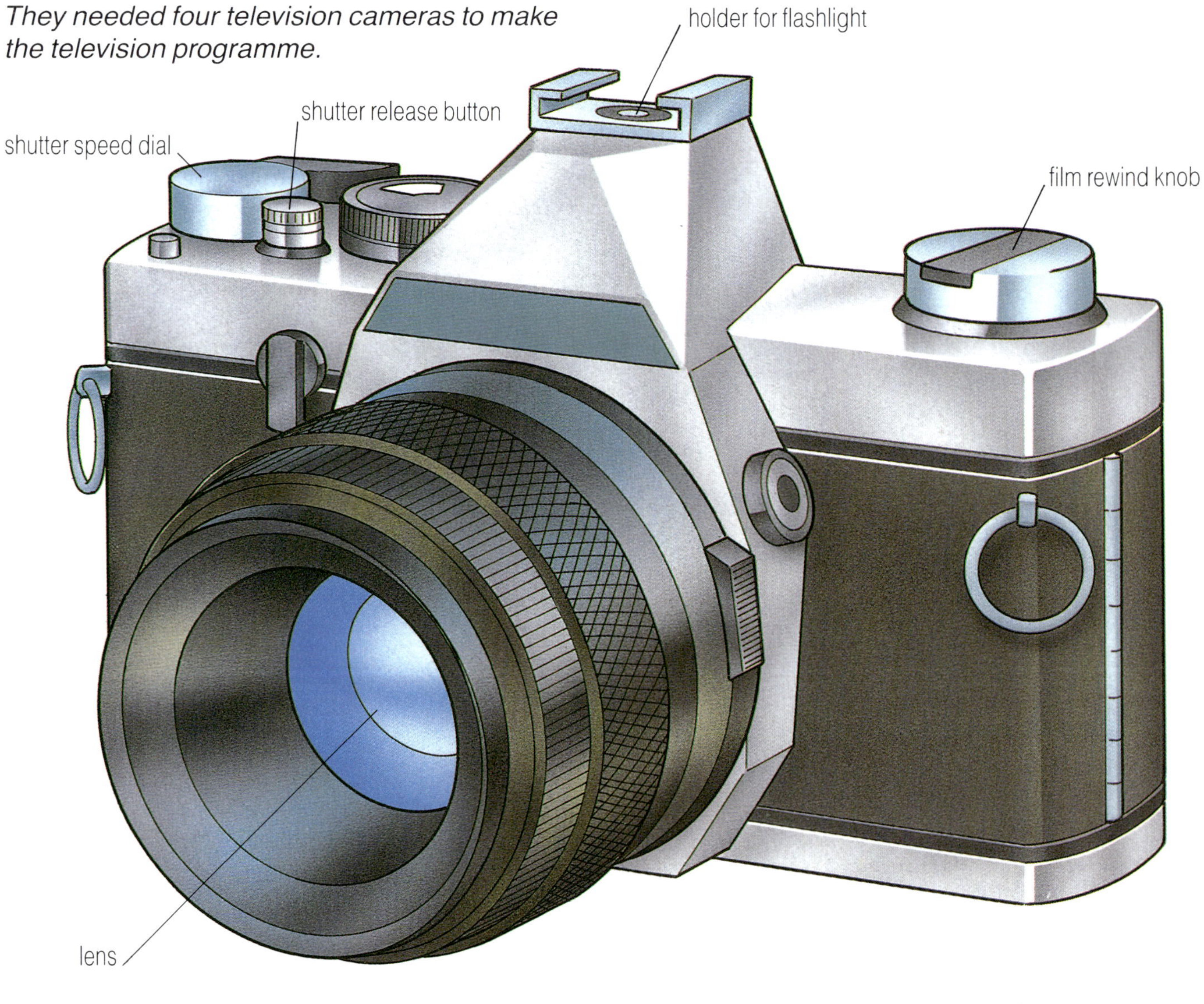

The back of a camera

How light passes through a single-lens reflex (SLR) camera

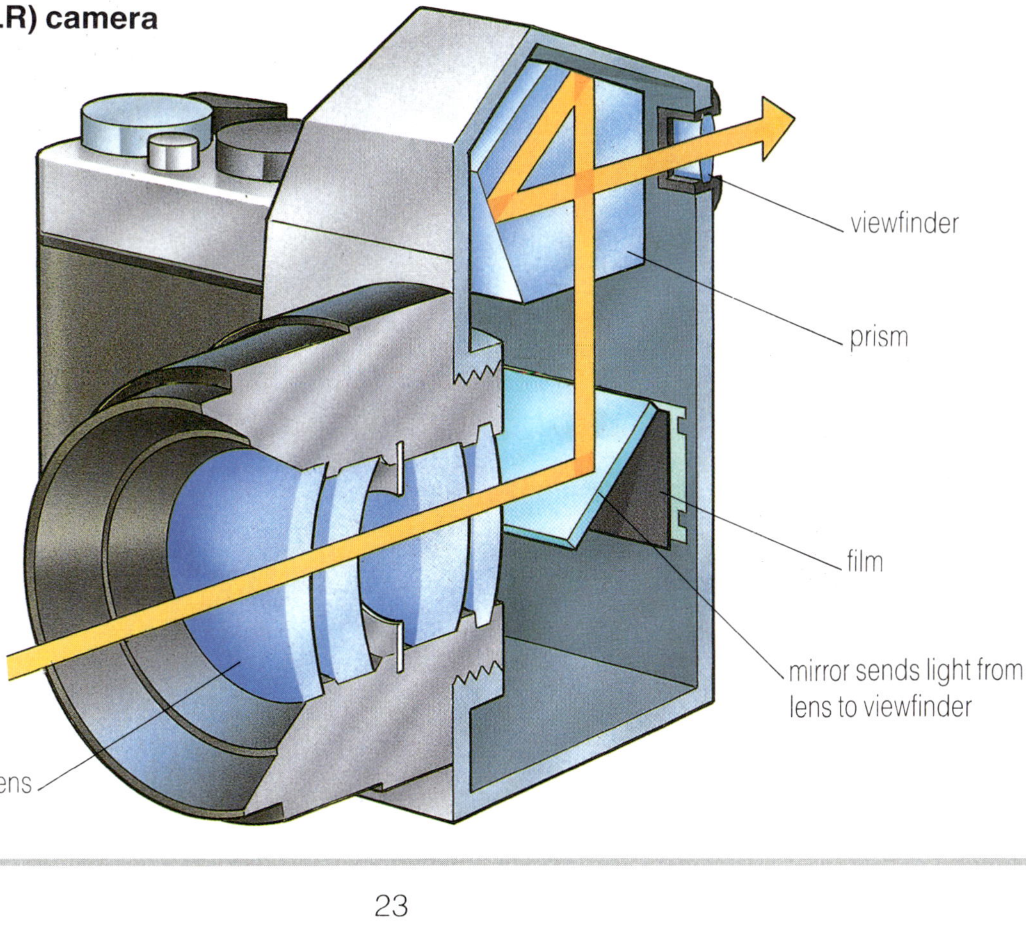

carbon *noun*
Carbon is a chemical **element**. It is a **non-metal**. All living things are made up from **compounds** which contain carbon. Fossil fuels, such as oil, contain carbon.
Diamonds and charcoal are two different forms of carbon.

carbon cycle ► page 25

carbon dioxide *noun*
Carbon dioxide is a colourless **gas**. It has no smell and can dissolve in water. Carbon dioxide is released into the air when animals **respire** and when **fossil fuels** burn.
Fizzy drinks and fire extinguishers contain carbon dioxide.

carrier wave *noun*
A carrier wave is a kind of radio **signal**. The wave carries information from a **transmitter** to a **receiver**. Sound and picture signals alter the strength and **frequency** of the carrier wave.
Radio transmitters broadcast carrier waves.

cassette *noun*
A cassette is a thin, plastic case which contains a long strip of **magnetic tape**. The tape is wound on a spool. When the cassette plays inside a **video** or a tape recorder, the tape winds on to another spool.
She placed a music cassette in the tape recorder.

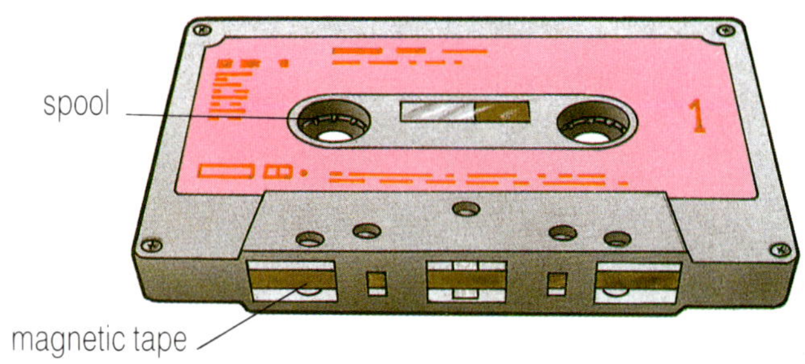

cast iron *noun*
Cast iron is a kind of **iron**. It is dark grey, hard and **brittle**. Objects of cast iron are made by pouring **molten** iron into hollow moulds.
Some parts of car engines are made from cast iron.

catalyst *noun*
A catalyst is a substance which helps to speed up a **chemical reaction.** The catalyst itself is not used up during the reaction.
Chemical factories use catalysts in the manufacture of plastic.

cathode ray tube *noun*
A cathode ray tube is a glass tube which makes pictures from electric signals. An **electron gun** inside the tube fires **electrons**. These make the screen at one end of the tube glow. Cathode ray tubes are used in televisions and visual display units.
The picture on the television screen is made by a cathode ray tube.

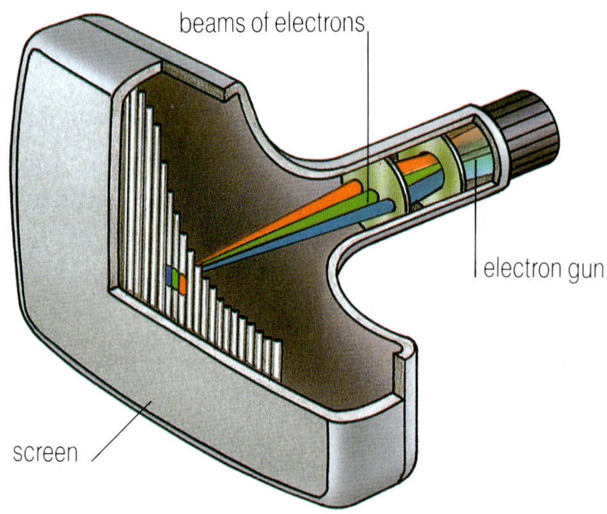

caustic *adjective*
Caustic is a word which describes some chemical **substances**. A caustic substance burns and destroys skin and flesh.
He wore rubber gloves while pouring out the caustic soda.

cell ► page 26

cell membrane *noun*
The cell membrane is a layer which surrounds the contents of a **cell**. The membrane allows some **substances**, like water, to pass in and out of the cell.
The cells of all living things have a cell membrane.

carbon cycle *noun*
The carbon cycle is a term which describes the movement of carbon between living things and **carbon dioxide** in the air. In the carbon cycle, plants take in carbon dioxide and give out oxygen during **photosynthesis.** Animals take in oxygen and give out carbon dioxide during **respiration**.
The carbon cycle includes the burning of fossil fuels such as coal, oil and natural gas.

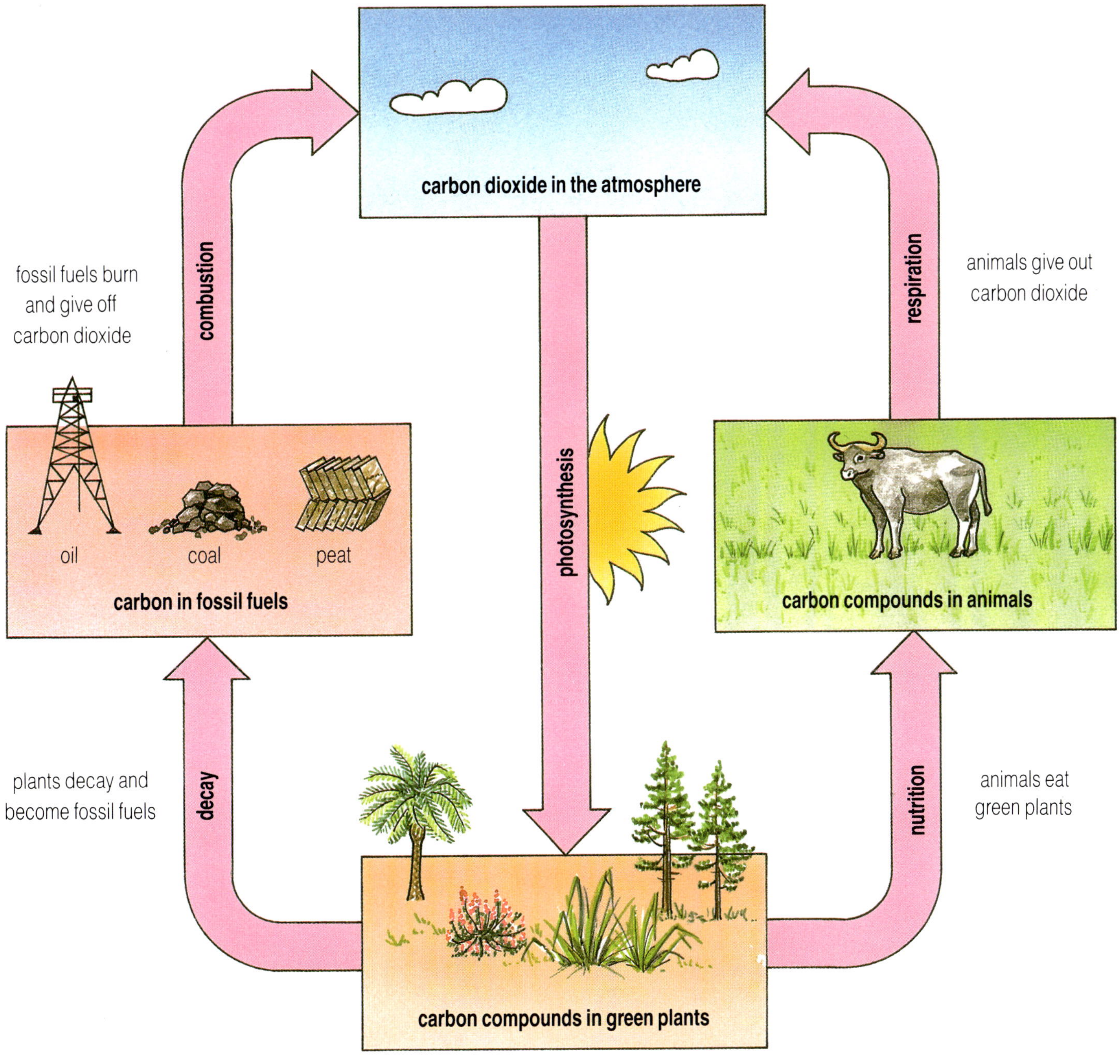

cell *noun*

1. A cell is a single, tiny part of all living things. It is made of a substance called **protoplasm**. Some simple plants and animals contain only one cell. Trees and humans contain millions of cells.
She looked through the microscope to see the cells in the leaf.

2. A cell is a device which helps to make an **electric current**. A simple cell contains two pieces of different metals and a chemical liquid or damp paste.
When two or more cells are connected together, they make a battery.

simple cell

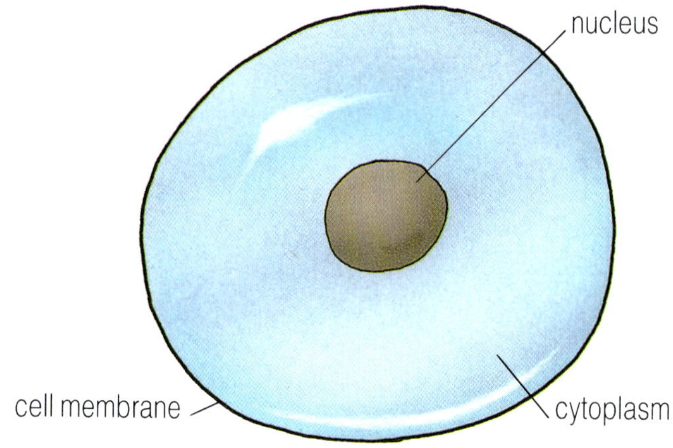

plant cell

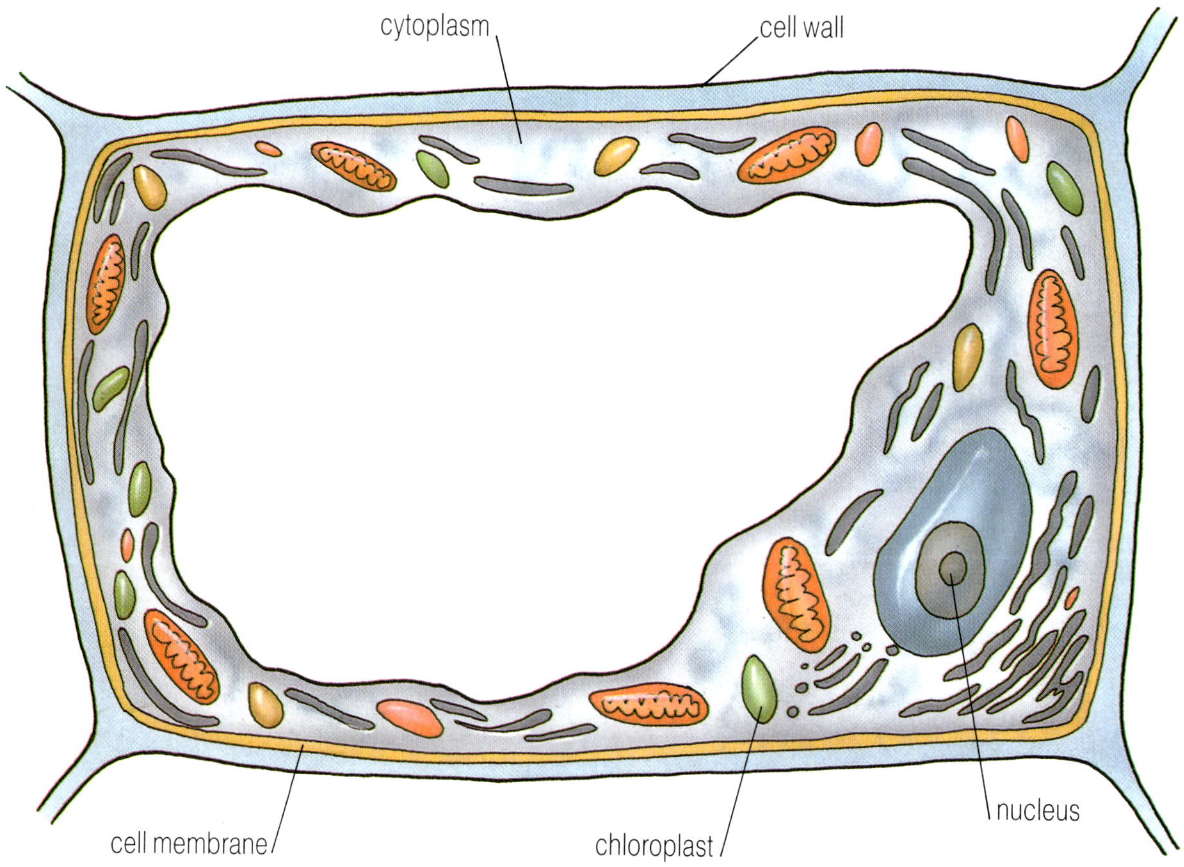

animal cell

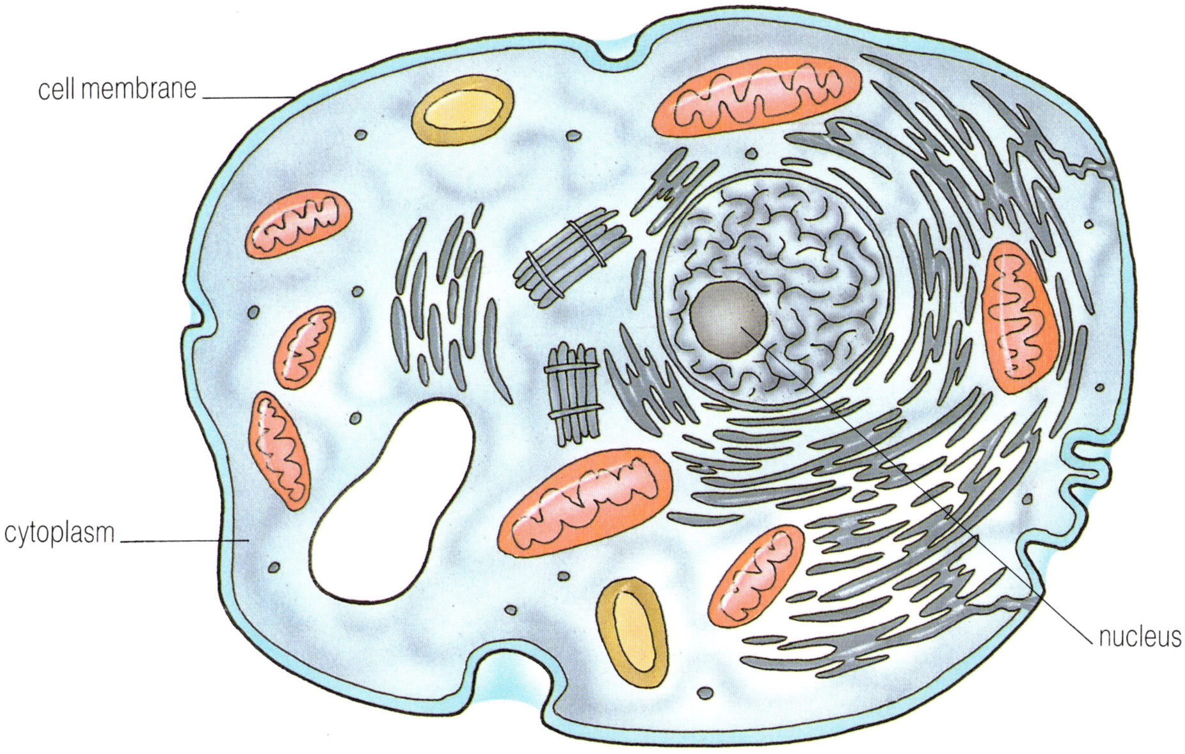

other kinds of cell

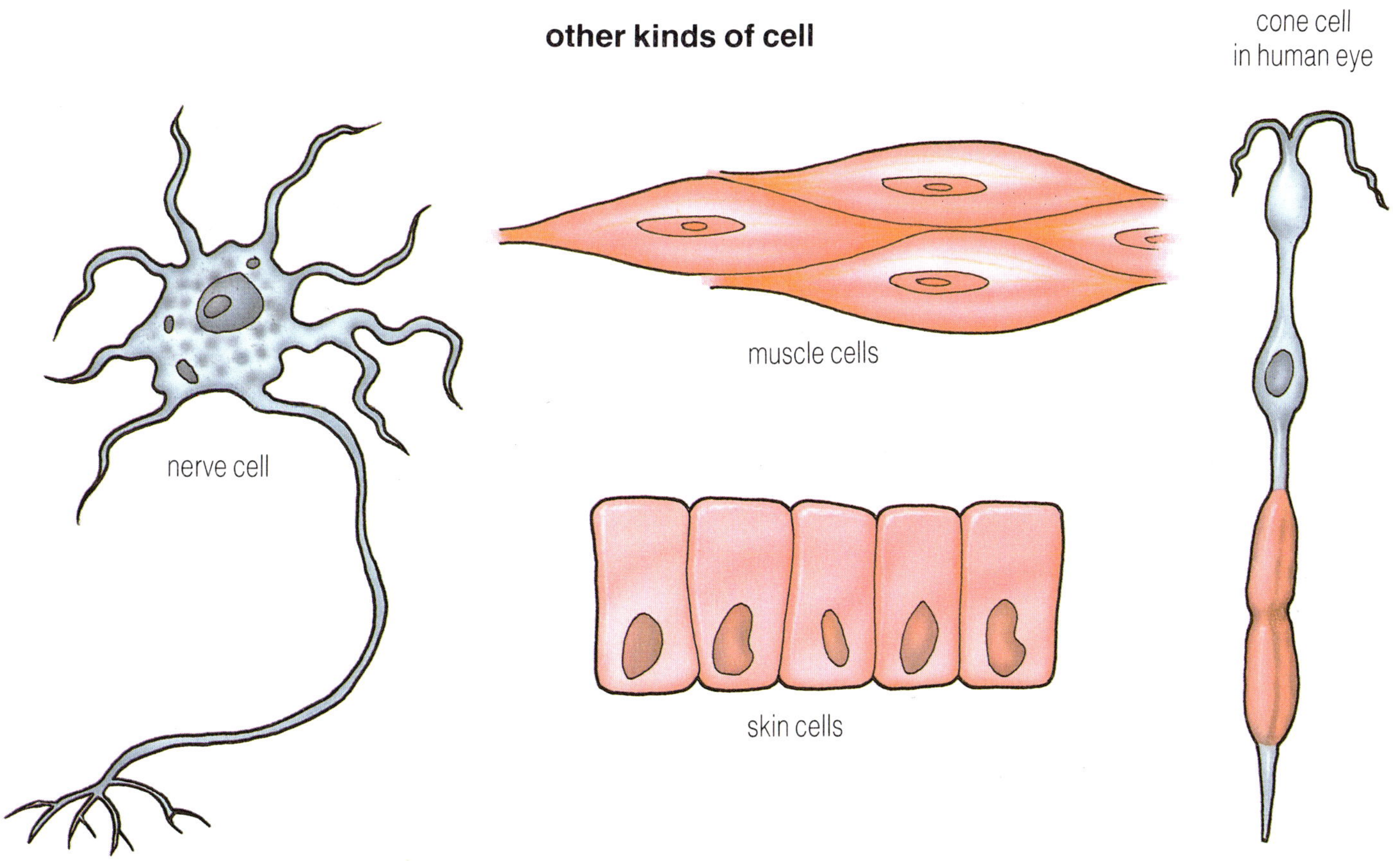

Celsius *adjective*
Celsius is a word which describes a **unit** used to measure temperature. Many thermometers have a **scale** which is marked in **degrees** Celsius, or °C for short. Water boils at 100 degrees Celsius (100°C), and freezes at 0 degrees Celsius (0°C).
Scientists all over the world use the Celsius scale to measure temperature.

centi- *prefix*
Centi-, or c for short, is placed in front of a **unit** of measurement. It divides the unit by 100. One **centimetre** is one-hundredth of a metre.
The carton contained 75 centilitres of orange juice.

centigrade *adjective*
Centigrade is a word which describes a **unit** used to measure temperature. Many thermometers have a **scale** which is marked in **degrees** centigrade. The centigrade scale is exactly the same as the **Celsius** scale.
Scientists now talk about the Celsius scale instead of the centigrade scale.

centilitre *noun*
A centilitre, or cl for short, is a **unit** of measurement. It is used to measure **volume**. There are 100 centilitres in 1 litre. There are 10 millilitres in 1 centilitre.
The bottle contained 75 centilitres of milk.

centimetre *noun*
A centimetre, or cm for short, is a **unit** of measurement. It is used to measure length. There are 100 centimetres in 1 metre. There are 10 millimetres in 1 centimetre.
The ruler was 10 centimetres long.

central processing unit *noun*
A central processing unit, or CPU for short, is a part of a **computer**. It uses a **program** to change **data** that pass through it.
The central processing unit passes information to the printer.

CFC ► chlorofluorocarbon

chain reaction *noun*
Chain reaction is a term which describes a kind of change. Chain reactions happen in nuclear **power stations**. Here, the **atoms** of uranium fuel are split, releasing **neutrons** and **nuclear energy**. The neutrons then split other atoms which release more neutrons and energy. This sequence of splitting is called a chain reaction.
The chain reaction in a nuclear reactor gives off a lot of heat.

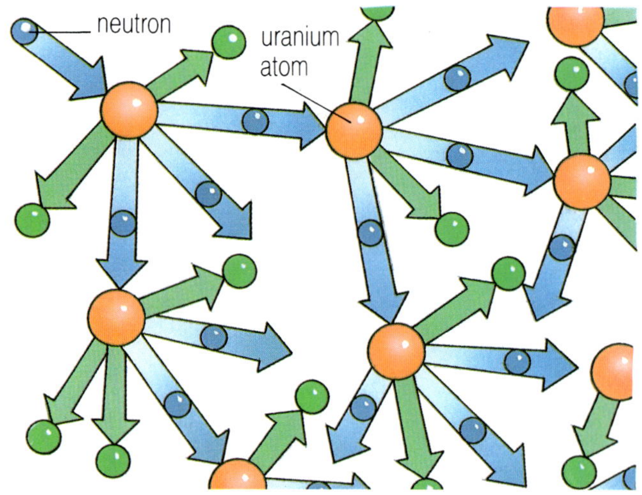

characteristic *noun*
Characteristic is a word which describes the parts, the shapes or the behaviour of living things. These characteristics help us to recognize different living things and to sort them into groups.
Walking upright on two legs is a characteristic of human beings.

charcoal *noun*
Charcoal is a black **solid** which contains **carbon**. It is made by heating wood in a closed space with no air. Charcoal is used as a filter to clean gases and liquids. It is also used as a fuel.
He added more charcoal to the fire in the barbecue.

charge ► electric charge

chassis *noun*
A chassis is a kind of metal plate or frame which helps to support the other parts of a machine or vehicle. The chassis in a truck is made from steel tubes. The chassis in a computer supports the **circuit boards**.
The car's engine and the axles are supported by the chassis.

chemical *noun*
A chemical is a single **substance** which is **pure**. Chemicals may be **elements** or **compounds**.
Bicarbonate of soda, calcium and oxygen are different kinds of chemical.

chemical energy *noun*
Chemical energy is a kind of **energy** which is stored inside **chemicals**. The chemical energy in a fuel changes to **heat energy** when the fuel burns. The chemical energy in a battery changes to **electrical energy** when a circuit is complete.
Chemical energy in food helps our bodies to keep warm and to move about.

chemical reaction *noun*
A chemical reaction is a kind of change. This change causes **atoms** in **chemicals** to rearrange themselves to make new chemicals. A chemical reaction takes place when chemicals are heated or mixed together. It can also happen when an **electric current** passes through the chemicals.
Chemists use a chemical reaction to change oil into soap.

chemistry *noun*
Chemistry is a scientific subject. It is the study of **chemical reactions**. A chemist is a person who studies chemistry.
Chemistry helps us to make many new and useful substances.

chip ► **silicon chip**

chlorine *noun*
Chlorine is a chemical **element**. It is a yellow, poisonous **gas** which dissolves in water. Chlorine makes water safe to drink. It is important in the manufacture of some kinds of plastic, medicine and disinfectant.
They added chlorine to the water in the pool.

chlorofluorocarbon *noun*
A chlorofluorocarbon, or CFC for short, is a **compound**. It is made up from **chlorine,** fluorine and **carbon**. Chlorofluorocarbons are used in refrigerators and aerosols, and to help make some plastics.
Scientists think that chlorofluorocarbons damage part of the Earth's atmosphere.

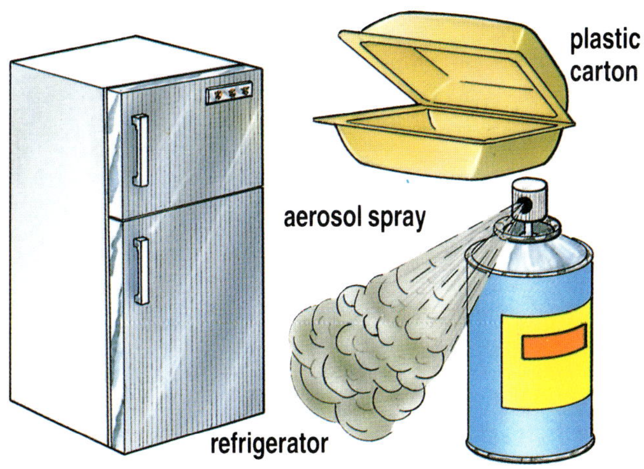

chromium *noun*
Chromium is a hard, silvery **metal**. It does not **corrode**. Chromium can be mixed with iron to make stainless **steel.**
Many gardening tools are made from steel which contains chromium.

circuit ► **electric circuit**

circuit board *noun*
A circuit board is a **device** which is part of a radio, a television or a computer. It is a plate which is made of **glass fibre** and is covered with thin copper strips. These strips join together electrical **components.** A circuit board is also called a printed circuit.
She made the computer work again by plugging in a new circuit board.

circuit breaker *noun*
A circuit breaker is a kind of electric **switch**. It is connected to an **electric circuit** and switches off the **electric current** if too much current flows through the circuit.
He mended the fault and then switched on the circuit breaker again.

circular *adjective*
Circular is a word which describes a kind of shape. A circular shape is perfectly round.
The Sun has a circular shape.

circumference *noun*
The circumference is a measurement of length. It is the distance around the outside of a circle.
The circumference of the circle was 40 centimetres.

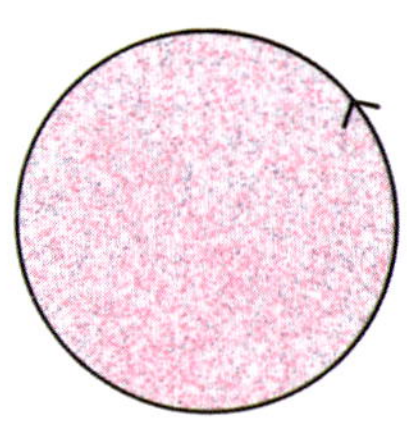

civil engineer *noun*
A civil engineer is a person who helps to design and build roads, bridges and tunnels. Civil engineers need to know about different **materials** and how and where to use them.
A civil engineer designed the new bridge over the river.

clamp *noun*
A clamp is a kind of **tool** which holds things together. You can tighten a clamp by turning a **screw** or **bolt**, or by pressing a **lever**.
The clamps held the two pipes together.
clamp *verb*

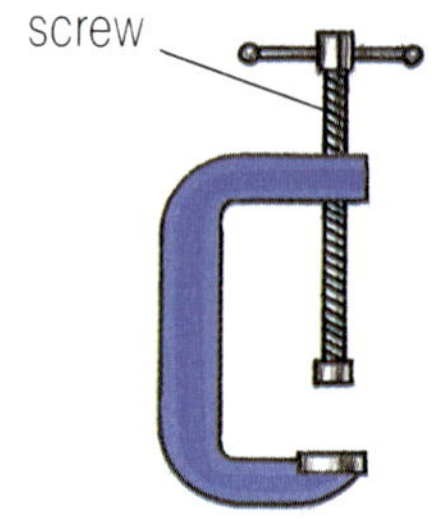

class *noun*
A class is a group of living things. All the living things in the same class have similar **characteristics**. Classes are part of the system of **classification** which is worked out by biologists.
Humans, horses, whales and dogs are grouped together in a class called mammals.

classification ► page 31

clockwork motor *noun*
A clockwork motor is a kind of **machine**. A clockwork motor stores energy when its spring is wound tightly with a key. This energy is used to turn wheels. Clockwork motors often power small toys and clocks.
She wound up the clockwork motor in the model car.

classification *noun*
Classification is the system which scientists use to sort different plants and animals into groups. Each group contains living things which have similar **characteristics.** Classification helps biologists to sort living things into five main groups called **kingdoms**. *The five kingdoms are animals, plants, fungi, protista and monera.*

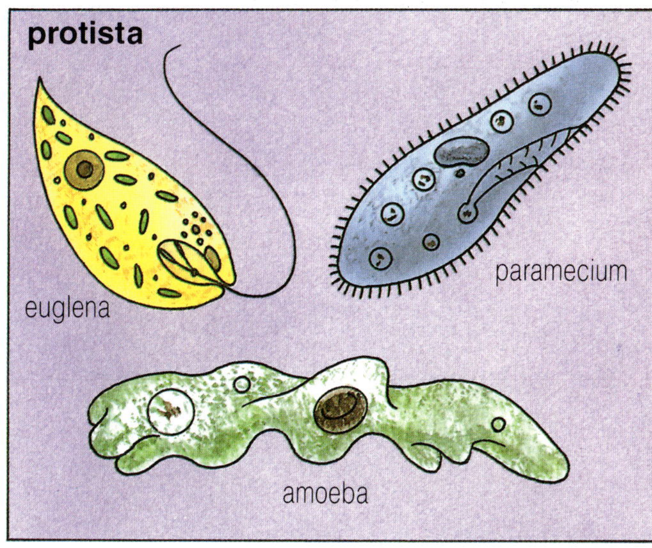

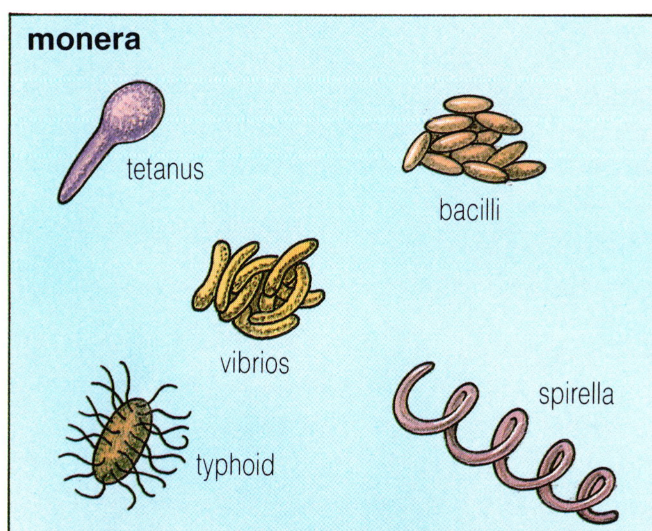

coal *noun*
Coal is a black, solid **fossil fuel** which is found under the ground. It burns with a hot flame. Coal is used in **power stations** and for heating and cooking in homes.
Many power stations burn huge amounts of coal to heat the boilers.

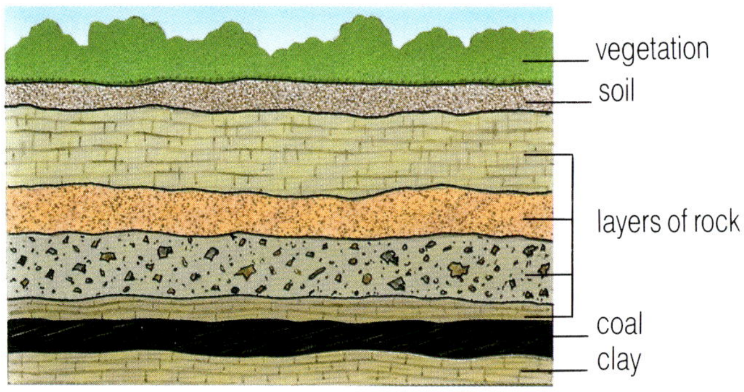

coal gas *noun*
Coal gas is a mixture of different kinds of **gas**. It is made when coal is heated in a closed space with no air. Coal gas contains **methane**, **hydrogen** and **carbon monoxide**.
Coal gas burns with a yellow flame.

coal tar *noun*
Coal tar is a thick, black **liquid**. It is a **by-product** which is made when coal changes into **coke**. Coal tar contains many useful **chemicals**.
The coal tar flowed through the pipe and into the tank.

cobalt *noun*
Cobalt is a very hard and silvery **metal**. It is mixed with iron to make cobalt **steel**. This is used in the manufacture of hard cutting tools such as drills.
The cobalt is mixed with liquid iron inside the furnace.

code *noun*
A code is a language made up of a group of **signals**, **symbols**, letters or numbers. It is a way of storing information. **Binary digits** make up the code which controls computers.
The code which the computers use means that they can send messages to each other.

cog *noun*
A cog is a small piece of **metal**. Cogs stick out around the outside edge of a **gear**. The cogs on one gear fit together with the cogs on another gear.
The gear had 20 cogs around its outside edge.

cog wheel *noun*
A cog wheel is a wheel with **cogs** around its outside edge. The cogs on one cog wheel usually connect with the cogs on another cog wheel.
The machine contained ten cog wheels.

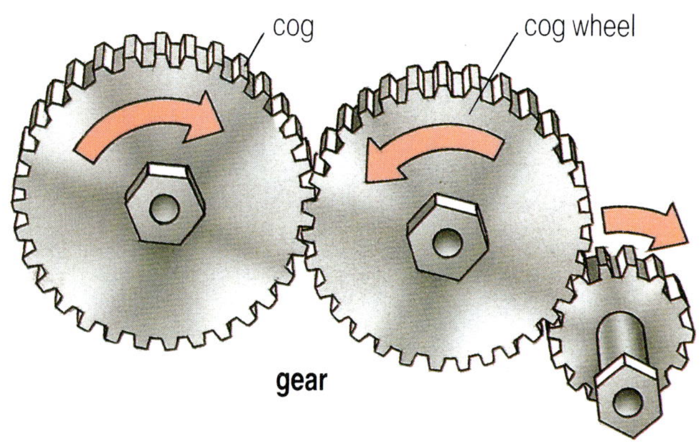

coil *noun*
A coil is a word which describes a shape. A coil is made when a length of wire, rope or other material is wound round many times in a circle.
There were 500 turns in the coil of wire.

coke *noun*
Coke is a dark grey **solid**. It is a **by-product** which is made during the manufacture of **coal gas**. Coke is used in **blast furnaces** to help make iron.
Coke is poured into the top of a furnace.

combust *verb*
Combust is a word which means the same as **burn**. A substance combines with oxygen when it combusts, giving out heat and waste products.
Wood combusts and leaves a pile of ashes.
combustion *noun*

command *noun*
A command is a kind of coded message. It tells a machine, such as a **computer** or space **satellite,** to behave in a special way.
She sent a command to the satellite to switch on its television camera.

communications *noun*
Communications is a word which describes all the different ways of sending messages from one place to another, or from one living thing to another. Communications between humans may involve talking and writing. It is often helped by **telecommunications**.
Two animals often communicate through their sense of smell.
communicate *verb*

commutator *noun*
A commutator is a device which is found inside some electric **motors**. It helps an **electric current** to flow from a fixed part to a moving part of a machine.
The commutator spins around inside the electric motor.

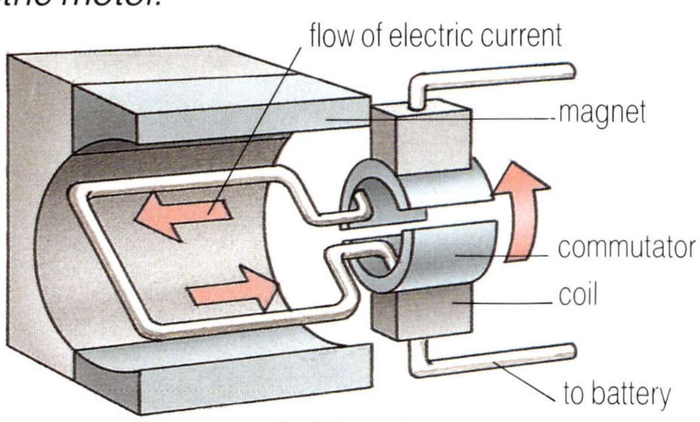

electric motor

compass *noun*
A compass is an instrument which helps people to find their way from one place to another. A **magnetic** compass contains a small magnet which can turn. The magnet, which is sometimes shaped like a needle, always points towards the Earth's **magnetic poles**.

They used a compass to find out which road led to the south.

component *noun*
A component is one part of a larger object. **Machines** and **engines** contain many different components. Radios contain **electronic** components.
The components of the clockwork motor include wheels and a spring.

compound *noun*
A compound is a kind of **chemical** substance. Compounds contain **atoms** of different **elements** which are joined together. Water, salt and sugar are examples of different compounds.
Water is a compound which is made up from two hydrogen atoms and one oxygen atom.

compress *verb*
Compress is a word which describes how a substance can be squeezed to make it smaller. Gases are much easier to compress than liquids. It is almost impossible to compress solids.
He used a pump to compress the gas in the container.
compressed *adjective*

compressor *noun*
A compressor is a kind of **machine** which is used to **compress** a gas. The compressor increases the **pressure** of the gas.
A compressor helps to send air down to a diver at the bottom of the sea.

computer ▶ page 34

computer-aided design *noun*
Computer-aided design, or CAD for short, is a way of using a **computer** to help design objects. It is used to design motor cars, buildings, bridges and machines. Computer-aided design can show what an object will look like and how it will behave when it is built.
Computer-aided design is helping to design a new high-speed aeroplane.

computer *noun*
A computer is an **electronic** machine which can solve problems very quickly. Information is fed into the computer and is stored in a **memory.** The information is changed into a form which we can read by the computer's **program**.
At the supermarket, a computer works out how much food is sold each day.

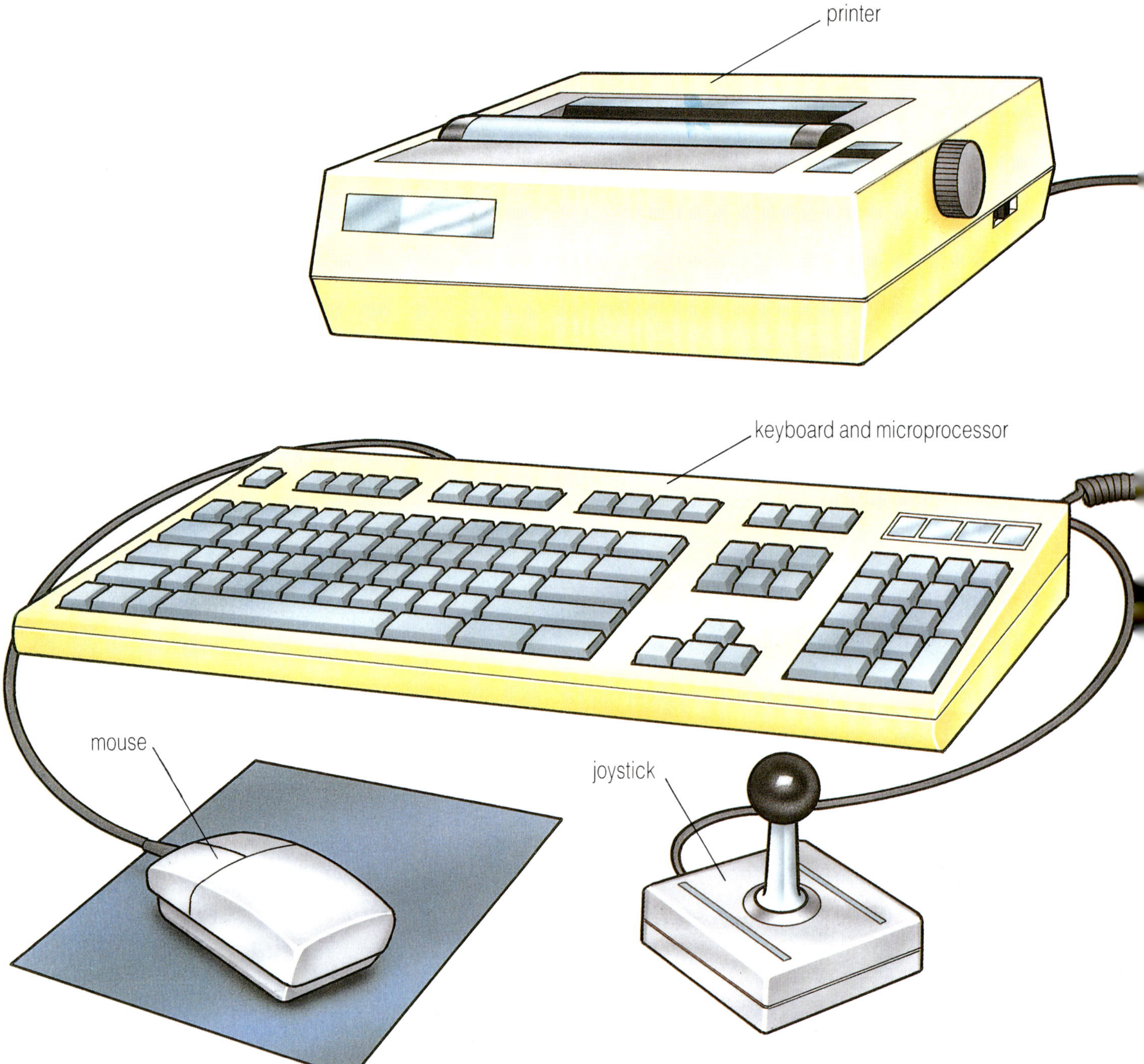

monitor
screen
disk drive
hard disk
floppy disk

concave *adjective*
Concave is a word which describes a kind of shape. A concave shape bends inwards to make a hollow. The opposite of concave is **convex**.
The inside of a bowl has a concave shape.

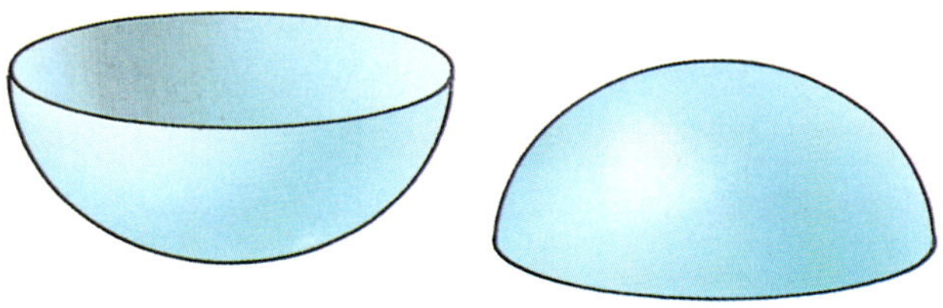

concentration *noun*
Concentration is a word which describes how much of a solid is **dissolved** in a liquid. If you stir 5 grams of salt into 1 litre of water, this makes a salt solution. The concentration of the solution is 5 grams per litre.
The concentration of sugar in lemon juice is low.

condensation *noun*
1. Condensation is a kind of **liquid**. When steam or another **vapour** cools, condensation forms.
Condensation runs down the inside of the cold windows in the kitchen.
2. Condensation is a word which describes how a **vapour** changes into a liquid. Condensation happens when a vapour cools.
In power stations, condensation turns the water vapour back into a liquid.

conduct *verb*
Conduct is a word which describes how substances allow **heat** or **electricity** to move through them. A metal rod which is warmed at one end will conduct heat through its length to its other end. Wires conduct electricity around an **electric circuit**.
Some metals, such as copper, conduct heat and electricity well.

conduction *noun*
Conduction is a word which describes how **heat** or **electricity** moves through a substance. The substance does not move, but it **conducts** the heat or electricity.
Heat flows along the metal rod by conduction.

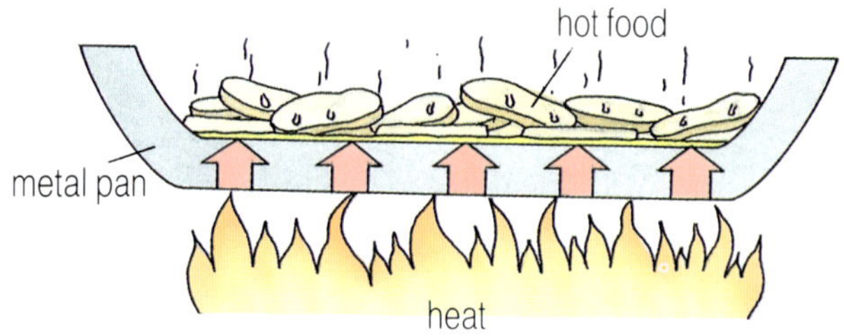

conductivity *noun*
Conductivity is a word which describes how well a substance allows **heat** or **electricity** to pass through it.
Copper has a high conductivity, but wood has a low conductivity.

conductor *noun*
A conductor is any **substance** that allows heat or electricity to flow easily through it.
Copper is a good conductor of heat and electricity.

cone *noun*
A cone is a solid shape. It has a flat, **circular** base and sloping sides. The sides rise up from the base and meet at a point called the vertex.
The top of the rocket is shaped like a cone.
conical *adjective*

conical flask *noun*
A conical flask is a kind of **apparatus.** It is a container which holds liquids. It has a round, flat bottom, sloping sides and a narrow neck.
A **scale** is usually marked on the flask to measure the **volume** of liquid inside it.
He poured the liquid into the conical flask.

connection *noun*
A connection joins together the different **components** in an **electric circuit**. Connections are made by clips, plugs and sockets, by **clamping** wires together or by using **solder**.
The light bulb has two connections on its metal end.

constant *noun*
A constant is a **quantity** which never changes and so it always has the same value. A **unit** of measurement will change when you **multiply** or **divide** it by a constant. The opposite of a constant is a **variable**.
If you multiply a number of hours by the constant 60, the answer will be a number of minutes.

contract *verb*
Contract is a word which describes how a substance becomes smaller or shorter. Most **gases, liquids** and **solids** contract when they cool. The opposite of contract is **expand**.
The metal railway line contracts in cold weather.

control rod *noun*
A control rod is a device which is built into a **nuclear reactor**. It controls the **power** of the reactor. Control rods are long, thin rods which slide in and out of the **core** of the reactor. They are made of a material that can absorb the **neutrons** in **atoms**.
The engineer moved the control rods into the reactor to stop it overheating.

control unit *noun*
A control unit is a device which is found inside a **machine**. It makes the machine behave correctly. A person decides which buttons to press or which levers to move on the control unit. Some control units contain small **computers**.
He used the control unit to work the crane.

convection *noun*
Convection is a word which describes how **heat** moves through a liquid or a gas. The liquid or gas moves and carries the heat with it.
In a heated room, the warm air rises by convection.

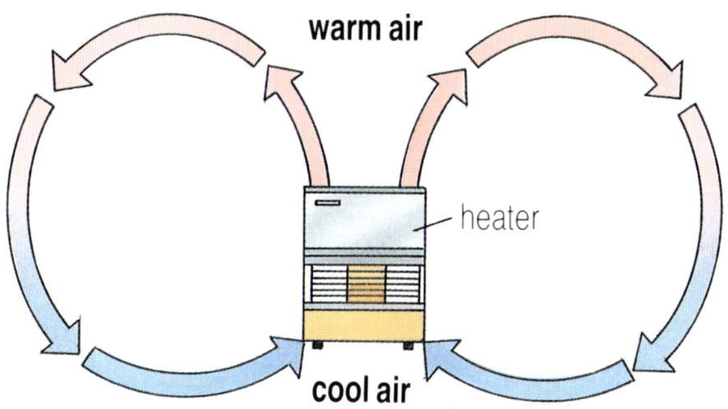

convex *adjective*
Convex is a word which describes a kind of shape. A convex shape bends outwards to make a bulge. The opposite of convex is **concave**.
The outside of a bowl has a convex shape.

coolant *noun*
A coolant is a substance which flows around the hot parts of a machine and cools them. A coolant may be a **liquid** or a **gas**.
Water is the coolant in some car engines.

cooling tower *noun*
A cooling tower is part of a **power station**. Cooling towers are built from concrete. Hot water from the **turbines** sprays down inside the cooling tower. The cold air in the tower cools the hot water, which is then used as a **coolant**.
A cooling tower may be over 50 metres tall.

copper *noun*
Copper is a chemical **element**. It is a soft, red-brown **metal**. Copper is used to make pipes and electric wires. When copper is mixed with other metals, it makes **alloys** such as **brass** and **bronze**.
You can easily bend a copper rod with your hands.

core *noun*
Core is a word which describes the centre part of a solid object. Apples, **nuclear reactors**, **electromagnets** and planets all have a core.
Scientists think that the core of the Earth is made up of a liquid metal.

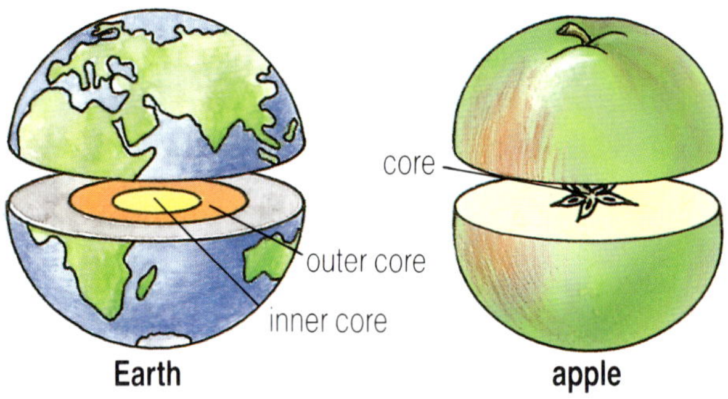

counterweight *noun*
A counterweight is a heavy weight inside a **machine**. It balances against a heavy moving part of the machine. The counterweight makes it easier to move the heavy part.
The lift goes up as the counterweight comes down.

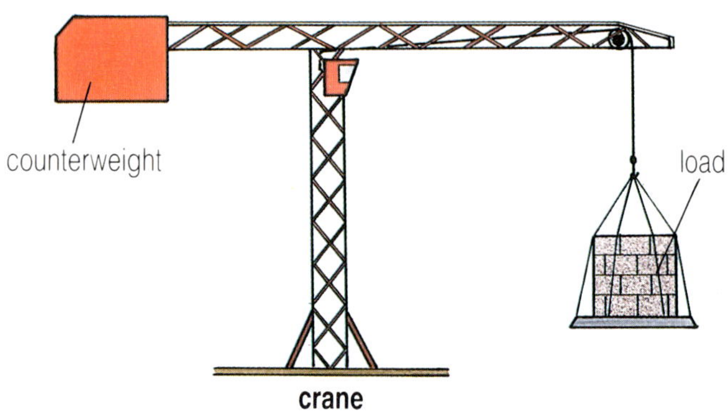

CPU ► central processing unit

cracking *noun*
Cracking is a word which describes how **heat** breaks down a substance. Cracking is used in **oil refineries** to make petrol and other useful chemicals from **petroleum**.
At the oil refinery, cracking only takes place when the oil vapour is very hot.

crankshaft *noun*
A crankshaft is a part of a **machine**. It is a long rod which changes an up-and-down movement into a round-and-round movement. The pedals on a bicycle join onto a crankshaft which drives the back wheel.
Most car engines contain a crankshaft.

crude oil ► petroleum

crystal *noun*
A crystal is a kind of **solid**. It looks like a piece of glass with straight edges. All the crystals of a particular substance are the same shape. Crystals of different substances are different shapes.
A crystal of sugar looks like a tiny cube.
crystalline *adjective*

cube *noun*
A cube is a solid shape. It has six square sides which are all the same size.
This box is a cube, with each side measuring 5 centimetres in length.
cubic *adjective*

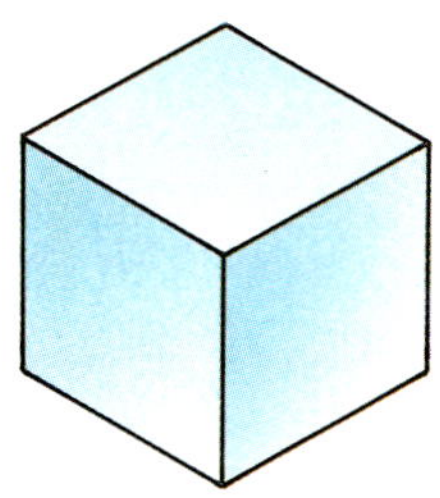

current ► electric current

cylinder *noun*

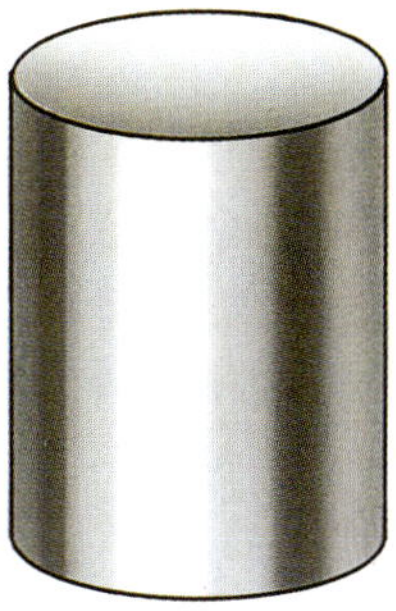

1. A cylinder is a solid shape. It has two ends which are flat and **circular**. The ends are parallel and they are joined by a curved surface. This surface makes the side wall of the cylinder.
A can of soup is a cylinder shape.

2. A cylinder is part of a **machine**. It is a hollow tube and has a **piston** which moves up and down inside it. **Internal combustion engines** and **steam engines** contain cylinders.
The hot steam rushes into the cylinder.

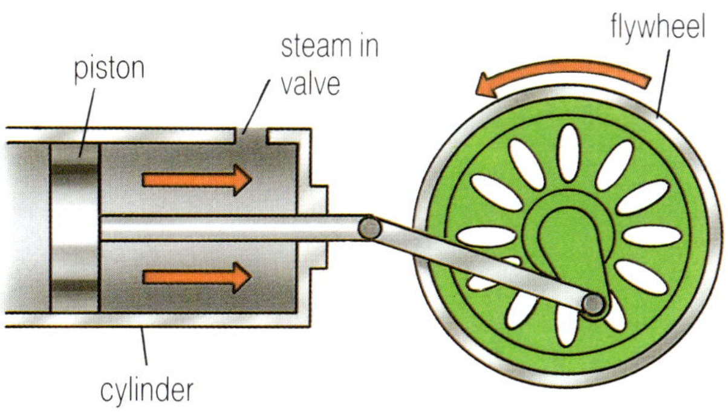

steam engine

cytoplasm *noun*
Cytoplasm is a **substance** which is part of all living things. It is found in every **cell**, lying between the **nucleus** and the **cell membrane**. The cytoplasm contains the main parts of the cell.
Cytoplasm looks like grey jelly.

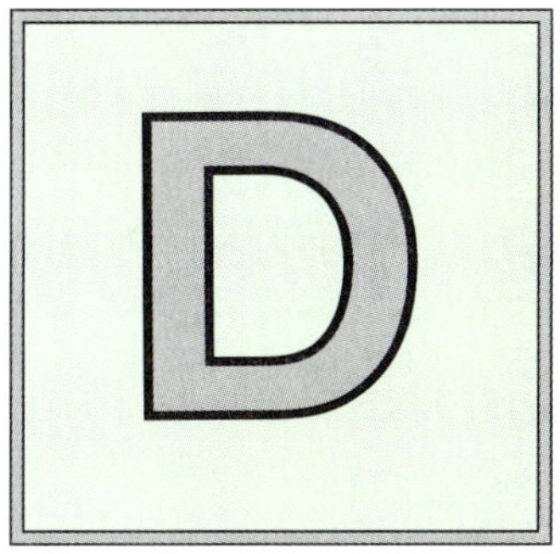

dam *noun*
A dam is a large, very strong wall. It is built across a river to block the flow of water. A lake builds up behind the dam. The water in the lake can be used for making **hydro-electric power** or for growing crops.
A dam was built to provide water for the people in the city.

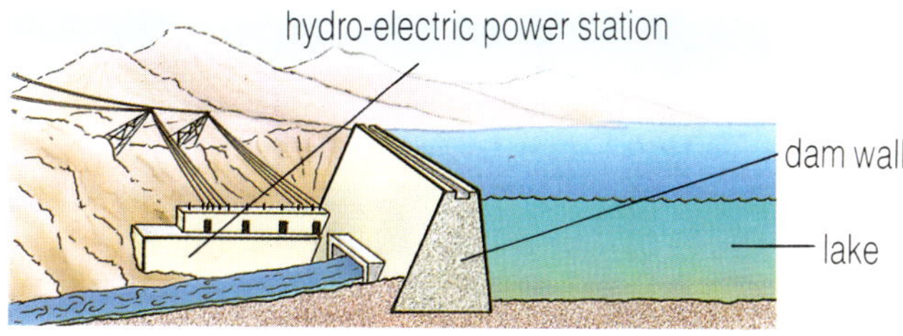

data *plural noun*
Data is a plural word which means facts or information. People and **computers** use data to solve problems and to answer questions. Data are fed into a computer through the **keyboard** or from a **disk** or **tape**. The data can then be stored in the computer's **memory**.
Data from this computer tell us what the weather will be like tomorrow.

database *noun*
A database is a large collection of facts or information. It is usually stored inside a **computer**. The computer can find each fact very quickly.
This database contains millions of telephone numbers and addresses.

decay *verb*
Decay is a word which describes how things break down into smaller parts. **Radioactive atoms** decay and give off **radiation**. Plants and animals rot and decay when they die.
Dead leaves fall off the trees and decay.

decelerate *verb*
Decelerate is a word which means to slow down. The opposite of decelerate is **accelerate**.
He pressed the brake pedal and the car decelerated.
deceleration *noun*

decibel ► page 41

decimal *adjective*
Decimal is a word which describes counting in tens. Decimal counting uses the **base** 10. In decimal counting, 1,234 means 1 thousand, 2 hundreds, 3 tens and 4 units.
The decimal system of counting is used all over the world.

degree *noun*
1. A degree is a **unit** for measuring **temperature**. It is measured in degrees **Celsius** or in degrees **Kelvin**.
The temperature of boiling water is 100 degrees Celsius.
2. A degree is a **unit** which measures **angles**. There are 360 degrees in one circle.
A right angle measures 90 degrees.

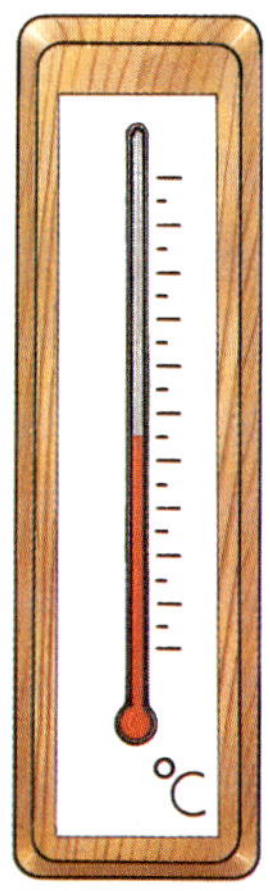

thermometer

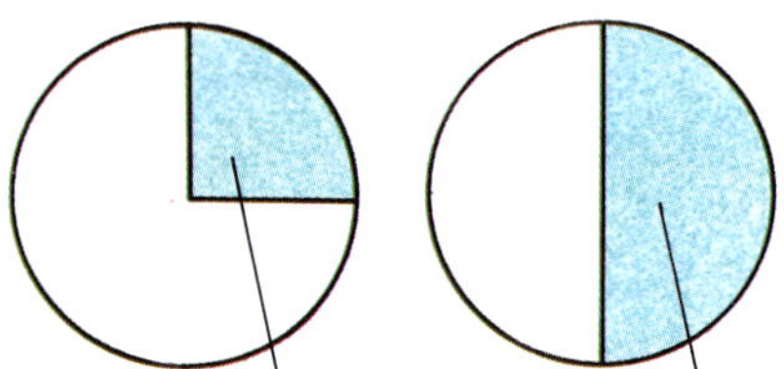

dehydration *noun*
Dehydration is a word which describes the removal of water from a substance. Dehydration takes place when a substance is heated, because the water escapes as **steam**.
Dehydration made the shiny crystals crumble into a powder.
dehydrate *verb*

density *noun*
Density is a kind of measurement. It measures the **mass** of 1 cubic metre of a substance. The **unit** of density is kilograms per cubic metre (kg/m^3). Density helps to compare the heaviness of different substances.
The density of oil is less than the density of water, so oil floats on water.

deposit *noun*
A deposit is a kind of layer which builds up on a solid surface. A deposit of dust from the air forms on furniture. When water **evaporates** from a solution, a deposit of a solid substance is formed.
A deposit of salt is left when sea water boils away in a pan.
deposit *verb*

desalination *noun*
Desalination is a word which describes the removal of salt from sea water. The sea water must be **distilled** to make it safe for drinking or for watering plants.
In countries where there is little rain, drinking water is made by desalination.
desalinate *verb*

desiccator *noun*
A desiccator is a kind of **apparatus**. The desiccator contains a chemical which removes water from a substance. A desiccator will stop a substance absorbing water from the air.
She put the damp powder inside the desiccator to remove the water.
desiccate *verb*

deuterium *noun*
Deuterium is a **gas** which is very similar to **hydrogen**. It is sometimes called heavy hydrogen. One atom of deuterium is made up of one **proton** and one **electron**. It is used in some **nuclear power stations**.
Sea water contains a very small amount of deuterium.

decibel *noun*
A decibel, or dB for short, is a **unit** of measurement. It measures the loudness of sound. The sound of a jet aeroplane taking off measures about 120 decibels. The purr of a cat measures about 10 decibels.
Music can damage your hearing if it measures more than 130 decibels.

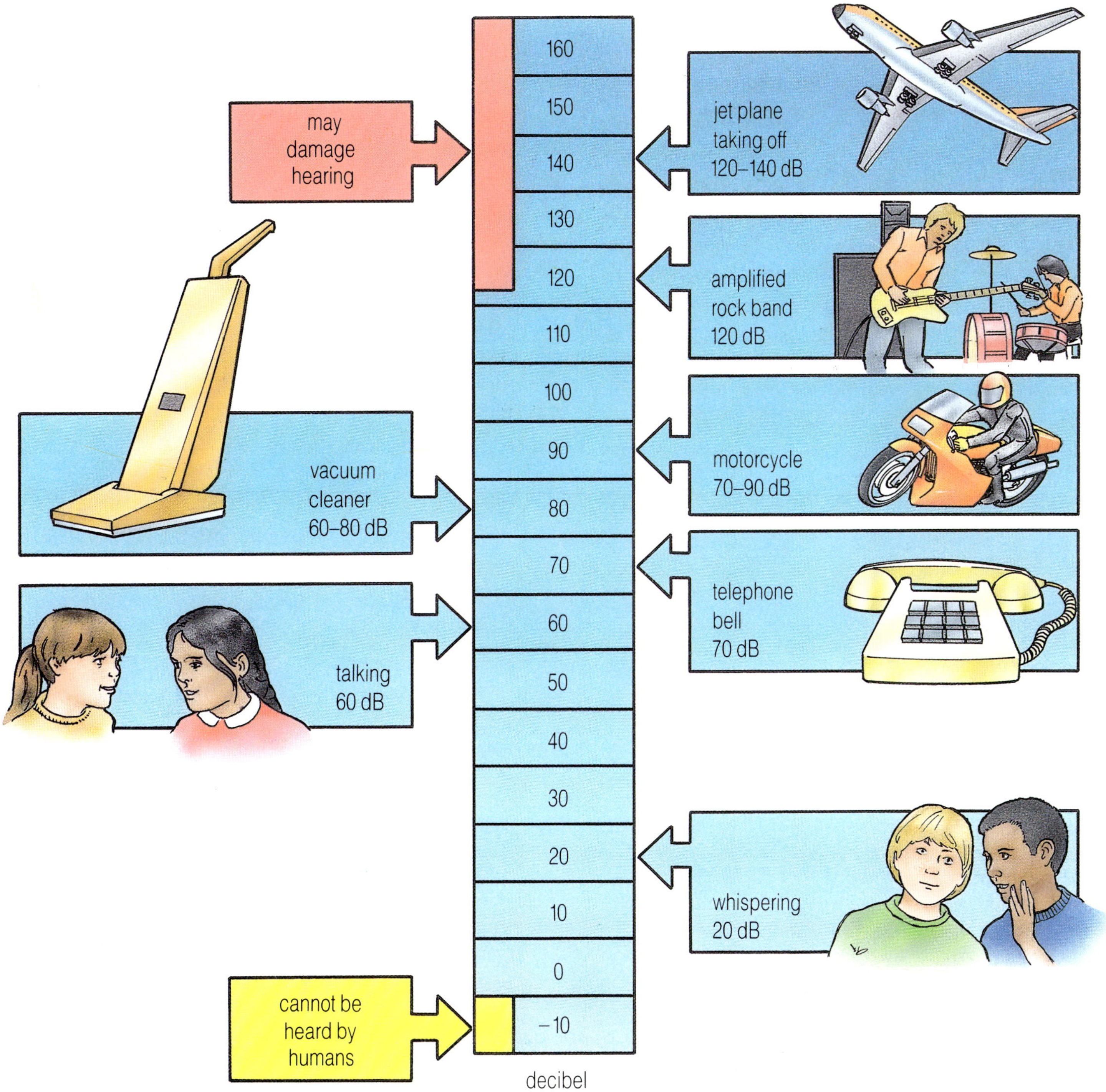

device *noun*
A device is a small, manufactured object. Hinges, **pulleys**, electric motors, switches and lamps are different kinds of device. When several devices are connected together, they make up an **appliance**.
A television set contains many different kinds of device.

diagonal *noun*
A diagonal is a straight line which can be drawn across a shape from one corner to another.
If you draw a diagonal across a square, you will cut the square into two triangles.

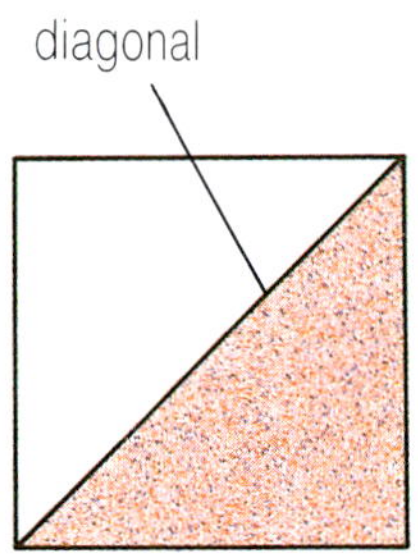

dial *noun*
A dial is a device which is used on a measuring instrument. A dial is usually round like the face of a clock. A hand or needle on the dial points towards a **scale** marked around the outside. **Analogue meters** and **gauges** have dials.
The dial on the weighing machine showed him the weight of the parcel.

diameter *noun*
A diameter is a straight line. It is drawn across a circle and passes through the centre of the circle.
The diameter of the circle is 5 centimetres.

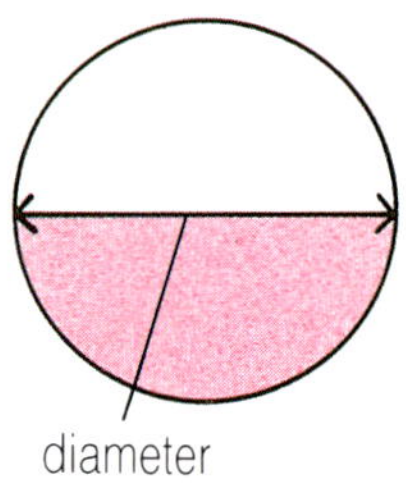

diaphragm *noun*
1. A diaphragm is a flat sheet of muscles. It lies under the lungs in some mammals.
Your diaphragm moves downwards when you breathe in air.
2. A diaphragm is a thin, flat sheet of material. Inside a telephone **receiver**, there is a diaphragm which is **vibrated** by electric signals. This vibration makes sounds that we can hear.
When you talk into the microphone, this makes the diaphragm move.

diesel engine *noun*
A diesel engine is a kind of **internal combustion engine**. Air is heated in cylinders inside the engine. **Diesel oil** sprays into the hot air and burns to make energy.
The ship is powered by a diesel engine.

diesel oil *noun*
Diesel oil is a liquid **fuel** which is made from **petroleum**. Diesel oil powers **diesel engines**.
The driver fills the truck's fuel tank with diesel oil.

diffusion *noun*
Diffusion is a kind of movement. It is the movement of **atoms** and **molecules** in gases and liquids. The diffusion of gases is faster than the diffusion of liquids. When perfume is spilled or sprayed, its molecules are spread through the air by diffusion.
Diffusion makes the drop of ink spread through the beaker of water.
diffuse *verb*

digit *noun*
A digit is a number, or **numeral**. Each of the ten numerals 0, 1, 2, 3, 4, 5, 6, 7, 8 and 9 is a digit. The number 428 has three digits — 4, 2 and 8.
The third digit in the number 694562 is 4.

digital *adjective*
Digital is a word which describes anything that uses numbers. **Data** flow through a digital **computer** in a stream of numbers. The opposite of digital is **analogue**.
A digital watch shows the time in numbers.

dilute *adjective*
Dilute is a word which describes a kind of **solution**. Only a small amount of solid or liquid has **dissolved** in a dilute solution. The opposite of dilute is **concentrated**.
He made a dilute sugar solution by stirring a spoonful of sugar into a bucket of water.

dimension *noun*
A dimension is a measurement, such as **length** or thickness. A straight piece of string has one dimension. A flat sheet of paper has two dimensions. A box has three dimensions.
The dimensions of this page are 270 millimetres high and 217 millimetres wide.

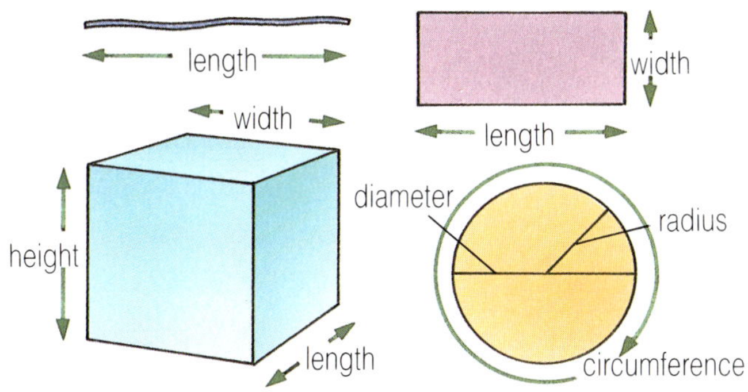

diode *noun*
A diode is a part of some **electric circuits**. Most diodes are shaped like a small **cylinder** with a thin wire joined to each end. **Electricity** can flow in one direction only through a diode.
This radio set contains six diodes.

direct current *noun*
Direct current, or DC for short, is a kind of **electricity**. It flows steadily through wires in one direction only. **Batteries** send direct current through **electric circuits**. The opposite of direct current is **alternating current**.
Direct current lights up my flashlight.

disc *noun*
A disc is a solid shape which is round, thin and flat.
A coin is shaped like a disc.

disk ► **floppy disk** and **hard disk**

disk drive noun
A disk drive is part of a **computer**. It operates the **hard disk** or the **floppy disk** and sends **data** and **programs** into the computer.
She put a floppy disk into the right-hand disk drive of her computer.

dissolve *verb*
Dissolve is a word which describes how some solids disappear when they are added to a liquid. Salt dissolves in water to make a salt **solution**.
Grease dissolves in petrol, and sugar dissolves in warm water.

distil *verb*
Distil is a word which describes how a liquid can be made **pure**. If a liquid is boiled in a **flask,** pure **vapour** rises off it and passes into a pipe. The pipe is kept cold so that the vapour cools as it passes through and then turns into a liquid.
They distilled the sea water to remove the salt and make pure water.
distillation *noun*

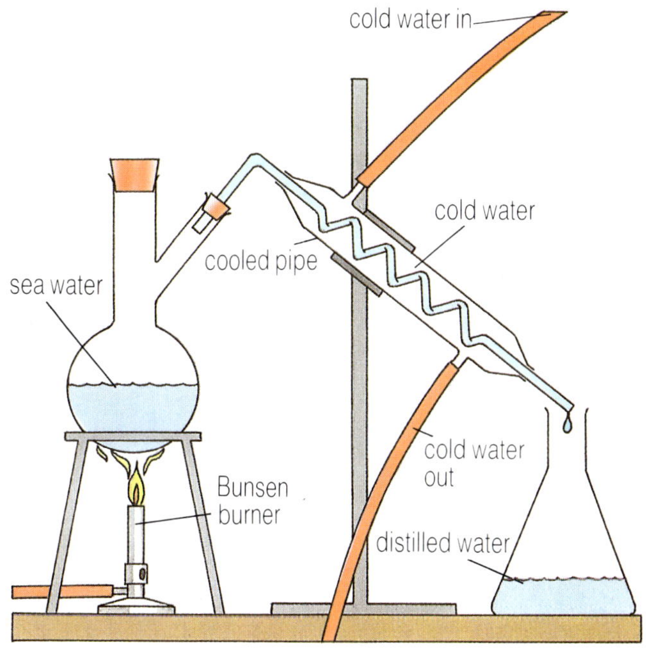

distilled water *noun*
Distilled water is **pure** water which does not contain any **dissolved** substances.
Distilled water can be made from sea water.

diverge *verb*
Diverge is a word which describes how two lines spread out in different directions from the same point. The opposite of diverge is **converge**.
The two lines diverge to form the letter V.

division *noun*
1. A division is a group of living things. All the plants in the same division have special **characteristics**. A division is similar to a **phylum**. They are both part of the system of **classification** which has been worked out by **biologists**.
Lilies, beans and corn are grouped together in the division called flowering plants.

2. Division is a word which describes how living **cells** reproduce. A cell grows larger and then splits down the middle, making two new cells.
Division makes two new cells which are exactly the same as each other.

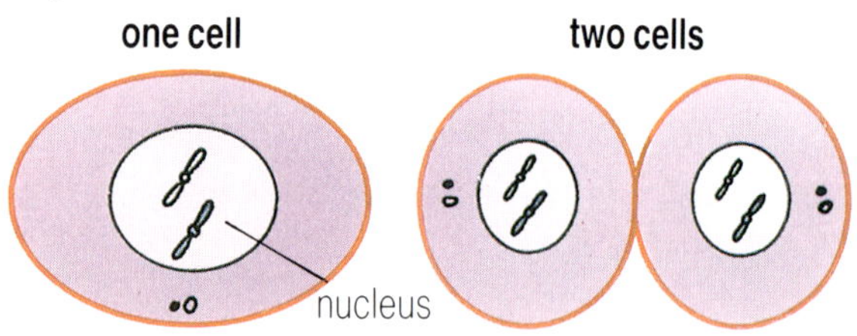

3. Division is a kind of **arithmetic**. It is a way of solving problems with numbers. The sign for division is ÷. Division can work out how to share 12 objects between 4 people.
$12 \div 4 = 3$ each. The opposite of division is **multiplication**.
She used division to share the sweets equally between her friends.
divide *verb*

drag *noun*
Drag is a kind of **force** which pulls things back as they try to move. The air moving round a cyclist causes drag. Drag makes a stone fall slowly through water. Air causes less drag than water.
Drag slows the parachute as it falls to the ground.

drive ► **disk drive**

dry cell *noun*
A dry cell is a kind of electric **battery**. It makes an **electric current** flow around an **electric circuit**. Dry cells have two **electrodes**. Between these electrodes is a damp paste made from chemicals.
She fitted the dry cells into her flashlight.

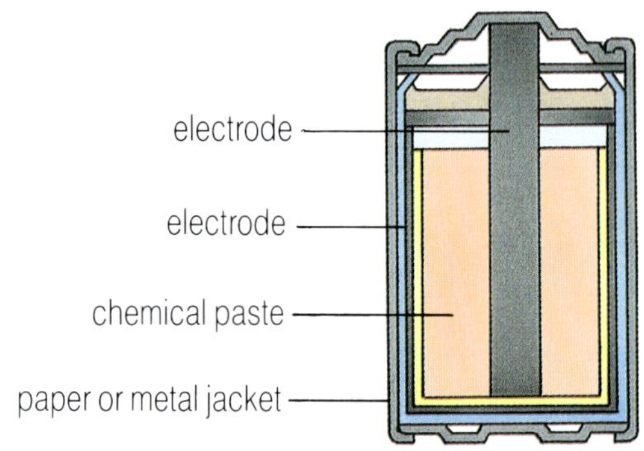

dry ice *noun*
Dry ice is a **solid**. It is made from **carbon dioxide** which has been frozen at −78 degrees Celsius. Dry ice changes from a solid into carbon dioxide gas without first becoming a liquid.
Dry ice stops ice cream from melting.

ductile *adjective*
Ductile is a word which describes how easily some **metals** can be stretched. **Copper** is a ductile metal which can be stretched to make thin wire. The opposite of ductile is **brittle**.
The machine stretched the ductile metal and made it thinner without breaking it.

dynamo *noun*
A dynamo is a kind of **machine**. When a shaft on the dynamo spins, an **electric current** is made to flow through an **electric circuit**.
A dynamo is also called a **generator**.
The dynamo on the bicycle lights up the front and rear lamps.

E

earth wire *noun*
An earth wire is found inside electric **cables.** It is a part of the **electricity** supply in a house. It is also found in the cables which lead from electric appliances. If there is a fault, the earth wire leads the **electric current** safely away.
He connected the earth wire from the kettle to the electric plug.

echo *noun*
An echo is a **sound** which is reflected. When a loud, sharp sound hits a hard surface, the sound is reflected as an echo. **Radio waves** can also be reflected as echoes. **Echo-location** machines use echoes.
She heard the echo of her voice five seconds after she shouted.

echo-location *noun*
Echo-location is a way of using an **echo** to find hidden objects. Sound waves or radio waves which bounce off an object, return as echoes. These echoes help to show where the object is located. **Radar** and **sonar** are two different kinds of echo-location.
He used echo-location to find the shoal of fish.

efficiency *noun*
Efficiency is a word which describes how well a **machine** is working. Machines use up one kind of **energy** and give out another kind of energy. A machine which only wastes a small amount of energy has a high efficiency.
The efficiency of most motor cars is very low.
efficient *adjective*

effluent *noun*
An effluent is a substance. It is made up of a liquid, a gas or solid **particles** and can cause **pollution.**
The liquid effluent flows out of the factory and into the river.

effort *noun*
Effort is a kind of **force**. It is the push or pull which makes things move or change shape.
The small boy lifted the heavy load with a great amount of effort.

egg *noun*
1. An egg is a tiny cell which is found inside female animals and plants. A **fertilized** egg is a single **cell**. In an animal, a fertilized egg will grow into a new living thing called an **embryo**. In a plant, the egg will become a seed.
A human egg is about the size of a full stop.
2. An egg is a round or oval body which is laid by birds, insects and reptiles. It has a shell or thick skin around the outside for protection. Food is stored inside the egg. In a **fertilized** egg, this food surrounds the **embryo** and helps it to grow.
A female frog lays hundreds of eggs each year.

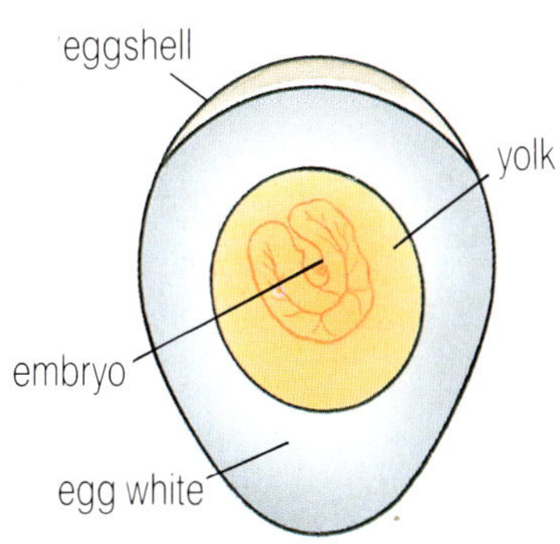

bird's egg

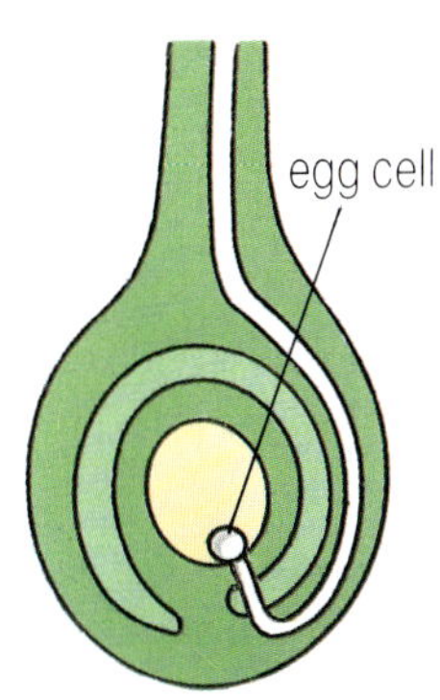

plant ovary

electric charge *noun*
Electric charge is **electricity** that is held within or released by something. All atoms contain particles which have either a **negative** or a **positive** electric charge. An electric charge which flows through a material is called an **electric current**.
The electric charge in the clouds caused a flash of lightning in the sky.

electric circuit *noun*
An electric circuit is a path along which an **electric current** flows. Circuits are usually made from copper **wires** or **cables** which link electrical **components** together.
The electric circuit joined the battery to the bulb.

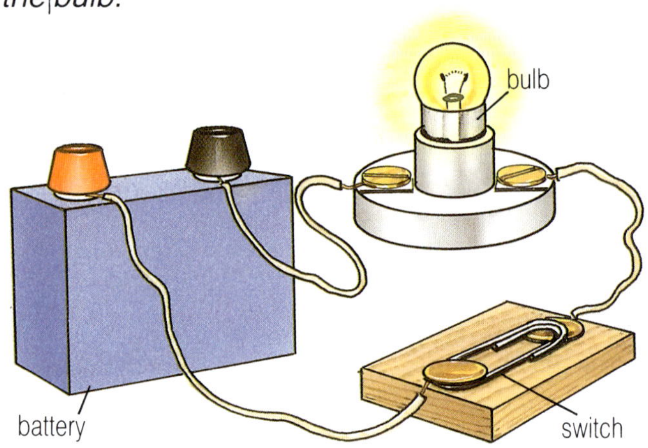

electric current *noun*
An electric current is a flow of **electricity**. It is made up of **electrons** which flow through a **conductor**. A **battery** or a **generator** makes the electric current flow.
An electric current flows through the lamp when it is switched on.

electricity *noun*
Electricity is a kind of **power** or **energy**. Lightning is electricity at work in its natural form. Electricity is also used to power radios and televisions and in electric lamps, motors and heaters. An **electric current** is electricity which flows in an **electric circuit**.
Electricity lights up the street lamps in cities and towns.

electro- *prefix*
Electro- describes anything which uses **electricity**. Electrochemistry is the study of how electricity flows through **chemicals**.
Electromagnetism is the subject which looks at electricity and magnetism.

electrode *noun*
An electrode is part of an electric **battery**. An **electric current** leaves the battery through the **positive** electrode and enters the battery through the **negative** electrode.
The two electrodes in some batteries are made from different metals.

electrolysis *noun*
Electrolysis is a word which describes how electricity can make a **chemical reaction** happen. An electric current passes through a solution or through a **molten** solid. New substances are made around the **electrodes**.
Aluminium metal is made by electrolysis.

electrolyte noun
An electrolyte is a **liquid** or a **solution** which conducts an electric current. **Batteries** contain an electrolyte. The solution used in **electroplating** is an electrolyte.
An electrolyte contains water and special chemicals.

electromagnet *noun*
An electromagnet is a special **coil** of wire. It is wound around an iron or steel rod. The rod becomes **magnetic** when an **electric current** flows through the wire.
Electric bells and electric motors contain electromagnets.

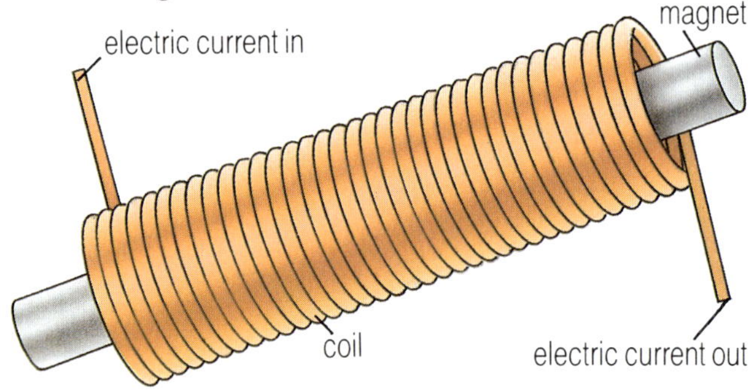

electromagnetic radiation *noun*
Electromagnetic radiation is a kind of **energy**. It is made up of electrical energy and magnetic energy. The radiation travels as electromagnetic **waves**, which move at 300,000 kilometres per second. The different kinds of wave make up the **electromagnetic spectrum**.
Electromagnetic radiation brings programmes to our radio and television sets.

electromagnetic spectrum ► page 48

electromagnetic waves ► **electromagnetic radiation**

electron *noun*
An electron is a tiny speck of **matter.** It is a kind of **particle**. Everything in the world is made up of electrons, together with **protons** and **neutrons**. Electrons have a **negative charge**.
An electron is too small to see, even with a very powerful microscope.

electron gun *noun*
An electron gun is a device which is found inside a television set or an **electron microscope**. It uses **electricity** to fire a beam of **electrons**. An electron gun helps to form the picture on the television screen.
An electron gun contains a red-hot coil of wire.

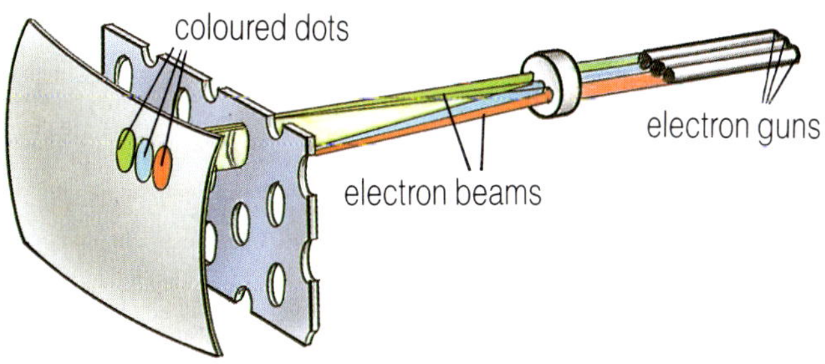

electron microscope *noun*
An electron microscope is an instrument. It is a kind of **microscope** which uses beams of **electrons** to make an object appear bigger. The electrons are fired from an **electron gun**.
An electron microscope magnified the cell 200,000 times.

electronic *adjective*
Electronic is a word which describes devices such as radios, televisions and **computers**. These contain electronic **components** which use streams of **electrons**. The electrons carry electric **signals** and information.
The doctor used an electronic scanner to look inside the patient's head.

electronics *noun*
Electronics is a **scientific** subject. It is the study of how **electrons** flow through different materials. Electronics helps scientists to invent and develop new kinds of **electronic** devices.
Electronics helps to pass all kinds of messages around the world quickly.

electroplating *noun*
Electroplating is a way of coating one **metal** with a thin layer of another metal. Each metal is dipped into **electrolyte**. The thin coat forms when an **electric current** passes between the two metals.
Electroplating coats the metal spoon with a layer of gold.

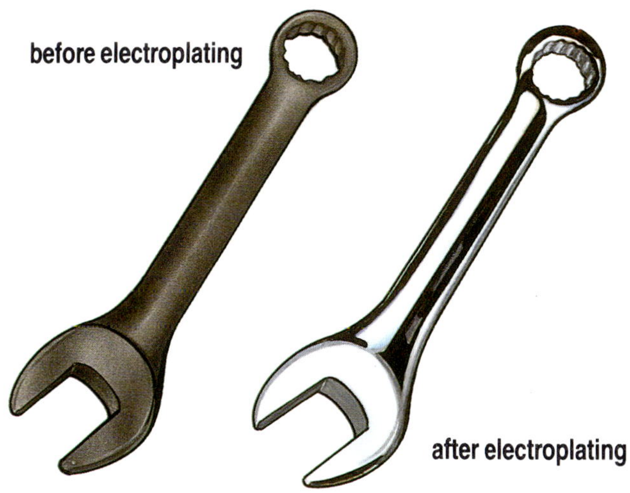

element *noun*
An element is a simple substance. It can be a **solid**, a **liquid** or a **gas**. An element contains **atoms** which are all of the same type. There are about 100 different elements.
Everything in the world is made up of elements which join together.

electromagnetic spectrum *noun*
The electromagnetic spectrum is a chart which lists all the different kinds of **electromagnetic radiation**. These different kinds of radiation are arranged in order of their **frequency** or their **wavelength.**
The electromagnetic spectrum includes X-rays, ultraviolet waves and radio waves.

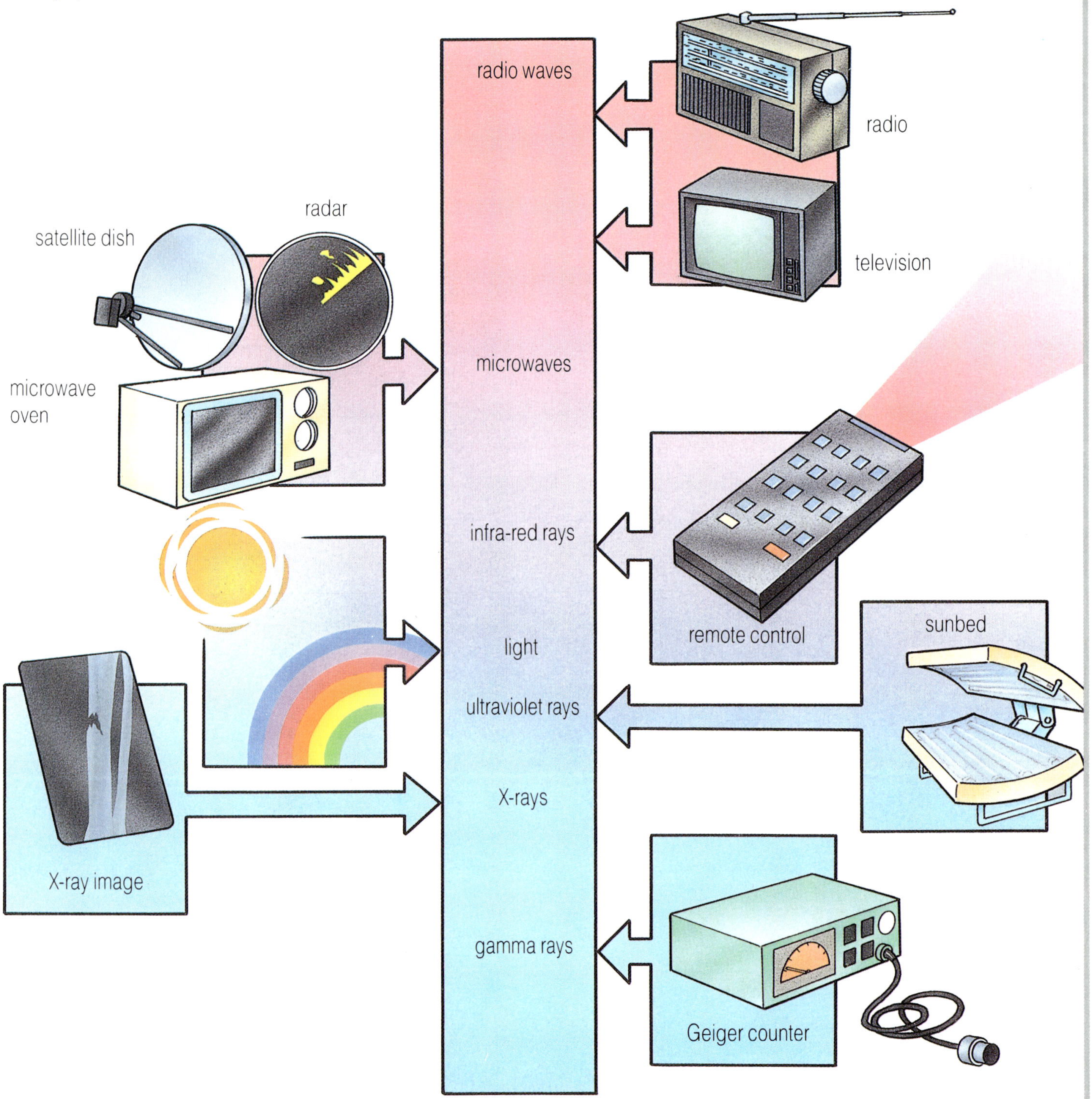

ellipse *noun*
An ellipse is a flat shape. It is the result of making a slanting cut through a **cone**. If you pull a **circular**, plastic hoop from opposite sides, you will make an ellipse.
The Moon travels around the Earth in an ellipse.
elliptical *adjective*

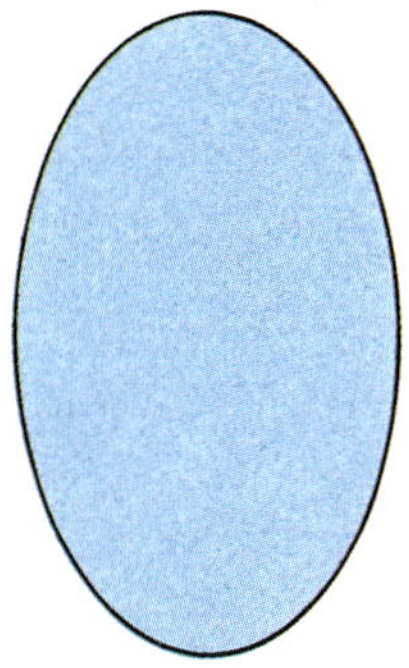

embryo *noun*
An embryo is a living thing. In animals, it is a very young baby growing inside its mother, or a young animal growing inside an **egg**. In plants, an embryo is the tiny plant inside a seed. The plant has not yet started to grow.
The chick inside a hen's egg is an embryo.

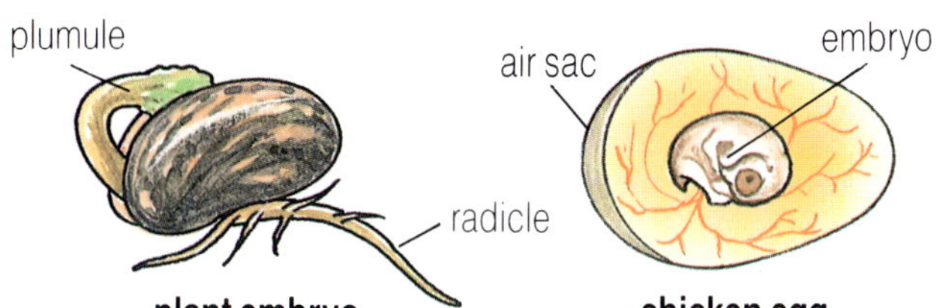

plant embryo **chicken egg**

emit *verb*
Emit is a word which describes how something, such as **light** or **sound**, streams out from a place. A hose emits a jet of water. A loudspeaker emits sound.
The street lamp emits a bright yellow light.

emulsion *noun*
An emulsion is a mixture of two **liquids** which do not usually mix. One of the liquids in the emulsion is split up into tiny droplets.
Milk is an emulsion of water and droplets of fat.

energy *noun*
Energy is needed in order to carry out **work**. Energy makes things happen. There are many different kinds of energy: **light**, **electricity**, **potential** and **kinetic** energy, **heat** and **nuclear** energy.
An electric kettle changes electrical energy into heat energy.

engine *noun*
An engine is a **machine** which uses energy from a fuel to spin a **shaft**. **Steam engines** and **internal combustion engines** are two different kinds of engine.
The engine powers the motor car.

enzyme *noun*
An enzyme is a chemical **compound**. Enzymes are found inside living things. They help **chemical reactions** to happen.
An enzyme changed the milk into cheese.

equation *noun*
An equation is a way of writing numbers in **mathematics**. Both sides of an equation say the same thing using different numbers and letters. An equation always has two sides with an equals sign (=) between them. An equation is used to help work out problems.
The equation $d = w \times 7$ tells us how many days (d) are in a certain number of weeks (w).

equilibrium *noun*
Equilibrium is a word which describes something that is balanced. A lake is in equilibrium when the amount of water flowing into it is the same as the amount of water flowing out of it.
The weight and the balance pan were in equilibrium.

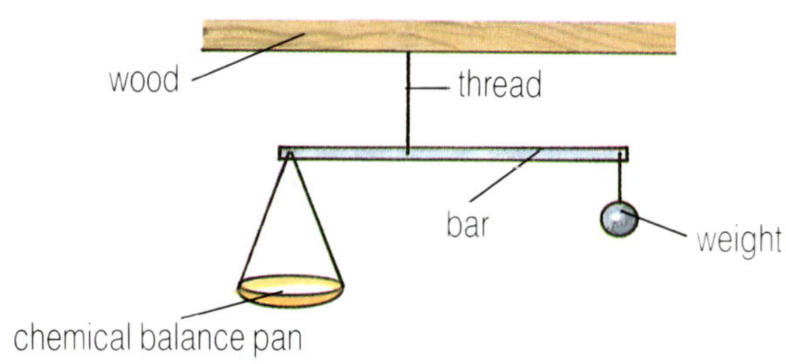

in equilibrium

ethanol *noun*
Ethanol is a colourless **liquid**. It is an **alcohol** which mixes with water. Ethanol burns easily and has a fruity smell. When yeast **ferments** sugar, ethanol is created.
Ethanol can dissolve many substances which do not dissolve in water.

ether *noun*
Ether is a colourless liquid which burns very easily. It **evaporates** very quickly. If you breathe too much ether **vapour**, you will become unconscious.
Ether will dissolve grease and oil.

evaporate *verb*
Evaporate is a word which describes how a **liquid** changes into a **gas** or **vapour**. Heat helps liquids to evaporate. Liquids evaporate most quickly when they **boil**. Water, for example, turns into steam when it boils.
The wet washing on the line became dry as the water evaporated in the hot sunshine.

evolution ► page 52

exhaust ► **exhaust gas**

exhaust gas *noun*
Exhaust gas is the mixture of waste gases which comes out through the exhaust pipe of an engine. The exhaust gas from an **internal combustion engine** includes carbon monoxide, **carbon dioxide** and water.
Steam is the exhaust gas from a steam engine.

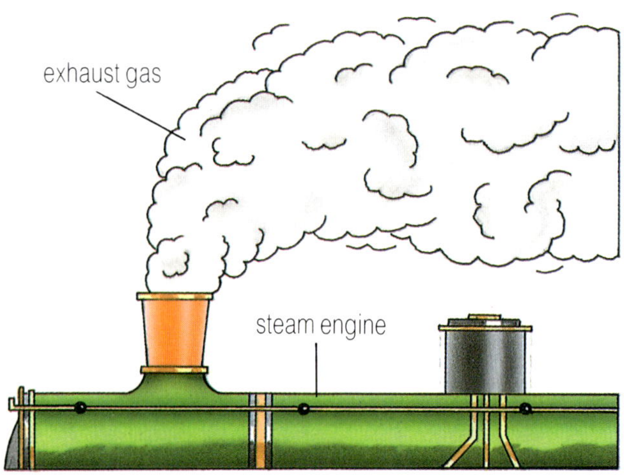

expand *verb*
Expand is a word which describes how a substance becomes bigger. Most **gases**, **liquids** and **solids** expand when they are heated. The opposite of expand is **contract**.
The air in a balloon expands when heated.

experiment *noun*
An experiment is a kind of **test**. Scientists use **apparatus** to do experiments with objects, materials and living things. Experiments help scientists to understand how things work or behave.
The experiment showed what happens to seeds when they are left to grow in the dark.

eyepiece *noun*
An eyepiece is a part of a camera, a **microscope** or a **telescope**. You place your eye against the eyepiece to see the **image**. Eyepieces contain **lenses**.
He looked through the eyepiece on the camera before taking a photograph.

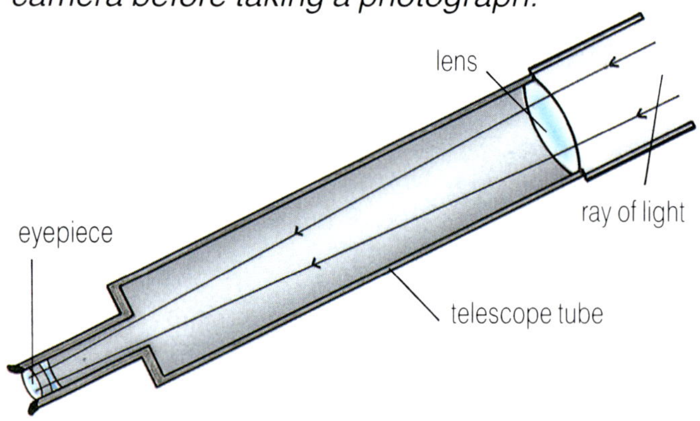

F

facsimile ► fax

factor *noun*
A factor is a whole number. It will **divide** exactly into another number. The number 3 is a factor of 9 but not a factor of 10.
The factors of 12 are 1, 2, 3, 4, 6 and 12.

Fahrenheit *noun*
Fahrenheit, or F for short, is a **unit** which measures **temperature**. Water boils at 212 degrees Fahrenheit (212°F) and it freezes at 32°F.
Scientists no longer use the Fahrenheit scale to measure temperature.

fallout *noun*
Fallout is made up of tiny, solid **particles** and **gases**. The particles spread all around the world after an atom bomb or a **nuclear reactor** has exploded. Fallout is **radioactive**.
Wind blew the fallout away from the explosion.

family *noun*
A family is a group of living things. All the living things in the same family have special characteristics. Families are part of the system of **classification** which biologists have worked out.
Tigers, lions and leopards are grouped together in the cat family.

fauna *noun*
Fauna is a word which describes all the animals found in one place.
He made a list of the fauna that live in the lake.

fax *noun*
Fax is an abbreviation for facsimile. It is a message which is sent through the telephone network. A letter or picture is placed in one machine and an exact copy of it appears in a second machine.
She faxed a diagram from New York to Paris.

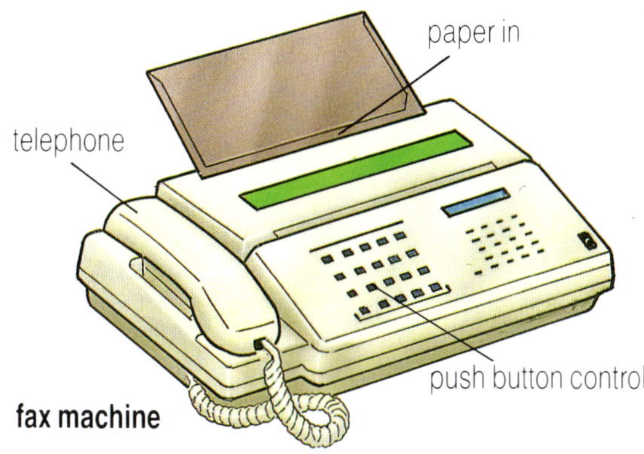

fax machine

ferment *verb*
Ferment is a word which describes a **chemical** change. Liquids, such as fruit juices, will ferment because they contain sugar. **Microbes** change the sugar into **carbon dioxide** and **ethanol**.
Grape juice ferments to make wine.

ferrous *adjective*
Ferrous is a word which describes **iron** or any **metal** which contains iron. Ferrous metals are **alloys** which contain large amounts of iron.
A magnet will pick up a piece of ferrous metal because it contains iron.

fertilization *noun*
Fertilization is a part of **reproduction**.
It usually takes place when a **cell** from a male plant or animal joins with a cell from the female plant or animal. In plants, this makes a seed. In animals, fertilization makes **eggs** or babies.
Fertilization makes the frog's eggs begin to grow into tadpoles.

evolution *noun*
Evolution is a **theory** which explains how living things may have slowly changed over millions of years. It tries to explain how plants and animals might have changed from their early forms millions of years ago to their present-day shapes and sizes.
Some scientists believe that birds evolved from reptiles which lived almost 400 million years ago.
evolve *verb*

the evolution of tusks and trunks

Modern elephants evolved from animals that lived millions of years ago. The tusks and trunks of early elephants developed in a variety of ways.

Deinotherium

Deinotherium lived in Africa about 30 million years ago. Its tusk-like front teeth were probably used for digging.

Gomphotherium

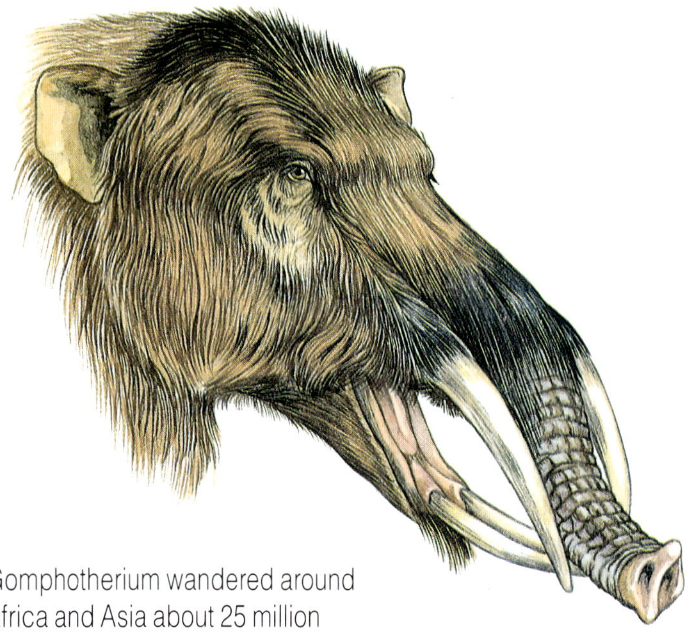

Gomphotherium wandered around Africa and Asia about 25 million years ago.

Mammoth

The tusks of some mammoths were four metres long. Mammoths became extinct about 10,000 years ago.

Primelephas

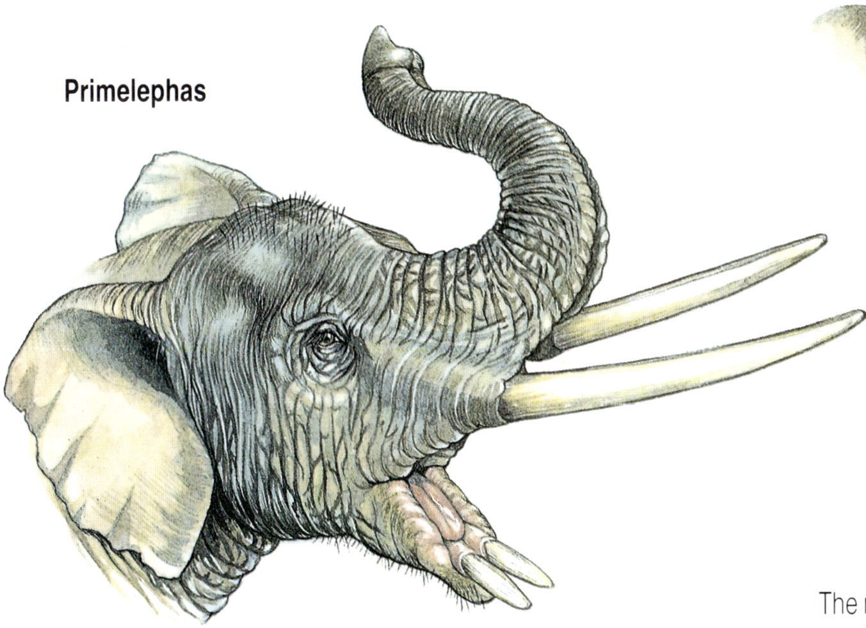

Primelephas was the most recent elephant ancestor to have four tusks.

African elephant

The modern African elephant uses its trunk like a hand. It also breathes and smells with its trunk, and uses it as a spray.

fertilizer *noun*
A fertilizer is a **substance** which is added to the soil. It helps plants to grow well. Artificial fertilizers are chemicals which contain **phosphate**, nitrogen or **potassium**.
Manure and compost are natural fertilizers.

fibre *noun*
A fibre is a long, thin length of material. Hair, wool and cotton are fibres. Nerve fibres carry messages around our bodies.
The machine spins the fibres together to make the thread.

fibre optics *noun*
Fibre optics is a special way of sending messages. Fibre optic **cables** are long strands of special glass. They carry messages which are made up from light. Fibre optics can carry more messages than ordinary cables.
Fibre optics carry telephone messages from one city to another.

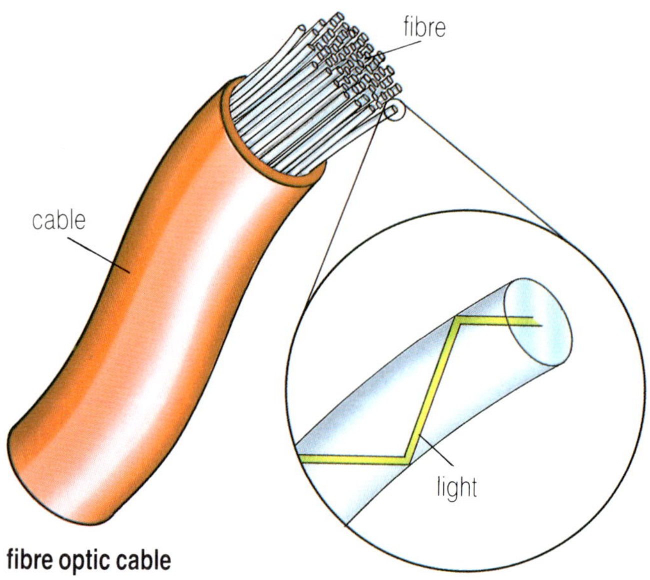

fibre optic cable

fibreglass *noun*
Fibreglass is a strong and very lightweight **solid**. It is made by mixing **fibres** of glass with a sticky, liquid **resin**. The resin sets and hardens.
Some sailing boats are made from fibreglass.

field of vision *noun*
Field of vision is a term which describes how far an animal can see around itself. Rabbits have a larger field of vision than humans. Our eyes point forwards but rabbits have eyes on the sides of their head.
Mice can spot danger behind them because they have a large field of vision.

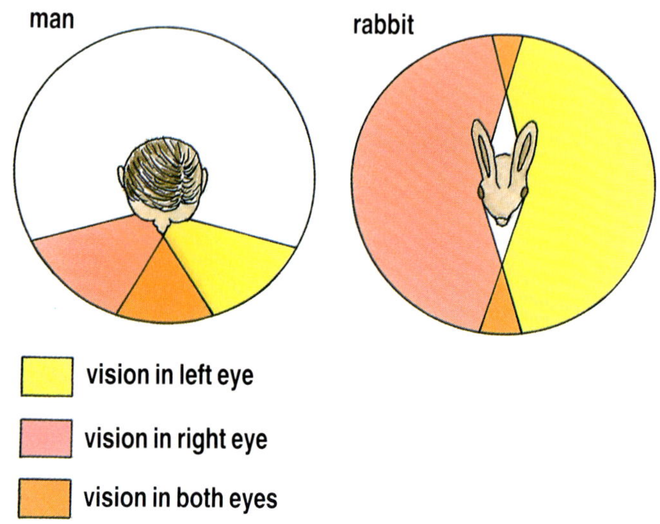

filament *noun*
1. A filament is another name for a **fibre**.
2. A filament is a thin **wire** which is found inside an electric light bulb. It is usually made from a **tungsten**. An **electric current** passes through the filament. This makes it glow white-hot and give off light.
If the filament breaks, the light will go out.

electric light bulb

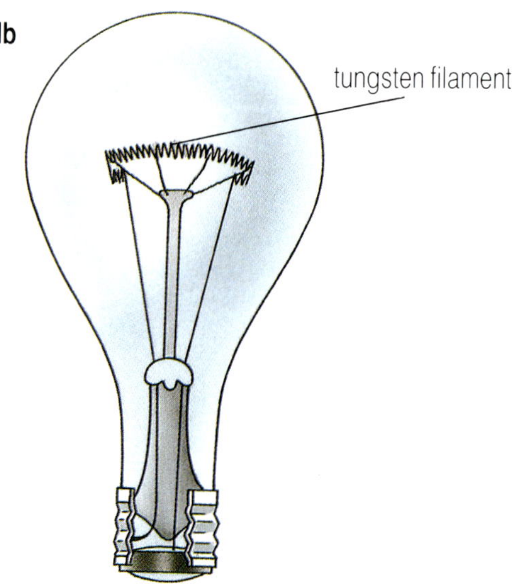

file *noun*
1. A file is a tool. It is a flat bar of steel with a handle. The bar is covered with tiny ridges or teeth. A file helps to shape or smooth pieces of wood or metal.
She scraped the file along the rough edge of the metal bar.
2. A file is a kind of store inside a **computer**. Each file contains a collection of **data** or a **program**. Files are stored on **floppy disks** or in the computer's **memory**.
The computer has hundreds of files in its memory.

filings *noun*
Filings are very small pieces of **metal**. They are about the size of grains of sand. Filings are made when a **file** scrapes along a piece of metal.
He sprinkled the iron filings on to the paper.

film *noun*
1. A film is a thin layer of a **solid** or a **liquid**. Oil floats on water as a thin film. A mirror is glass which is usually coated with a film of **aluminium**.
The meat is wrapped in plastic film.
2. A film is a flat strip of **plastic**. It is coated in **chemicals** which are changed by light. Cameras use films to record pictures.
She can take 24 pictures on the film in her camera.

filter *noun*
1. A filter is a kind of **apparatus** which helps to separate a mixture. The filter is made from a solid material which is full of tiny holes. The holes allow a liquid but not a solid to pass through.
She poured the dirty water through the filter to remove the grit.
2. A filter is a **disc** of coloured glass or plastic. It is placed over the **lens** of a camera. Filters remove different colours from **light**.
Grass is black if you look at it through a red filter.
filter *verb*

filter paper *noun*
A filter paper is a paper **disc**. The paper forms a **filter** when it is folded into a cone shape and placed in a **funnel**. The filter paper traps solid particles as a liquid soaks through it.
He poured the mixture on to the filter paper.

fission *noun*
Fission is a word which describes how something breaks into two or more parts. Fission in a living **cell** makes two new cells. Another kind of fission is **nuclear fission**.
Fission takes place when an animal cell divides into two.

flammable *adjective*
Flammable is a word which describes substances that can **burn**. A flammable substance can be a solid, a liquid or a gas.
Coal, petrol and natural gas are flammable substances.

flask *noun*
A flask is a kind of **apparatus**. It is a container which holds liquids. Flasks usually have a flat bottom, rounded sides and a long neck. A **scale** is usually marked on the side to measure the **volume** of the liquid.
He filled the flask with a clear, blue liquid.

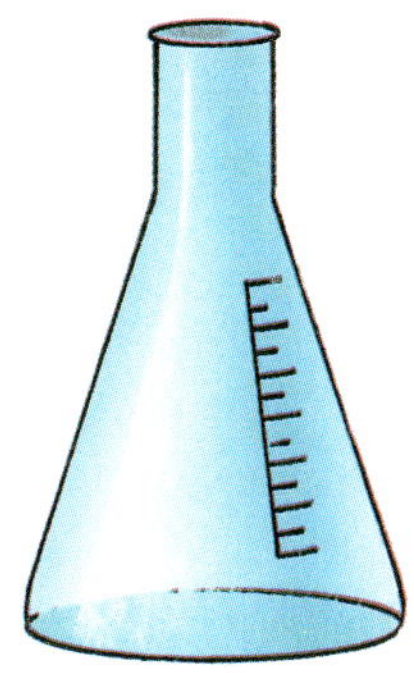

flexible *adjective*
Flexible is a word which describes a material which can bend without breaking. Paper and **polythene** are flexible.
Some raincoats are made of flexible plastic.

floppy disk *noun*
A floppy disk is a part of a **computer**. It is a **flexible**, plastic disc which is coated in **magnetic** particles. A floppy disk is surrounded by a stiff, plastic envelope. Floppy disks store **data** and **programs**.
She stored all the words of her story on to the floppy disk.

flora *noun*
Flora is a word which describes all the plants found in one place.
He is making a list of the flora that live in the forest.

flow chart ► page 57

fluid *noun*
A fluid is a **substance** which flows easily. All liquids and gases are fluids. Some powders become fluids when air blows through them.
The fluid escaped through the hole in the container.

fluoridation *noun*
Fluoridation is a word which describes how tiny amounts of **fluoride** are added to drinking water. Fluoridation helps to prevent tooth **decay.**
Fluoridation of the drinking water helps children's teeth to grow strong.

fluoride *noun*
Fluoride is a chemical **compound.** Different kinds of fluoride are added to toothpaste and drinking water. This helps to prevent tooth **decay**.
Most kinds of toothpaste now contain fluoride.

flywheel *noun*
A flywheel is a part of a **machine**. It is a heavy, metal **disc** which the machine spins round. The flywheel stores up **energy** which can be used later.
The spinning flywheel moves the toy motor car.

focus *verb*
Focus is a word which describes how to make a clear picture, or **image**. A control knob on cameras, telescopes, microscopes and video recorders helps to focus the picture.
She focused the camera to get a clearer picture of the insects.

food chain ► page 58

force *noun*
A force is a push or a pull. Forces do **work** and make things move or change their shape. One force can also cancel out another force by pushing against it. Different kinds of **energy** help to make forces.
The force of the wind tore the roof off the house.

forensic science *noun*
Forensic science is a **scientific** subject. A forensic scientist carries out **tests**, and searches for clues to help the police and lawyers. These clues help to show why an accident happened or which person committed a crime.
Forensic science helped the police to find out why the building burned down.

formula *noun*
1. A formula is a way of solving problems using numbers and letters. It is an **equation** that uses algebra and shows how to find an unknown answer from things that are known.
In the formula $A = L \times W$, A is the area, L is the length and W is the width.
2. A formula is a way of writing about a substance. It shows what kinds of **atom** are in a chemical **compound**. The formula for water is H_2O. This means that one **molecule** of water contains two atoms of hydrogen (H) and one atom of oxygen (O).
He used letters and numbers to write the formula of the chemical he had made.

flow chart *noun*
A flow chart is a kind of drawing or diagram. It is a way of showing a set of instructions that must be carried out in the correct order.
He followed the flow chart to help him to write a new computer program.

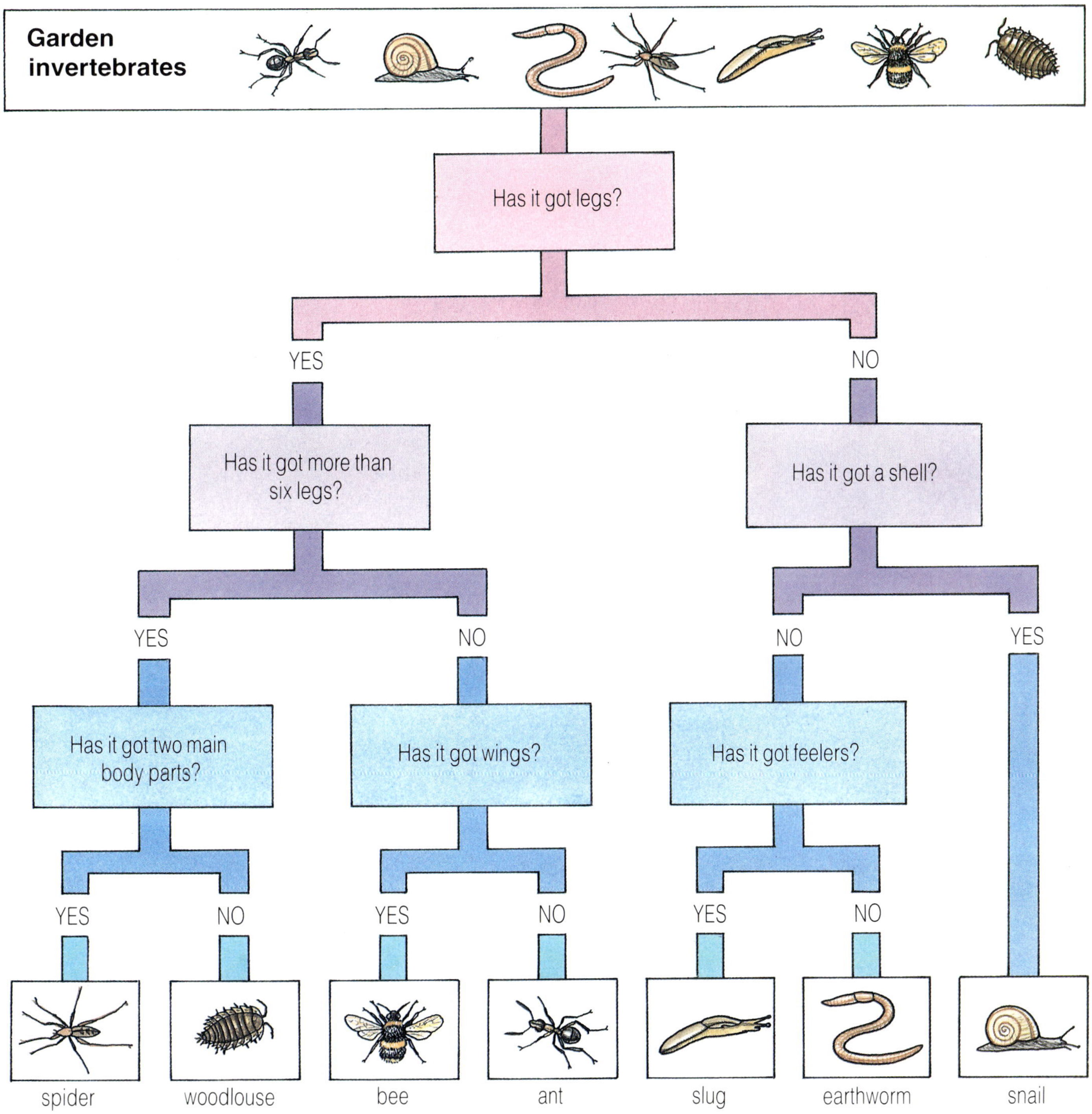

food chain *noun*
A food chain is a term which describes a group of living things that are dependent on each other. All the living things in a food chain depend on each other for food.
In the food chain, sheep eat the grass and then humans eat the sheep.

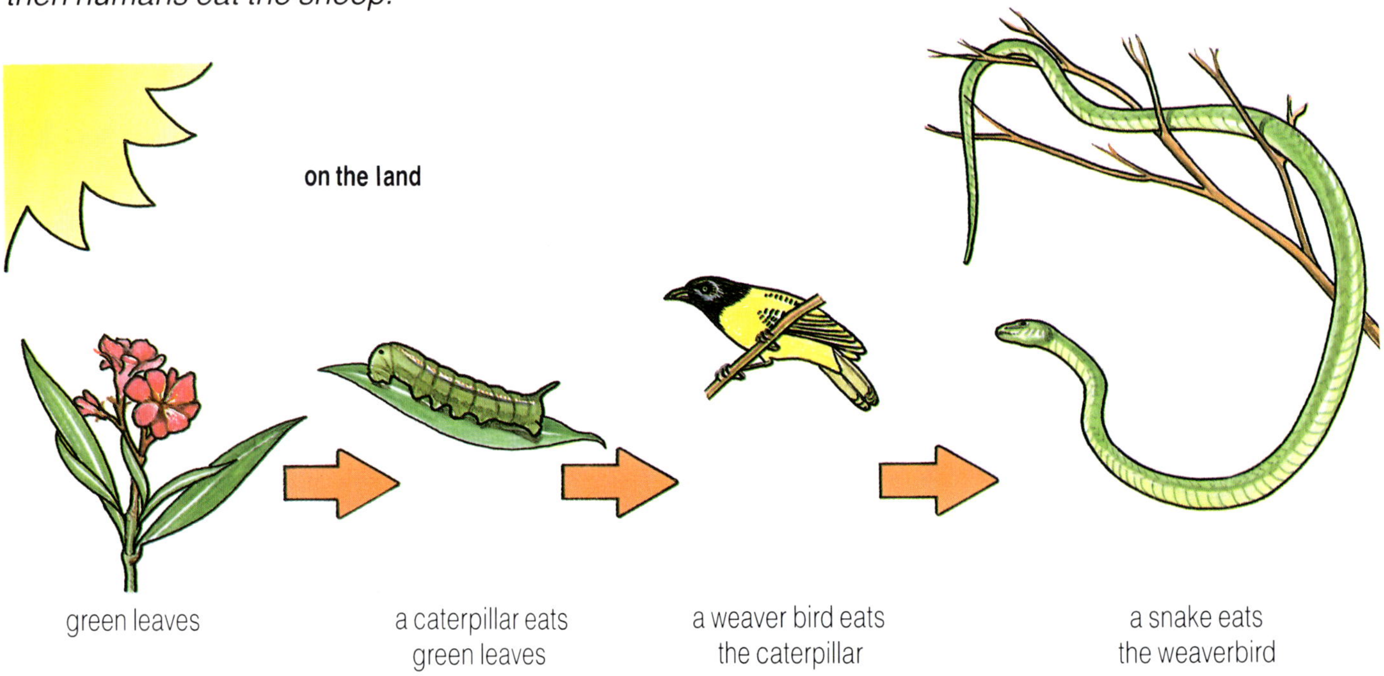

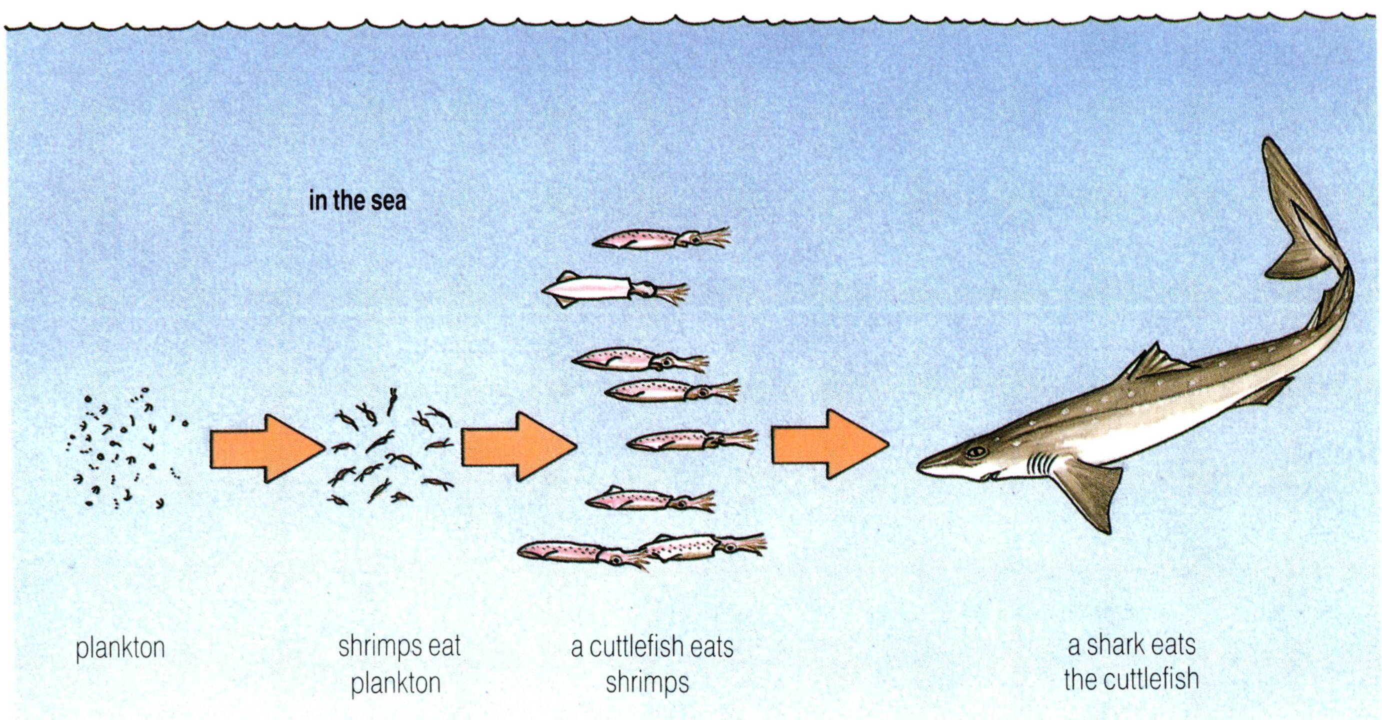

fossil fuel *noun*
A fossil fuel is a kind of solid, liquid or gas which is found under the ground. Fossil fuels were formed millions of years ago from buried plants and tiny animals. **Coal**, **petroleum** and **natural gas** are fossil fuels.
We burn fossil fuels in our power stations to make heat.

foundations *noun*
Foundations are a part of a building. The building sits on top of flat foundations which rest on solid ground. On sandy ground, raft foundations spread the **load** of the building. Pile foundations go deep into soft ground.
The builders made the foundations out of concrete.

flat foundations

raft foundations

pile foundations

four-stroke engine *noun*
A four-stroke engine is a kind of **internal combustion engine**. Each of the four strokes is a movement of a **piston** inside the engine. The pistons move up or down as fuel and air are sucked in (1), **compressed** (2), burned (3) and pushed out (4). These movements are repeated in a cycle to make **power**.
A four-stroke engine powers my motor car.

fraction *noun*
1. A fraction is a part of a whole thing. If you **divide** something into three equal parts, each part is called one-third. This fraction is written as $\frac{1}{3}$. Two of the parts together make up the fraction two-thirds, which is written as $\frac{2}{3}$.
The fraction $\frac{1}{4}$ is the same as one quarter.
2. A fraction is a **liquid**. Fractions separate from a liquid mixture during **fractional distillation**. Each fraction boils at a different temperature.
At the oil refinery, gasoline formed one of the fractions.

fractional distillation *noun*
Fractional distillation is a term which describes how a mixture of **liquids** is separated. The mixture boils and the **vapour** rises up inside a **fractionating column**. The vapour forms into different liquids at different levels in the column.
Fractional distillation helps to make petrol and kerosene.

fractionating column *noun*
A fractionating column is a tall tower. It is hot at the bottom and cooler at the top. There are trays at different levels in the column. Different liquids **condense** on these trays during **fractional distillation**.
A fractionating column in an oil refinery can be 30 metres high.

freeze *verb*
Freeze is a word which describes how a **liquid** changes into a **solid**. The liquid is cooled to a lower **temperature** and freezes into a solid. The **particles** in a liquid move about freely. When the liquid freezes, the particles stick firmly together.
When liquid water freezes, it makes solid ice.

freezing point *noun*
Freezing point is a **temperature**. A pure liquid **freezes** when it cools to its freezing point.
The freezing point of water is 0° Celsius.

frequency *noun*
Frequency is a word which describes how often something happens. The frequency of sea tides is usually twice every day. The frequency of an **alternating current** is measured in **hertz**.
The frequency of an adult's heartbeat is about 72 times a minute.

friction *noun*
Friction is a word which describes how two or more objects rub against each other. This rubbing will slow down the objects if they are moving. Friction between moving parts in **machines** makes the parts hot and wastes **energy**. A **lubricant**, such as oil, reduces the amount of friction between moving parts.
He skated easily because the friction between the ice and his skates was low.

fuel *noun*
A fuel is a substance which gives out **heat** when it is burned. **Fossil fuels**, such as petrol or fuel oil, burn in **engines** or **furnaces**. They give out energy which can be used. Fuels, such as **uranium**, help to generate electricity in **nuclear power stations.**
He lit the fuel and felt the heat with his hands.

fuel oil *noun*
Fuel oil is an oily **liquid**. It is made from **oil**. Fuel oil is used to power ships and is burned inside large **furnaces**.
The ship's engine burns 1,000 litres of fuel oil every hour.

fulcrum *noun*
A fulcrum is a part of a **lever**. It supports the lever, which moves or **pivots** around it.
The fulcrum is in the middle of the see-saw.

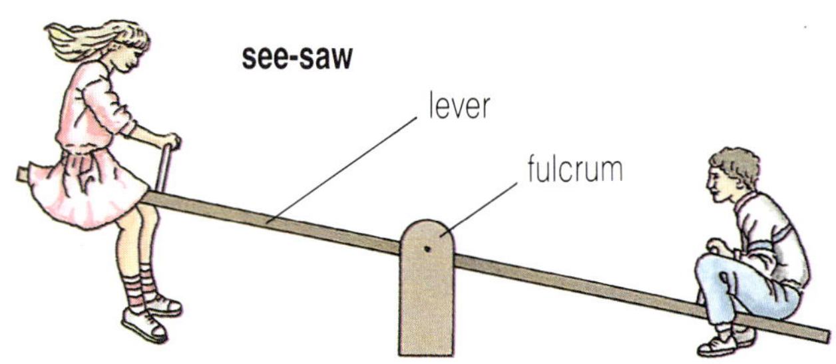

fungus (plural **fungi**) *noun*
A fungus is a kind of living thing. It is a plant which cannot make its own food. Fungi usually take in their food from dead plants. Mushrooms and toadstools are kinds of fungus.
The fungus is growing on the side of the dead tree.

funnel *noun*
A funnel is a pipe which is narrow at one end and wider at the other end. **Steam** and smoke escape from the funnel on a ship or a **steam engine**. Funnels are also used when pouring liquids into small openings.
She pours the petrol into the funnel on top of the petrol can.

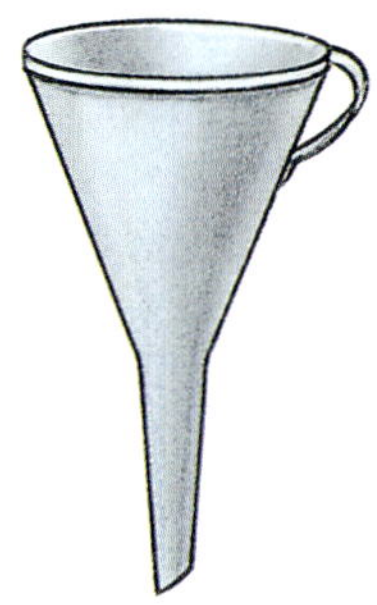

furnace *noun*
A furnace is a **machine** which heats things. It becomes hot by burning a **fuel**, such as gas, oil or coal, or by using **electricity**. The heat can melt metals, boil water or warm the air.
The heat inside the furnace makes it glow red-hot.

fuse *noun*
A fuse is a thin piece of wire. It is a part of an **electric circuit**. If there is too much current, the fuse becomes hot and melts. This safely switches off the electricity.
When the fuse breaks, all the lights go out.

fuse *verb*
Fuse is a word which means the same as **melt**. Ordinary salt **crystals** fuse when they are heated strongly. The salt becomes **molten** or liquid.
He fused the two metals together to make an alloy.

fusion ► **nuclear fusion**

G

galvanize *verb*
Galvanize is a word which describes a way of protecting **steel** and **iron**. Objects made from these metals are dipped into a tank of **molten** zinc. This gives them a coat of zinc which stops rusting.
They galvanized the steel nails to stop them rusting.

gamma ray *noun*
A gamma ray is a kind of **electromagnetic radiation**. Gamma rays are given off by atoms during **nuclear fission**. They can travel very large distances through the air.
If a gamma ray passes through one centimetre of lead, it loses half its strength.

gas *noun*
A gas is a kind of **substance**. All gases are usually kept in containers. A gas spreads out to fill the whole of its container. It is easy to **compress** a gas. **Oxygen** and **carbon dioxide** are two different kinds of gas.
Bubbles of gas float up through the water.
gaseous *adjective*

gas turbine *noun*
A gas turbine is a **machine**. It has a fan which sucks in and **compresses** air. A spray of liquid **fuel** burns in this air. Hot gases from the burning fuel rush through a **turbine**. The turbine blades spin a **shaft** which can then do **work**.
Two gas turbine engines power the jet aeroplane.

gasohol *noun*
Gasohol is a liquid **fuel**. It is a mixture of petrol and **alcohol**. The alcohol is made by **fermenting** sugar cane or grain.
In Brazil, some motor cars use gasohol as a fuel.

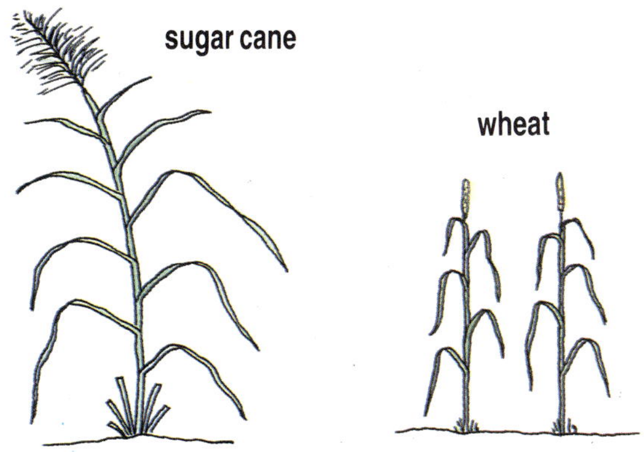

gasoline *noun*
Gasoline is a liquid which is made from **petroleum**. It is made by **fractional distillation** and **cracking**. Gasoline is used as a fuel in some kinds of **internal combustion engine**. Gasoline is another name for petrol.
She poured the gasoline into the fuel tank in the motor car.

gate *noun*
A gate is a part of a **computer**. It is a kind of switch which controls where the **electric currents** flow. This control makes the computer program work properly. **Integrated circuits** contain thousands of gates in a tiny space.
The gate allows the electric current to pass through.

gauge *noun*
A gauge is an instrument used for **measuring**. It has a dial or a **scale** which is marked with numbers. Different gauges can measure many things, such as **pressure**, length or thickness. Some gauges measure the amount of a substance in a container.
The rain gauge told us how much rain had fallen during the past week.

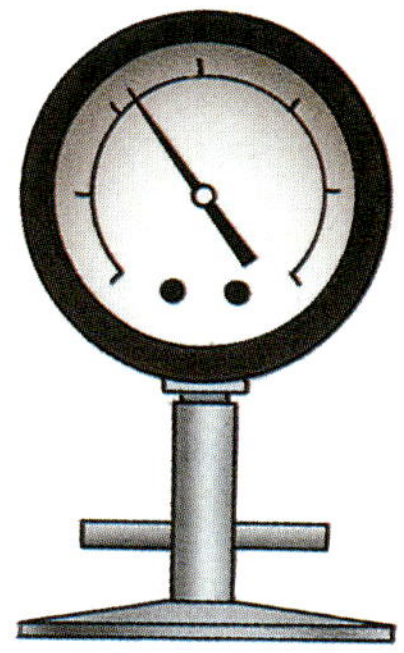
pressure gauge

gear *noun*
A gear is a kind of wheel. It has **cogs** around its outside edge. Gears fit together so that one gear turns another gear. Inside **machines**, gears of different sizes turn together at different speeds.
Gears help motor cars to travel at different speeds.

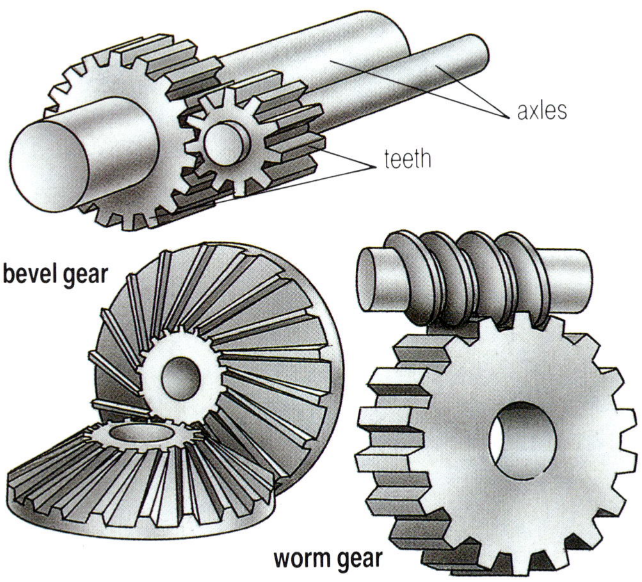

gearbox *noun*
A gearbox is a part of a **machine**. Inside a gearbox, a **shaft** spins a **gear** which fits with other gears. These gears can spin a second shaft at different speeds. The gearbox of a motor car is fitted between the engine and the wheels.
The gearbox contained six gear wheels.

Geiger counter *noun*
A Geiger counter is a **device** which measures **radiation**. It measures the strength of **alpha particles**, **beta particles** or **gamma rays**.
She held the Geiger counter near to the soil to measure the radiation.

gene *noun*
A gene is a part of all living things. Genes are found in the **nucleus** of every cell. **Fertilization** mixes male and female genes.
The genes inside our bodies control what we look like and how we grow.

generator ► page 64

genus *noun*
A genus is a group of living things. All the living things in the same genus have special characteristics. Each genus is part of the system of **classification** which biologists have worked out.
All these frogs are grouped together in the same genus.

geology *noun*
Geology is a **scientific** subject. It is the study of the rocks which make up the Earth, the other planets and the moons. A geologist is a person who studies geology.
Geology explains how the world may have been formed 4,500 million years ago.
geological adjective

geometry *noun*
Geometry is a part of **mathematics**. It is the study of shapes, such as cones, cubes, ellipses, graphs, hexagons, spheres and triangles. Geometry helps to solve problems in many different **scientific** subjects.
Geometry helped the engineer to design the strongest shape for the bridge.

glass *noun*
Glass is a hard **solid**. It is made by melting sand and **fusing** it with other chemicals. Pure glass is **transparent.** Many pieces of chemical apparatus are made of glass.
Beakers are made when hot, liquid glass is forced into a mould.

glass fibre *noun*
Glass fibre is a material which consists of fine threads of **glass**. These threads are very **flexible** and are woven into cloth. This can make fireproof clothing. Glass fibre also helps to make **fibreglass.**
Cloth which is made from glass fibre is very light and strong.

glucose *noun*
Glucose is a white, powdery **solid**. It is a kind of sugar. Animals digest some of their food into glucose. The glucose is used in **cells** to make **energy**.
Fruit juice contains large amounts of glucose.

glycerine *noun*
Glycerine is a colourless **liquid**. It is sweet and sticky and **dissolves** in water. It is found in all living things, usually as a part of fats and oils.
The hand lotion contained glycerine and water.

gold *noun*
Gold is a yellow **metal**. It is soft and **malleable** and very rare. Air, water and most **acids** and **alkalis** do not **corrode** gold. Jewellery, ornaments and electronic devices are made from gold.
He hammered the gold into a thin, flat sheet.

gradient *noun*
Gradient is a word which describes the steepness of a line on a **graph**. If the gradient is large, the slope of the line will be steep.
The gradient of the line on this graph is 2.

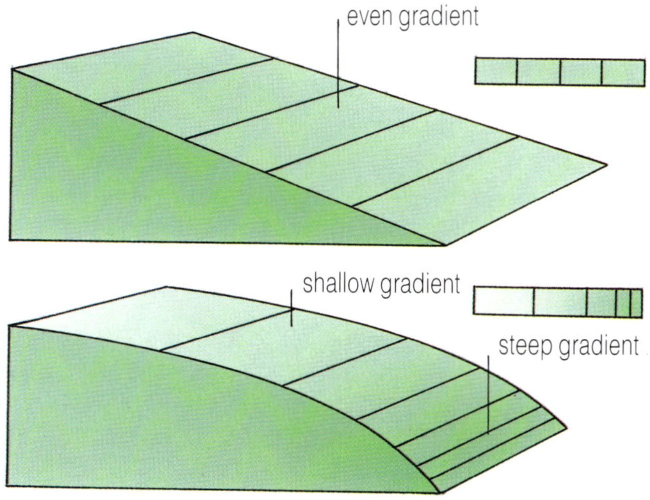

gram *noun*
A gram is a **unit** of measurement. It is used to measure **mass**. There are 1,000 grams in a **kilogram**. The abbreviation for gram is g.
The mass of the book was 250 grams.

graph *noun*
A graph is a kind of picture which makes it easy to understand two sets of numbers. Each number in one set is paired with a number in the other set. The numbers of one set are written on the vertical **axis**. The numbers of the second set are written on the horizontal axis.
The graph shows how the amount of water in the lake changes during the year.

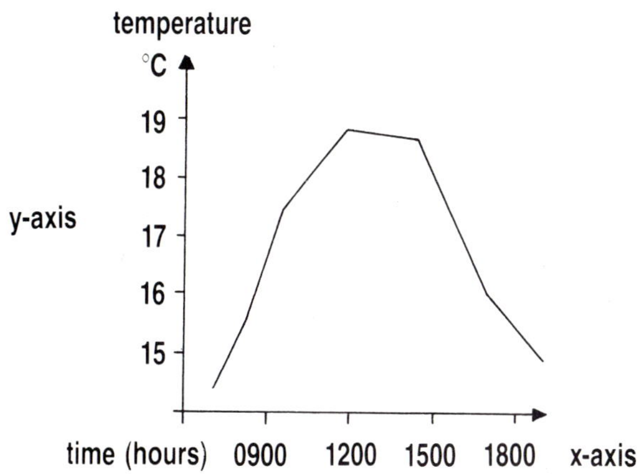

generator *noun*
A generator is a kind of **machine** for making electric power. It has a **shaft** which is turned by an engine or a **turbine**. When the shaft turns, an electric current flows in wires which are connected to the generator. **Alternators** and **dynamos** are two kinds of generator.
The electricity in our homes comes from a generator at the power station.
generate *verb*

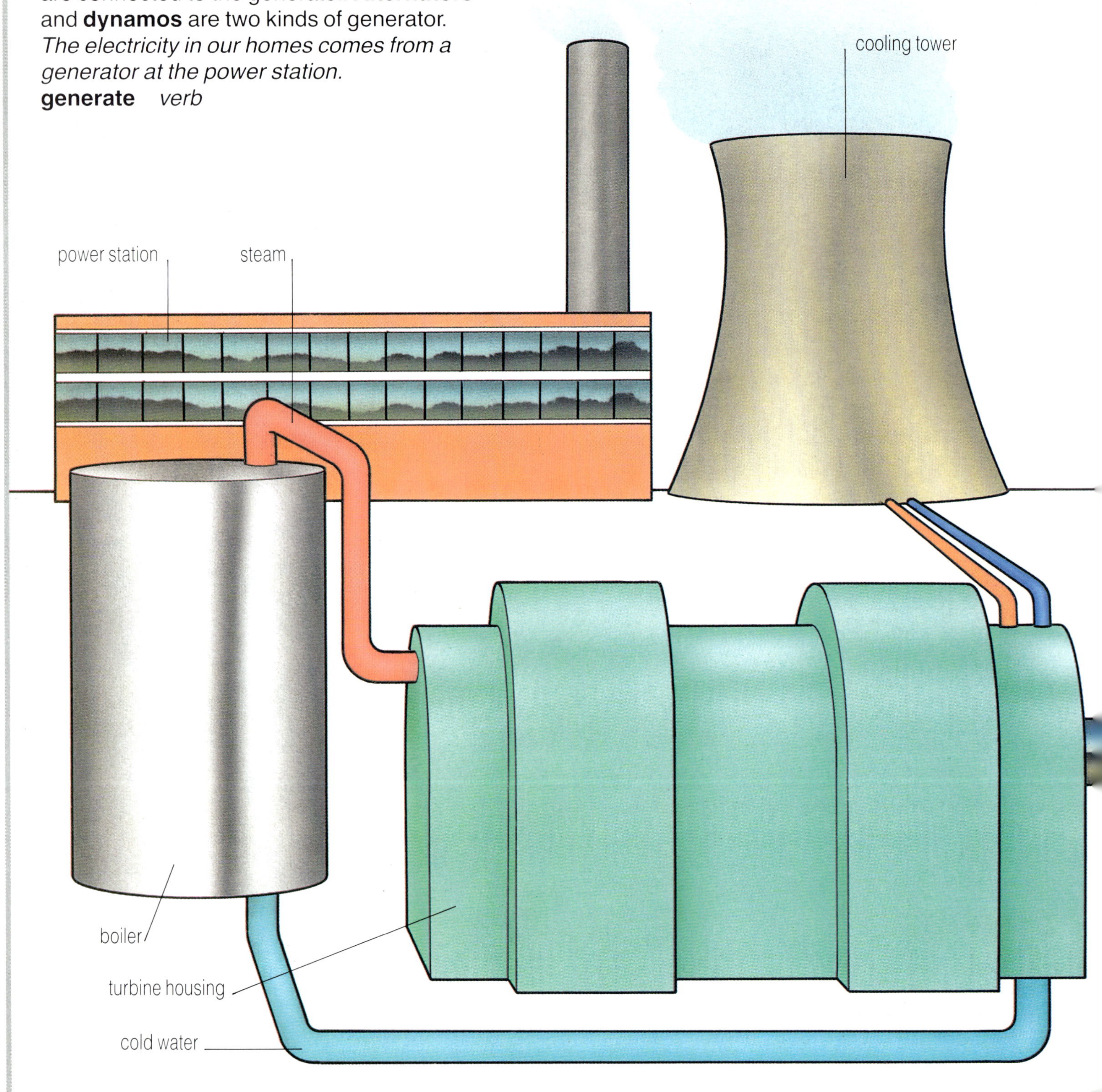

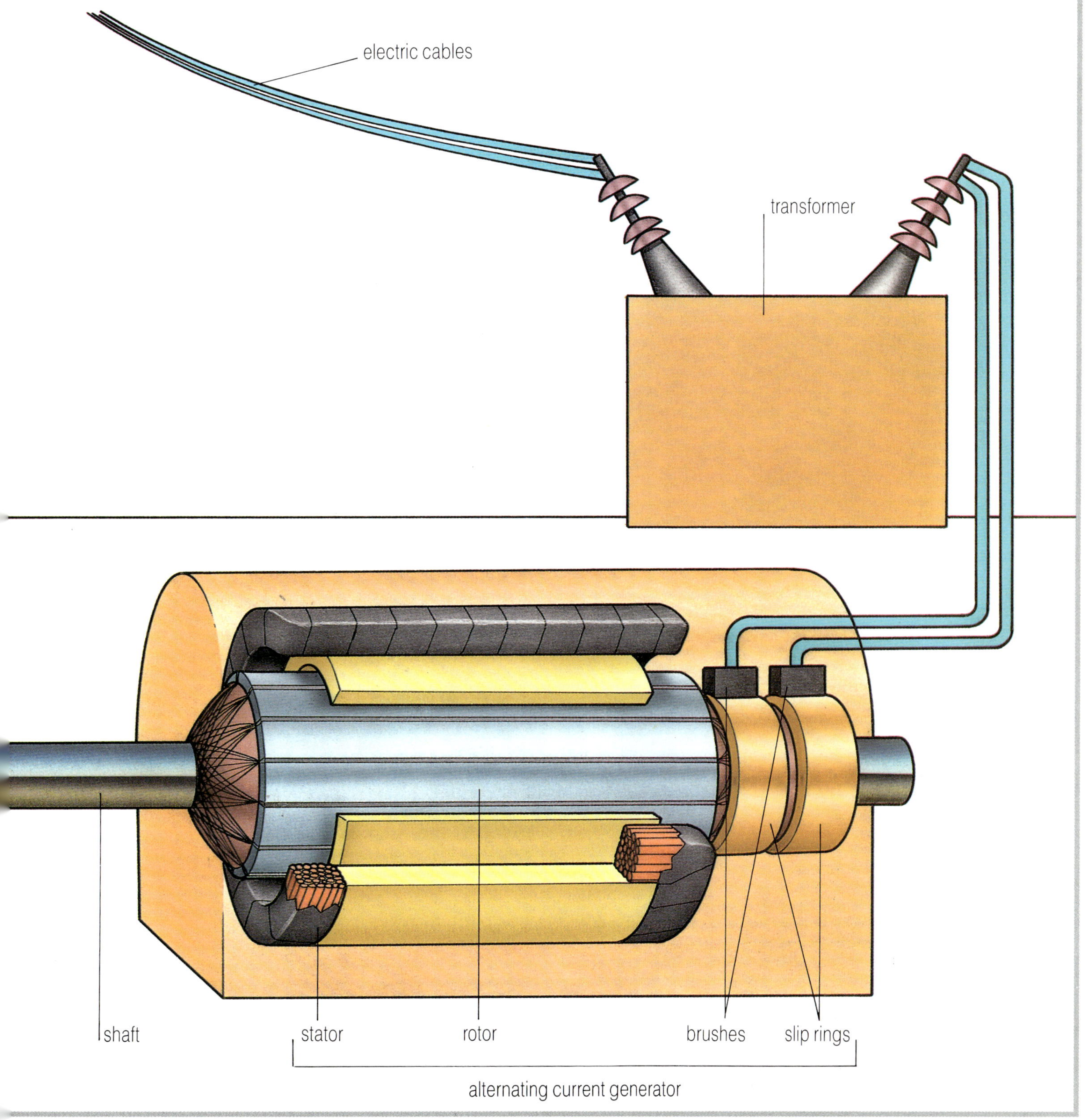
electric cables
transformer
shaft
stator
rotor
brushes
slip rings
alternating current generator

graphite *noun*
Graphite is a grey **solid**. It is a kind of **carbon** which is soft and slippery. It is used to make pencil leads and the **brushes** inside electric **motors** and generators.
She drew on the paper with the piece of graphite.

gravity *noun*
Gravity is a **force** which pulls objects towards each other. The gravity of the Earth pulls downwards on the **mass** of an object. This gives the object **weight**. There is no gravity in outer space, so objects in space have no weight.
The gravity of the Earth is six times stronger than the gravity of the Moon.

ground wire ► earth wire

gyrocompass *noun*
A gyrocompass is a kind of **compass**. It contains a heavy, metal **disc** or wheel which spins freely. The axis of the disc always points steadily in the same direction. Gyrocompasses contain **gyroscopes** and are found in ships and aeroplanes.
The gyrocompass helped the pilot to fly in the right direction.

gyroscope *noun*
A gyroscope is a heavy, spinning wheel. It has a large amount of **inertia**. This means that a gyroscope is difficult to tilt while it is spinning. **Gyrocompasses** contain gyroscopes.
He balanced the spinning gyroscope on the tip of his finger.

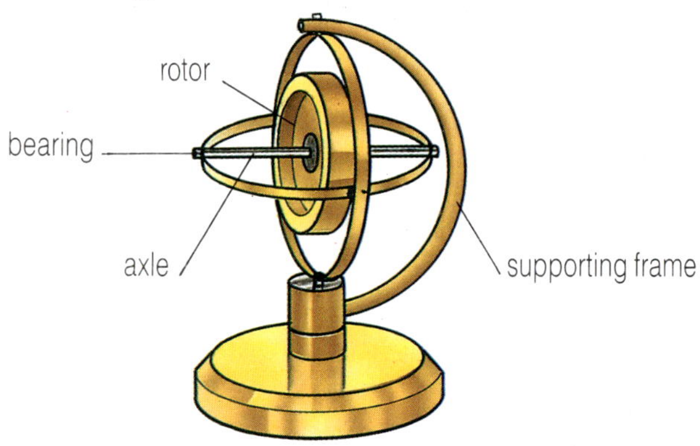

H

habitat *noun*
A habitat is a place where a particular kind of living thing is found. When describing a habitat, we talk about the non-living things that make up each habitat. Streams, rivers and lakes are three kinds of freshwater habitat.
Animals choose habitats where there is plenty of food for them to eat.

half-life *noun*
Half-life is an amount of time. It is the time taken for half the **atoms** in a **radioactive** substance to **decay**.
The half-life of uranium is 700 million years.

halogen lamp *noun*
A halogen lamp is a kind of electric light bulb. It gives out more light than an ordinary bulb. This is because it contains **iodine**, which allows the **filament** inside the bulb to be hotter and brighter.
The halogen lamp lit up the whole garden.

hard copy *noun*
Hard copy is information which is printed on to paper. The information usually comes from a **computer** or from a **fax** machine.
The printer made a hard copy of each page of the newsletter.

hard disk *noun*
A hard disk stores information inside some kinds of **computer**. Its surface contains **magnetic** material. Unlike a **floppy disk**, a hard disk cannot be removed from its computer.
The hard disk spins at high speed inside the computer.

hard water *noun*
Hard water is a word which describes some kinds of water. Chemical substances have **dissolved** in hard water. They are **salts** which contain **calcium** or **magnesium**. Soap does not lather easily in hard water and forms a **scum**.
The calcium in hard water helps children to grow healthy teeth.

hardware *noun*
Hardware is a word which describes all the **electronic** and **mechanical** parts of a computer. These parts include the **disk drives**, the **keyboard**, the **electronic** circuits and the **visual display unit.** A computer system is made up of both hardware and **software**.
He unpacked the computer hardware from the box and connected it together.

heat ► heat energy

heat energy *noun*
Heat energy makes cold things warmer. It makes the **particles** in **matter** move about more quickly. Combustion, nuclear fission and nuclear fusion all release heat energy. Heat energy is measured in **joules**.
He warmed his hands with the heat energy from the fire.

hectare *noun*
A hectare is a **unit** of measurement. It measures **area**. One hectare is the area of a square with sides 100 metres long. The abbreviation for hectare is ha.
The farm had 500 hectares of fields.

helium *noun*
Helium is a colourless **gas**. It is a chemical **element** which does not burn. Helium has a very low **density**.
The balloon was filled with helium to make it rise up in the air.

hertz *noun*
A hertz is a **unit** of measurement. It measures the **frequency** of **vibrations**, such as sound, and of **waves**, such as radio. A frequency of 500 hertz means 500 complete vibrations in each second. The abbreviation for hertz is Hz.
The frequency of the sound was 10,000 hertz.

hexagon *noun*
A hexagon is a flat shape which has six sides.
Snowflakes are shaped like hexagons.
hexagonal *adjective*

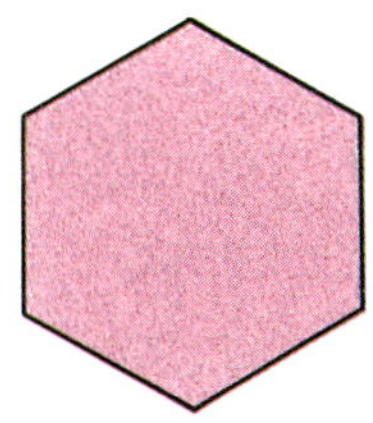

hi-fi *noun*
Hi-fi is the abbreviation for high fidelity. This term means that when you listen to recorded **sounds** from a loudspeaker or headphones, you hear sounds which are exactly like the original.
When you listen to modern hi-fi, it is just like being at a live concert.

hologram *noun*
A hologram is a kind of photograph. If you shine **laser** light at a hologram, it makes a special picture appear. The picture seems to be solid so that you can walk around it.
A hologram makes a picture even when it is cut into pieces.

hydro-electric power *noun*
Hydro-electric power is **electricity** which is generated by flowing water. Inside a hydro-electric power station, the water spins a **turbine** which drives an electric **generator.**
Hydro-electric power is generated in areas where fast rivers flow down from mountains.

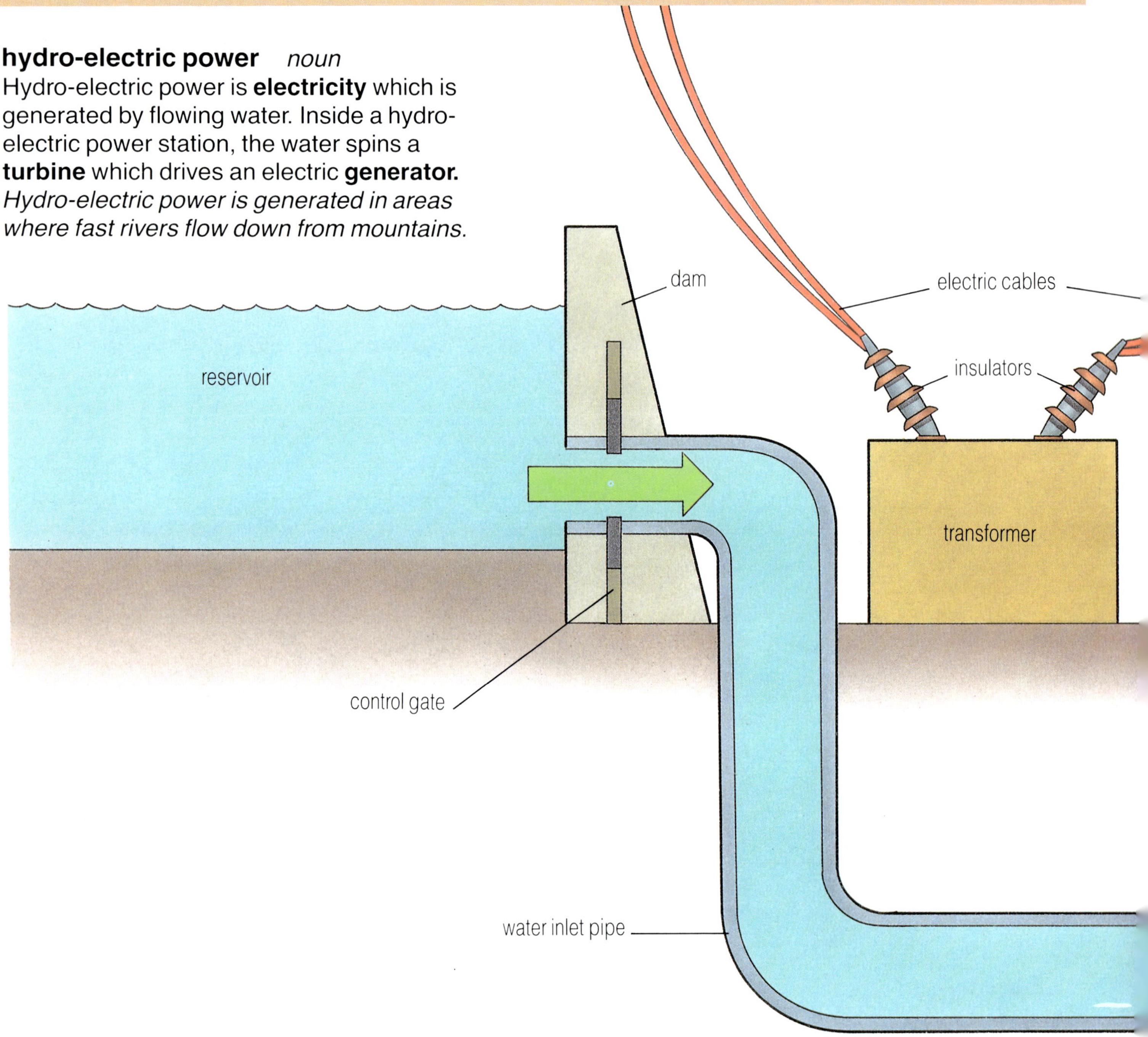

hydro-electric power station

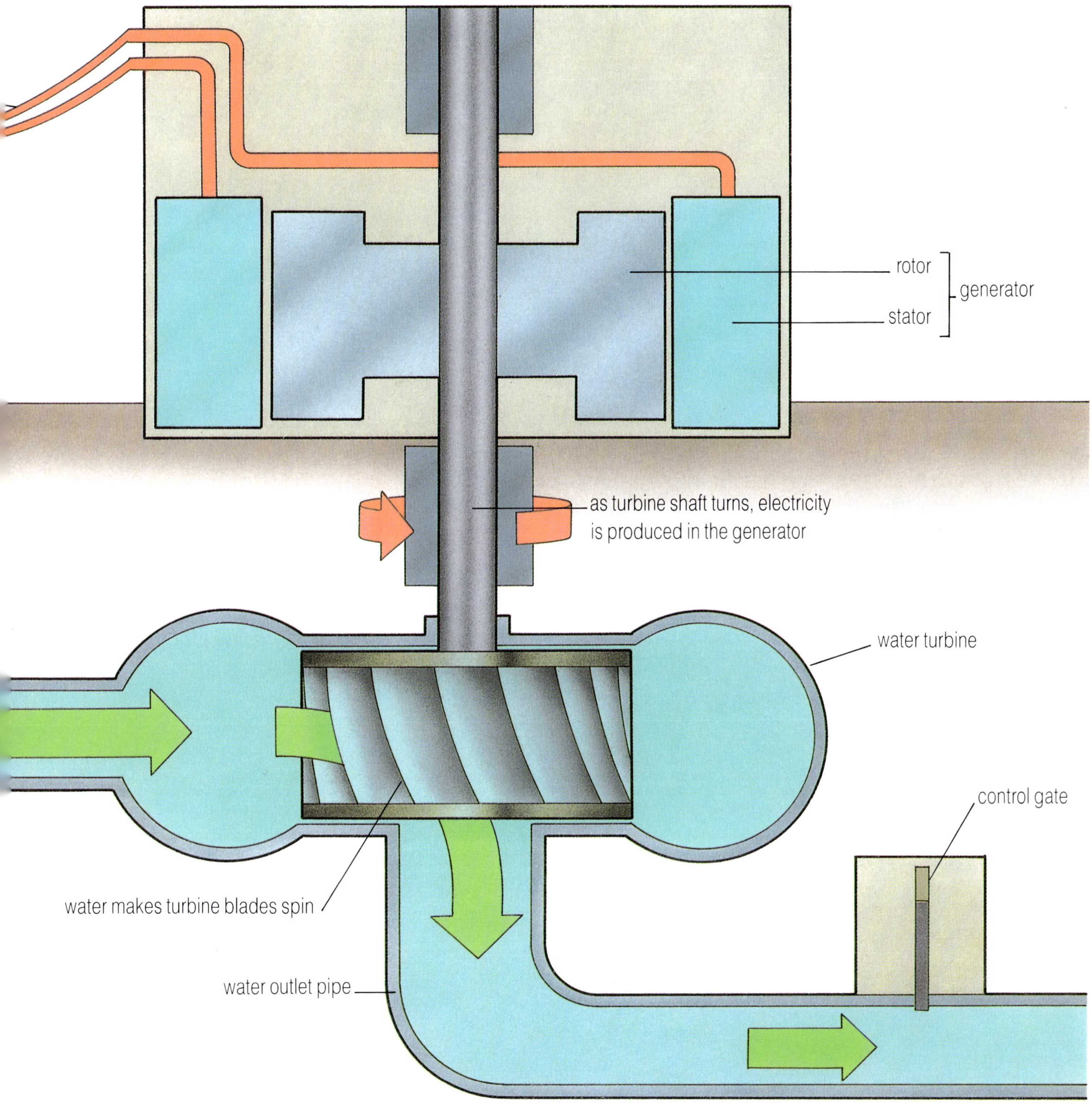
rotor
generator
stator
as turbine shaft turns, electricity is produced in the generator
water turbine
control gate
water makes turbine blades spin
water outlet pipe

horizontal *adjective*
Horizontal is a word which describes something that is flat and level. The floor in a room is horizontal. It does not slope. A horizontal line has a **gradient** of zero. The opposite of horizontal is **vertical**.
You are horizontal when you lie down flat on your bed.

horsepower *noun*
Horsepower is a **unit** of measurement. It measures how fast **work** is being done. A very strong person can work at a rate of 1 horsepower for only a short time. The abbreviation for horsepower is hp.
The power of the motor car engine is 100 horsepower.

hybrid *noun*
Hybrid is a word which describes some kinds of living thing. The parents of a hybrid are very different from each other. A mule is a hybrid because its mother is a horse and its father is a donkey.
The new kind of plant was a hybrid of two different flowering plants.
hybrid *adjective*

hydration *noun*
Hydration is a word which describes the addition of water to a solid substance. The substance stays solid and does not **dissolve**. The opposite of hydration is **dehydration**.
Hydration made the substance change from being colourless to blue.

hydraulic *adjective*
Hydraulic is a word which describes some kinds of **machine**. A hydraulic machine uses an oily liquid to transfer **power** from one place to another place. The liquid is under high **pressure** and forces a **piston** to move.
The hydraulic brakes slowed down the motor car.

hydrocarbon *noun*
A hydrocarbon is a chemical **substance**. It can be a solid, a liquid or a gas. Hydrocarbons are **molecules** which contain atoms of **carbon** and **hydrogen**. **Methane** and ethane are hydrocarbons.
The hydrocarbon burned with a sooty, yellow flame.

hydrochloric acid *noun*
Hydrochloric acid is a **liquid**. It is a strong **acid**. Hydrochloric acid gives off **hydrogen** gas when it **dissolves** metals.
He used hydrochloric acid to remove the rust from the steel plate.

hydroelectric power ► page 68

hydrogen *noun*
Hydrogen is a colourless **gas**. It is the simplest **element** and has the lowest **density** of all substances. One atom of hydrogen is made up of one **proton** and one **electron**.
Hydrogen is important in the manufacture of margarine.

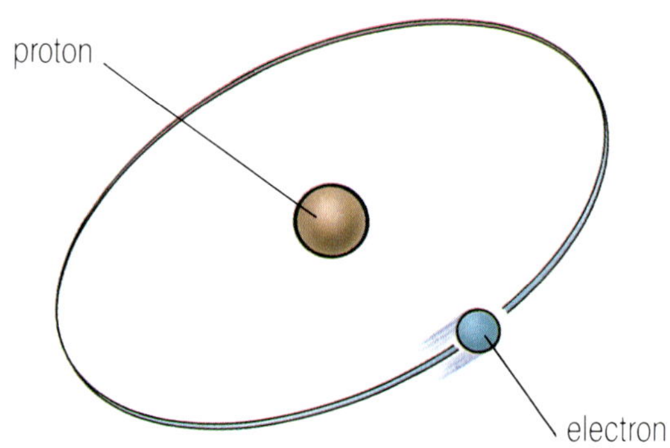

I

ignite *verb*
Ignite means to set light to something or to catch fire. A match ignites when it is struck against a matchbox. The lighted match can then ignite a **fuel**, such as **natural gas**.
The spark ignited the gas inside the oven.

image *noun*
An image is a kind of picture. You see an image when you look in a mirror, through a **lens** or at a **screen**. Images are made by **rays** of light.
She watched the image on the cinema screen.

impulse *noun*
An impulse is a push which is given to an object for a short amount of time. The impulse starts the object moving or makes it move more quickly.
The tennis racket gave an impulse to the ball.

impure *adjective*
Impure is a word which describes a **substance** that contains small amounts of other substances. These other substances are mixed in with it. The opposite of impure is **pure**.
The air was impure because it contained smoke from the factory.

indicator *noun*
An indicator is a **liquid** which can change its colour. It is added to a **solution** to test the solution. The colour of the indicator shows if the solution is an **acid,** an **alkali** or if it is **neutral**. Litmus is an example of an indicator.
She added two drops of indicator to the liquid to see if it was acid.

induce *verb*
Induce is a word which describes a way of making **electricity**. A **generator** contains a magnet and a spinning coil of wire. The magnet induces an **electric current** and makes it flow in the wire.
She induced an electric current in the wire by holding a magnet near it.
induction *noun*

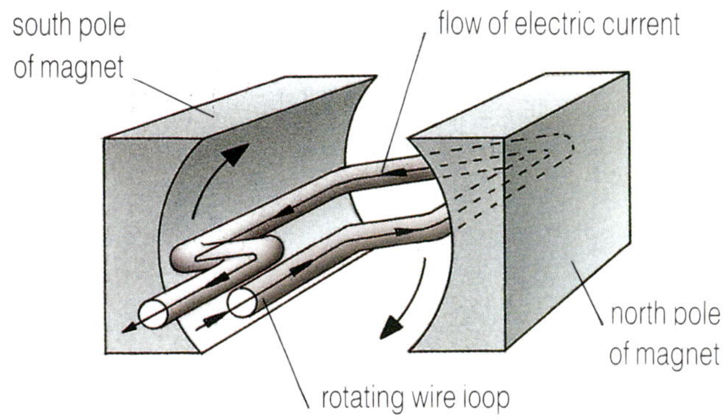

inert *adjective*
Inert is a word which describes a **substance** that does not burn and does not change when it is heated. It does not produce a **reaction** when it is mixed with other **chemicals**.
The inert gas helped to put out the fire.

inertia *noun*
Inertia is a word which explains why all objects need a push to make them move. If an object has a large **mass**, it will also have a large inertia. **Force** works against the inertia of an object and changes its speed or direction.
A truck has a larger engine than a motor car because it has more inertia.

inflammable ► **flammable**

information technology *noun*
Information technology is a **scientific** subject. It is the study of how to collect, use, move, store and display information. Information technology uses **computers**, **fax** machines, television and radio.
Many factories use information technology to control their machines.

infra-red *adjective*
Infra-red is a word which describes a kind of **light**. It is a part of the **electromagnetic spectrum**. You cannot see infra-red light but you can feel it as **radiant heat**.
Some snakes use infra-red light to hunt their prey in the dark.

inorganic *adjective*
Inorganic is a word which describes **substances** that do not usually contain **carbon**. The opposite of inorganic is **organic.**
Rocks and metals are inorganic substances.

input *noun*
Input is information which flows into a **computer**. It comes from **floppy disks**, **keyboards** and **joysticks.**
When you type the input into a computer, words appear on the screen.

insoluble *adjective*
Insoluble is a word which describes some solids, liquids and gases. An insoluble substance will not **dissolve** in a liquid.
Argon gas and sand are both insoluble in water.

insulator *noun*
An insulator is a substance which stops the flow of **heat** or **electricity**. We wear clothes to insulate our bodies and keep them warm. The plastic covering on some electric wires is an insulator and makes the wires safe.
Glass insulators stopped the electricity in the cables flowing through the metal tower.
insulate *verb*

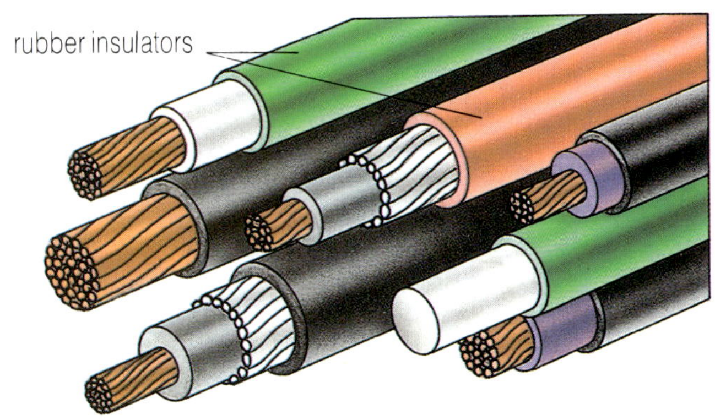

integrated circuit *noun*
An integrated circuit is an **electronic** device. It is a tiny piece of **silicon** which has **electric circuits** on its surface. An integrated circuit is sometimes called a chip or a microchip.
A powerful computer may contain as many as 15 integrated circuits.

internal combustion engine *noun*
An internal combustion engine is a kind of **engine**. Internal combustion engines may be petrol engines, diesel engines or gas turbines.
Fuel burns inside an internal combustion engine.

iodine *noun*
Iodine is a grey-black **solid**. It is a chemical **element**. Iodine does not melt into a liquid when it is heated. Instead, it turns into a purple gas. Iodine is used to make medicines, drugs and **halogen lamps**.
Iodine is found in some kinds of seaweed.

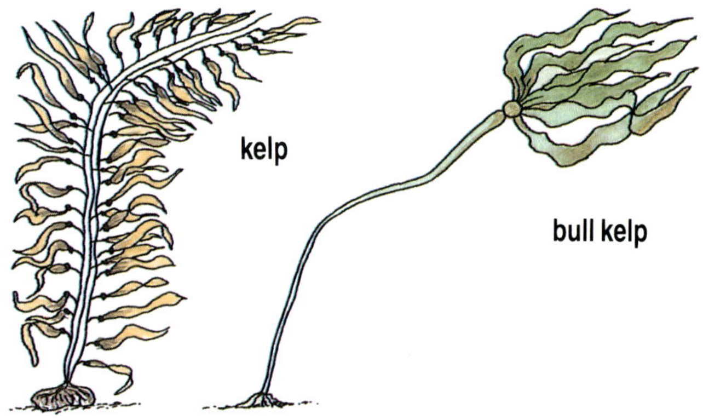

ion *noun*
An ion is a small **particle** found in many chemicals. Each particle has an **electric charge**. An ion with a **positive** charge is an atom which has lost one or more **electrons**. An ion with a **negative** charge is an atom which has gained one or more electrons. Batteries contain chemicals which are made up of ions.
A salt is made up from positive and negative ions.
ionize *verb*

iron *noun*
Iron is a chemical **element**. It is a dark-grey **metal**. Iron is usually mixed with other metals and **non-metals** to make **steel**. Magnets attract iron. It **corrodes** easily in damp air to make rust.
The magnet in the scrapyard picked up the huge pieces of iron.

isotope *noun*
An isotope is an **atom** which has extra **neutrons** in its **nucleus**. These neutrons often make the atom **radioactive**. Some isotopes are found naturally, but others are made in **nuclear reactors**.
Isotopes helped the engineers to find out where the underground pipes were leaking.

IT ► information technology

J

jet engine *noun*
A jet engine is the kind of **engine** which is usually fitted to aeroplanes. It is a **gas turbine** engine. A jet engine makes the aeroplane move by pushing a stream of hot gas in one direction. This push creates a **force** in the opposite direction.
Large aeroplanes have four jet engines.

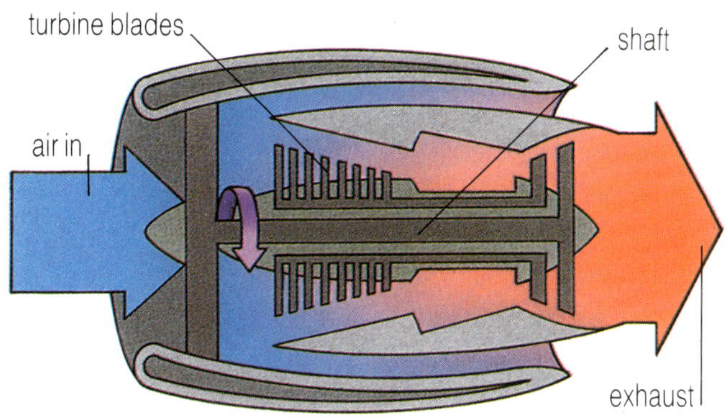

joule *noun*
A joule is a **unit** of measurement. It measures an amount of **energy**, such as **work** or heat. The abbreviation for joule is J.
The food that he ate every day contained 10 million joules of energy.

joystick *noun*
A joystick is a part of a **computer**. It is a straight handle connected to the computer by a **cable**. The joystick controls the picture on the **screen**.
The children moved their joysticks to play the computer game.

kingdom *noun*

A kingdom is a group of living things. All the living things in the same kingdom have special similarities. Kingdoms are part of the system of **classification** which biologists have worked out. Each kingdom can be divided into smaller and smaller groups. The animal kingdom is divided into **phylum**, **class**, **order**, **family**, **genus** and **species**. *Humans, mice, worms and fleas are all members of the animal kingdom.*

phylum

class

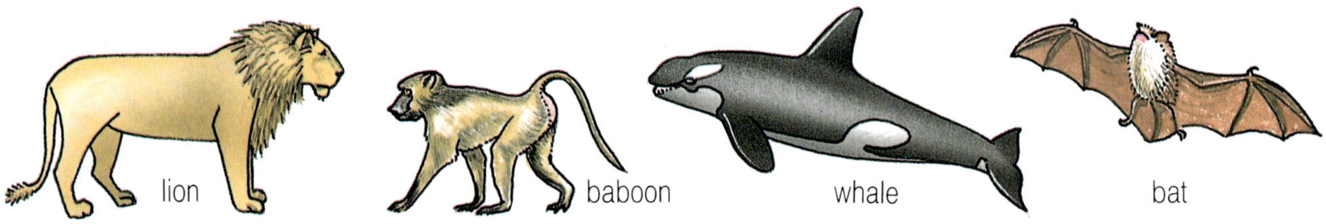

order

family

genus

species

ostrich

bat

kangaroo

hare

sheep

hare

sheep

pig

kangaroo

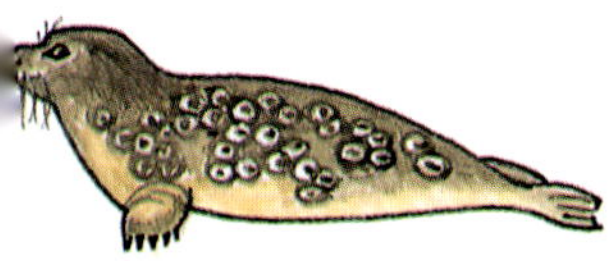
seal

bear

lynx

cat

K

kelvin *noun*
A kelvin is a **unit** of measurement.
It measures **temperature**. One kelvin is the same as one degree **Celsius**. Zero kelvin is the same as −273 degrees Celsius.
The temperature in outer space is about 4 kelvin.

kerosene *noun*
Kerosene is a liquid **fuel**. It is made from **petroleum** in an oil refinery. Kerosene does not burn as easily as gasoline. It is mainly used in **jet engines**.
The aeroplane carried 40 tonnes of kerosene in tanks in its wings.

keyboard *noun*
A keyboard is a part of a **computer**. It has rows of buttons, called keys. A number or a letter is marked on each key. When you press the keys, this sends **data** or instructions into the computer.
A computer keyboard has more than 50 different keys.

keypad *noun*
A keypad is a part of a **computer**. It is a small **keyboard** which has no more than 20 buttons or keys. A pocket **calculator** has a small keypad.
She worked out the problem by pressing the buttons on the keypad of the calculator.

kilo- *prefix*
Kilo- is placed in front of a **unit** of measurement. It multiplies the unit by 1,000. One kilometre is 1,000 metres. One kilogram is 1,000 grams. The abbreviation for kilo- is k.
They measured the distance between the two cities in kilometres.

kilobyte *noun*
A kilobyte is a **unit** of measurement.
It measures an amount of **data** or the size of the **memory** in a computer. A kilobyte is the same as 1,000 **bytes**.
My computer can store 500 kilobytes of data.

kilogram *noun*
A kilogram is a **unit** of measurement.
It measures **mass**. One kilogram is 1,000 **grams,** and 1,000 kilograms is 1 tonne. The abbreviation for kilogram is kg.
The packet of sugar had a mass of 1 kilogram.

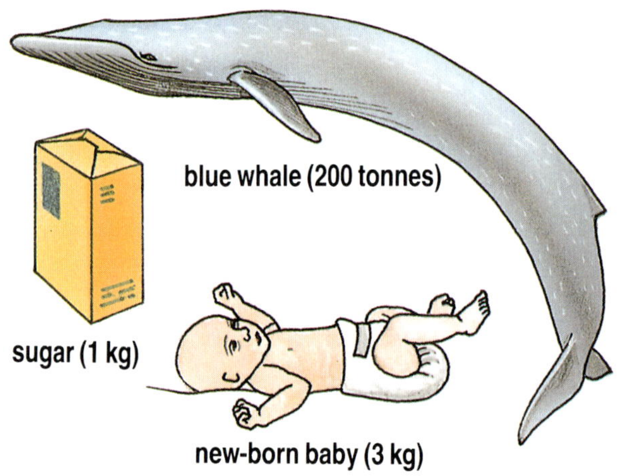

kilometre *noun*
A kilometre is a **unit** of measurement.
It measures **length.** One kilometre is 1,000 **metres**. The abbreviation for kilometre is km.
The distance around the world is about 40,000 kilometres.

kilowatt *noun*
A kilowatt is a **unit** of measurement.
It measures **power**. One kilowatt is 1,000 **watts**. The abbreviation for kilowatt is kW.
The electric heater had a power of 3 kilowatts.

kinetic energy *noun*
Kinetic energy is the **energy** which objects have when they are moving. If an object is heavy and moves quickly, it has a large amount of kinetic energy.
A slow motor car and a fast motorcycle have about the same kinetic energy.

kingdom ► page 74

krypton *noun*
Krypton is a chemical **element**. It is a colourless **gas** which does not burn. Krypton is used in some kinds of **fluorescent** electric lamps.
The air which we breathe contains very small amounts of krypton.

L

laboratory *noun*
A laboratory is a room where scientists or students do **experiments**. It usually contains tables or benches with sinks and water taps. The special **apparatus** and **chemicals** are stored in cupboards.
The physics laboratory contained a lot of apparatus for experimenting on electricity.

laminate *noun*
A laminate is a **solid**. It contains layers of substances that are stuck together. The **properties** of a laminate are different from the properties of the substances in it. **Fibreglass** is a tough laminate that contains hard **resin** and strong **fibres**.
The table top was made from a plastic and wood laminate.

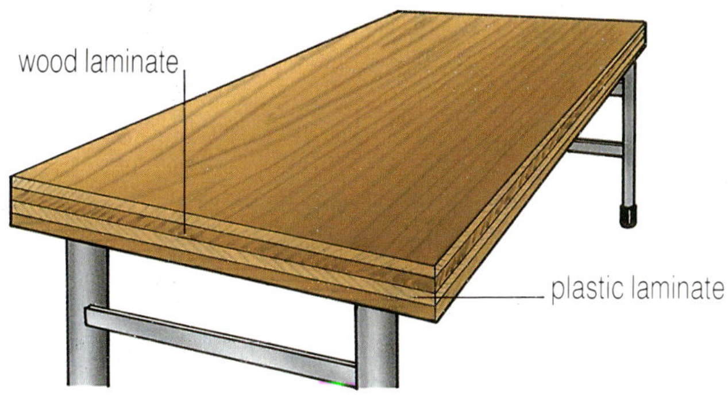

laser ► page 78

laser printer *noun*
A laser printer is a part of some **computers**. It prints very clear letters and pictures. A beam of **laser** light makes **images** on a drum. Ink powder sticks to the images. The drum prints the inky images on to paper.
A coloured picture came out of the laser printer.

laser *noun*
A laser is a **device** which produces a beam of very bright and powerful light. All the **photons** in laser light **vibrate** at the same speed. Lasers are used in medicine and in industry.
Scientists have used a laser to measure the distance between the Earth and the Moon.

endoscope

An endoscope is used in throat and stomach operations. The doctor looks through the eyepiece to inspect the inside of a patient's body. The laser at the end of the flexible tube can make delicate cuts, without having to open up the patient.

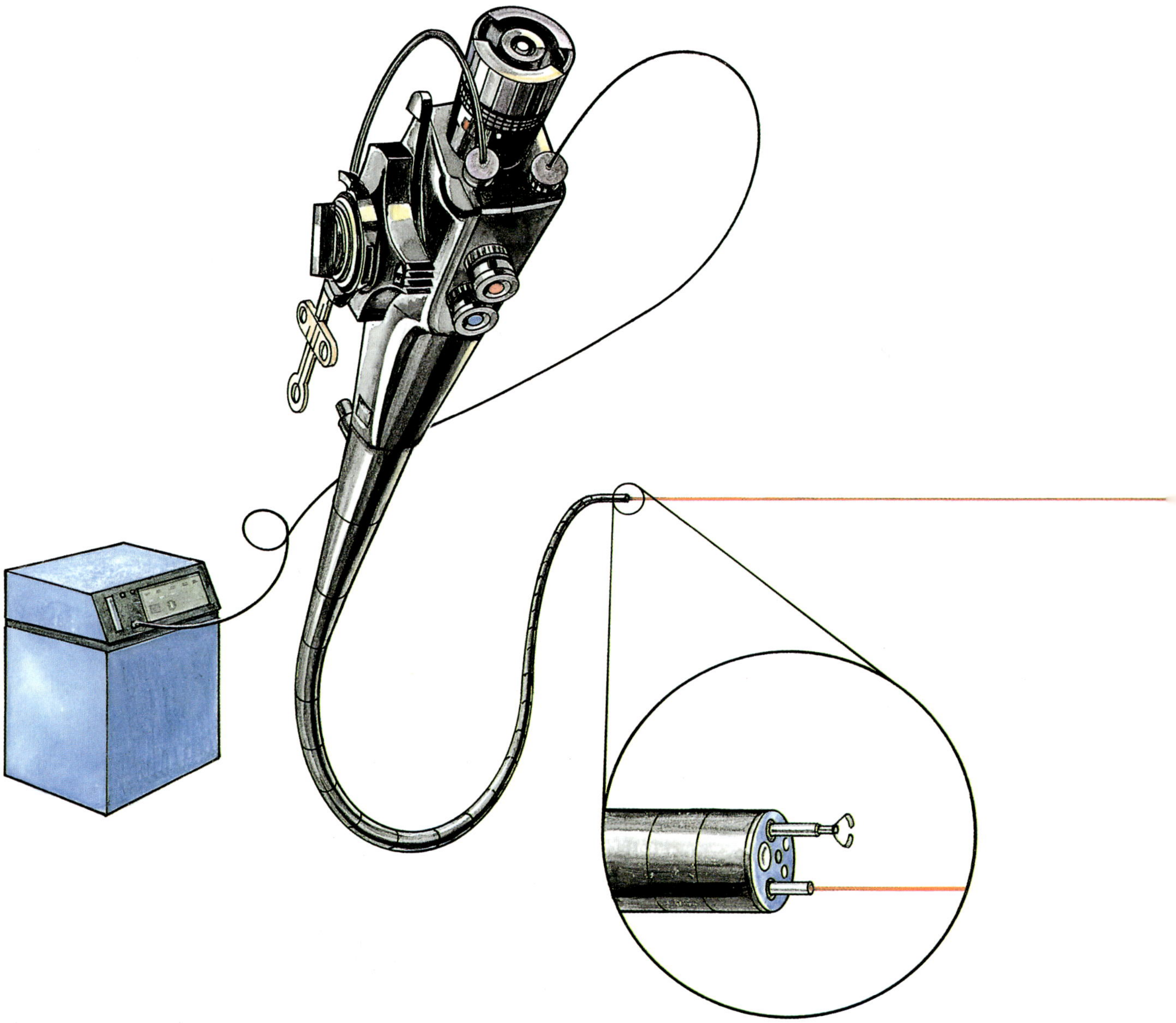

how a ruby laser works

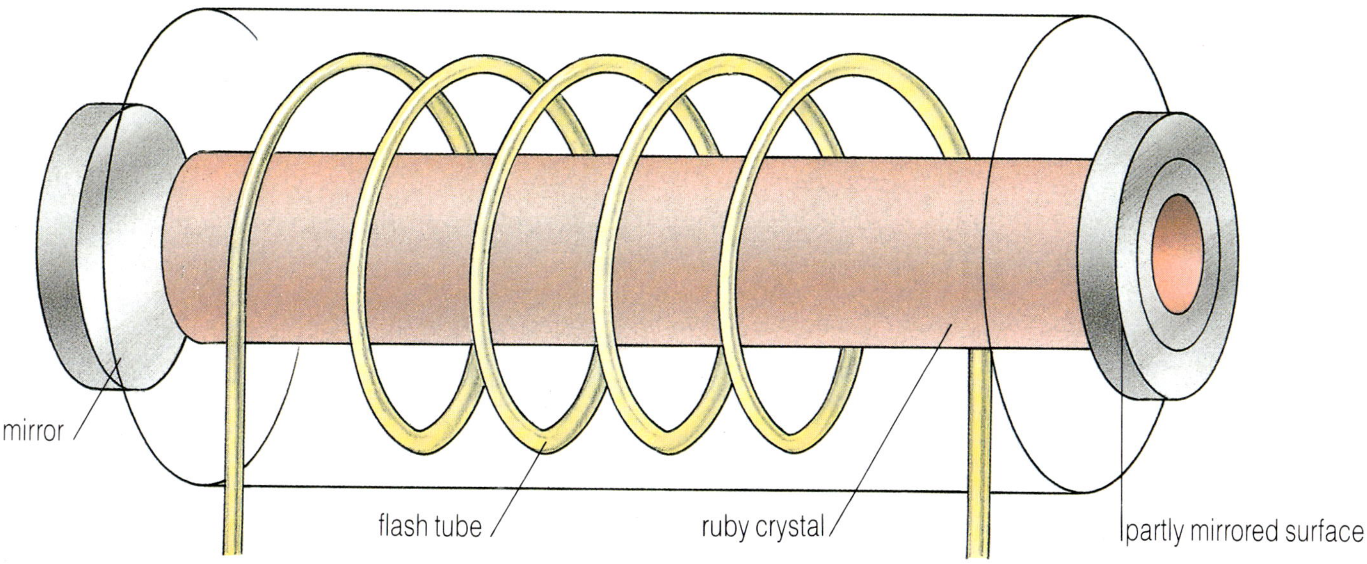

A powerful flash tube is coiled round a ruby crystal. The atoms in the ruby crystal contain some energy.

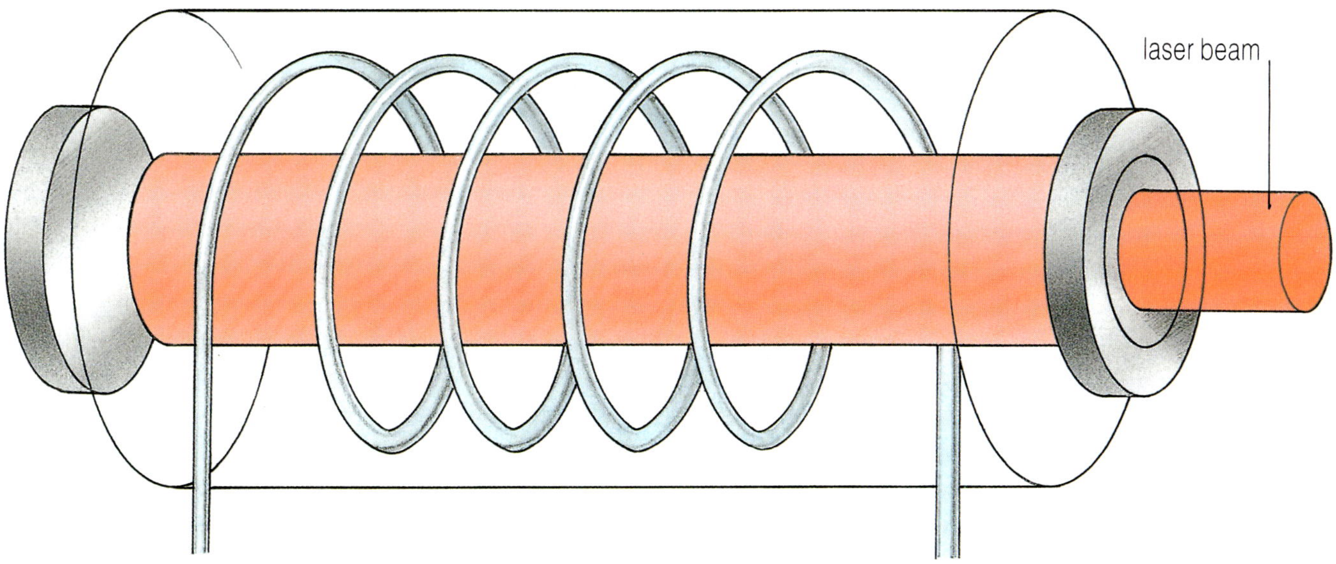

When a light shines through the ruby crystal, the atoms in the crystal become excited, so they have more energy. The excited atoms give off light.

The light is reflected by mirrors at each end of the tube, making other atoms release light energy, too. The intense light passes out of the tube as a burst of laser light.

lattice *noun*
Lattice is a word which describes the shape of a **crystal**. A lattice is the arrangement of the **atoms** or **ions** in the crystal. Different substances have crystals with different shapes. These crystals are made up of different shapes of lattice.
A salt crystal contains a lattice which is made up of cubes.

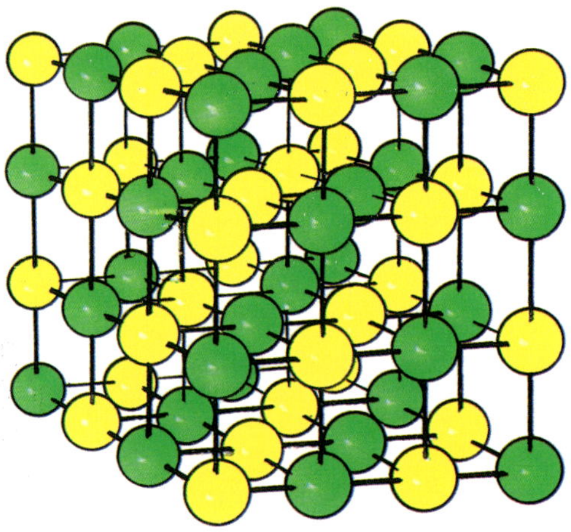

law *noun*
A law is a special kind of **theory** or rule. A law is a rule which is true everywhere. For example, the law of **gravity** says that objects will fall downwards towards the Earth.
The law of gravity was first stated more than 300 years ago.

lead *noun*
Lead is a chemical **element**. It is a grey **metal** which is soft and **ductile**. Lead has a high **density**. Lead helps to make **solder**, **accumulators** and gasoline for cars.
Thin sheets of lead keep roofs watertight.
You can bend a lead bar with your hands.

length *noun*
Length is a kind of measurement.
It measures distance in **millimetres**, **centimetres**, **metres** or **kilometres**.
The length of a box measures its longest side.
The length of a journey measures a twisting road as if it were a straight one.
The length of her ruler was 31 centimetres.

lens *noun*
A lens is a piece of clear glass or plastic with curved sides. **Concave** and **convex** lenses change the direction of **rays** of light. Spectacles, **telescopes** and **microscopes** contain lenses.
Her spectacles had glass lenses inside a plastic frame.

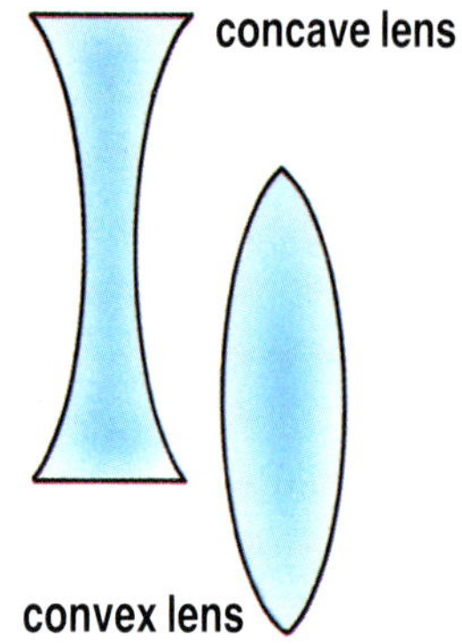

lever *noun*
A lever is a bar or rod which moves around a **fulcrum**. An **effort** is needed to move one end of the lever. This movement will move a **load** at the other end.
She pushed on the lever and lifted the heavy rock.

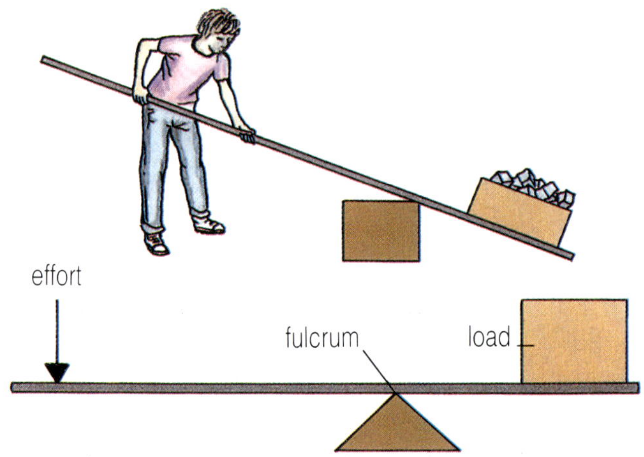

life cycle *noun*
Life cycle is a term which describes the different stages in the life of a living thing. Some animals change their appearance by **metamorphosis** during their life cycle.
The life cycle of a fly includes the egg, the larva, the pupa and the adult.

light *noun*
Light is a kind of **energy**. Light is made up of **electromagnetic waves** which we can see with our eyes. A **ray** of light travels through space in a straight line at 299,792 kilometres per second.
Light takes about eight minutes to travel from the Sun to the Earth.

lightning conductor *noun*
A lightning conductor is a thick **wire**. One end is fixed to the top of a building, and the other end is buried in the ground. A lightning conductor carries lightning safely away and stops damage to the building.
They fitted a lightning conductor to the tall building on the top of the hill.

limestone *noun*
Limestone is a **mineral**. It contains a chemical called **calcium carbonate**. Huge amounts of limestone help to make cement and iron.
A steel factory uses thousands of tonnes of limestone every week.

liquefy *verb*
Liquefy is a word which describes how a solid or a gas changes into a **liquid**. A gas liquefies when it is **compressed** or cooled. A solid liquefies when it is heated.
He liquefied the ice by warming it in his hand.

liquid *noun*
A liquid is a kind of **substance**. A liquid has a level surface and spreads out to fill the bottom of its container.
The liquid flowed out of the pipe and into the sea.

litmus *noun*
Litmus is a coloured dye. It is often used to coat special strips of paper called litmus paper. Litmus is an **indicator**. Blue litmus turns red when it is added to an **acid**. Red litmus turns blue when it is added to an **alkali**.
She poured the blue litmus into the vinegar to see how acid it was.

alkali turns red litmus blue   acid turns blue litmus red

litre *noun*
A litre is a **unit** of measurement. It measures **volume**. A box with sides which are 10 centimetres long holds 1 litre. There are 1,000 **millilitres** or 100 **centilitres** in 1 litre. The abbreviation for litre is l.
The petrol tank in his motor car held 35 litres of petrol.

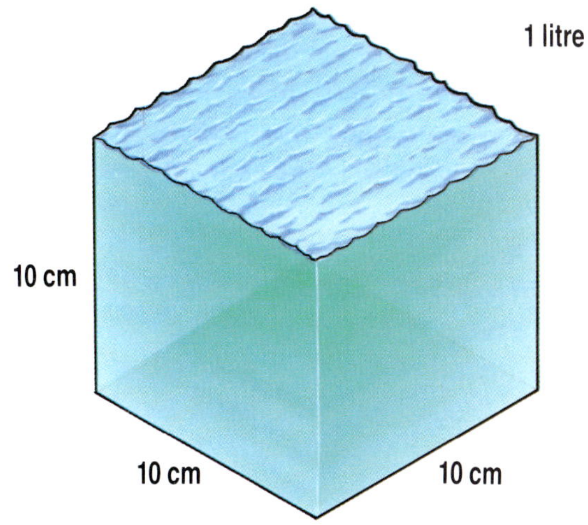

load *noun*
A load is a **weight**. It is the weight which a **force** pushes against. **Levers**, **pulleys** and other machines move loads. **Beams** and bridges support loads.
The engine in the crane lifted the heavy load of steel girders.

logic *noun*
Logic is a set of rules. It controls the way in which **computers** work and the way in which people think. Computer logic depends on how the logic **gates** inside the computer are connected together. People use logic to sort out information and solve problems.
If today is Wednesday, then logic tells us that in two days' time it will be Friday.

long waveband *noun*
The long waveband is a group of radio **signals**. It is part of the **electromagnetic spectrum**. Radio **transmitters** using the long waveband can send signals around the world.
The radio can receive programmes from other countries in the long waveband.

lubricant *noun*
A lubricant is a slippery liquid. Lubricants make moving parts slide smoothly against each other. **Oil**, grease and **graphite** are lubricants. They help to reduce the amount of **friction** in machines.
She poured 5 litres of lubricant into the engine of her motor car.
lubricate *verb*

luminous *adjective*
Luminous is a word which describes something that gives out **light**. The Sun, electric lamps and candles are all luminous.
He could tell the time in the dark because his watch had a luminous dial.

M

machine *noun*
A machine is a **device** which does **work**. There are six simple machines. These are the **lever**, the inclined plane, the **wheel** and **axle**, the wedge, the **screw** and the **pulley**. Together, these simple machines make up complicated machines, such as engines and gearboxes. Computers and other electronic devices are also called machines.
A crane is a machine which lifts heavy weights.

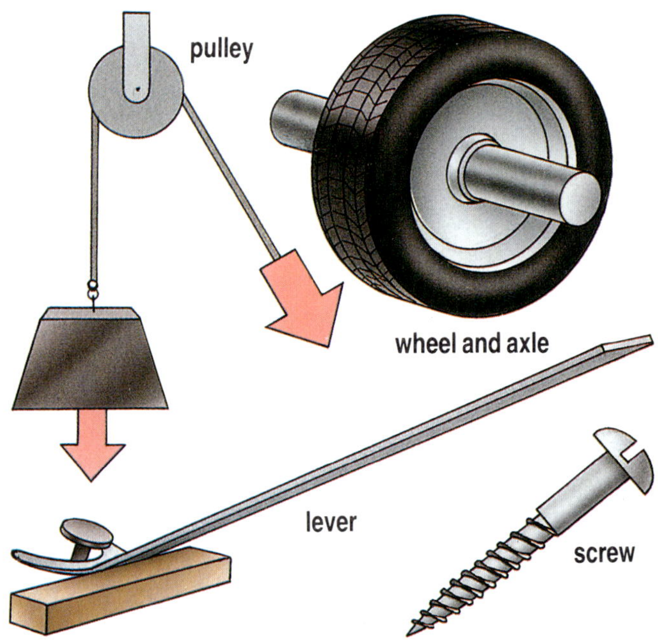

magnesium *noun*
Magnesium is a chemical **element**. It is a silvery **metal** which has a low **density**. Magnesium burns fiercely when it is heated. Aeroplanes are built from an **alloy** of magnesium and **aluminium**.
They made the magnesium from thousands of litres of sea water.

magnet *noun*
A magnet is an object which attracts other objects containing iron. Magnets are either **permanent magnets** or **electromagnets**. They have two **magnetic poles**. Magnets are found in electric motors, generators, compasses and magnetic tape.
A magnet will pick up steel paperclips.

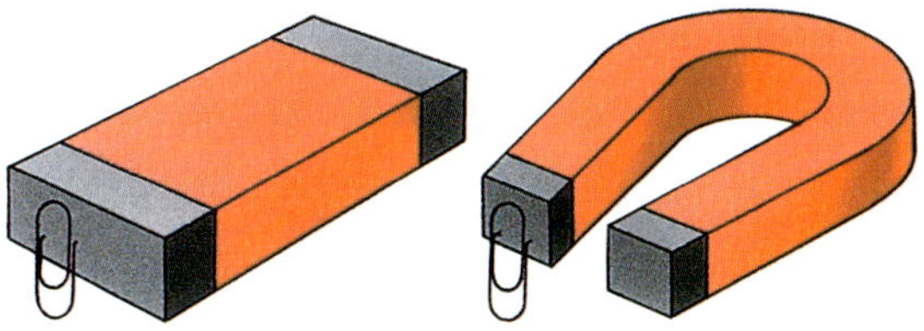

magnetic *adjective*
Magnetic is a word which describes a **magnet** or a material that is attracted by a magnet. Magnetic also describes things which use **magnetism**.
Telephones, loudspeakers and electric motors contain magnetic materials.

magnetic levitation *noun*
Magnetic levitation is a **force** which makes objects float in the air. Magnetic levitation powers special trains which are very fast and quiet. **Electromagnets** under these trains **repel** electromagnets in the track.
Magnetic levitation lifted the train 15 centimetres above the track.

magnetic pole *noun*
A magnetic pole is a part of a **magnet**. Each magnet has a **north pole** and a **south pole**. Iron **filings** are attracted to the poles and the lines of magnetic **force**. The magnetic force is strongest at the poles.
Bar magnets have a magnetic pole at each end.

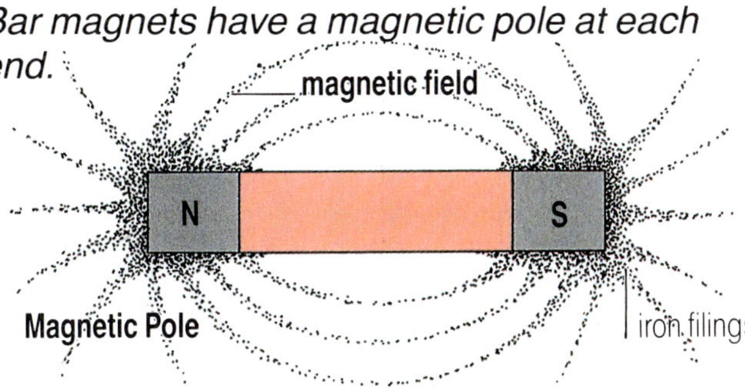

magnetic tape *noun*
Magnetic tape is thin **plastic** ribbon. It is coated with **magnetic** particles. Magnetic tape inside **cassettes** stores **computer programs**, **video** films and sound **signals**.
She recorded the television programme on magnetic tape.

magnetism *noun*
Magnetism is the **force** between two **magnets**. It makes two **south poles** or two **north poles** repel each other. Magnetism makes a north pole and a south pole attract each other.
Magnetism made the two magnets move towards each other.

magnify *verb*
Magnify is a word which describes how things are made to look bigger. **Telescopes**, **microscopes** and **magnifying glasses** magnify objects. They all contain **lenses** which make the **image** appear larger than the object.
She magnified the picture of the fly to see its feet more clearly.

magnifying glass *noun*
A magnifying glass is a kind of **lens**. It is a **convex** lens which is fixed to a handle. If you look at an object through a magnifying glass, the object appears larger and clearer.
He looked at the flower petals through a magnifying glass.

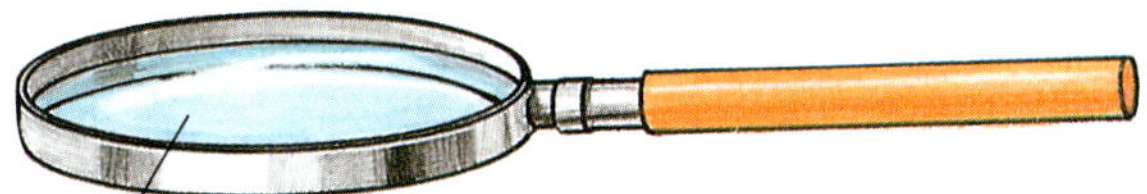

mainframe computer *noun*
A mainframe computer is the largest and most powerful kind of **computer**. Mainframe computers can fill a whole room. They are used by the head offices of banks and large companies.
A mainframe computer can work out the electricity bills for millions of homes.

malleable *adjective*
Malleable is a word which describes some **metals**. Malleable metals can be beaten or squeezed to make new shapes. **Copper** and **gold** are malleable metals.
He hammered the malleable metal to make it into a thin sheet.

mammal *noun*
A mammal is an **animal**. Mammals have hair and feed their young with milk. There are over 4,000 different **species** of mammal.
Humans, whales, kangaroos and rats are different kinds of mammal.

mass *noun*
Mass describes how much **matter** there is in an object. All objects have mass and take up space. Mass is measured in **kilograms**. When **gravity** pulls on the mass of an object, the object is said to have **weight**.
The mass of the table was greater than the mass of the chair.

material *noun*
Material is a word which describes different kinds of solid. Copper, skin, steel, plastic, wood and cloth are materials. Different materials fit together to make different objects.
An electric light bulb contains the materials glass, tungsten and brass.

mathematics *noun*
Mathematics is a subject which includes **arithmetic**, **geometry** and **algebra**. It helps us to understand and use measurements and observations. Mathematicians use **logic** to solve problems.
The children studied mathematics at school.

matter *noun*
Matter is anything which has **mass** and takes up space. The three types of matter are **solids**, **liquids** and **gases**.
Many scientists think that the Earth is made from matter which came from the Sun.

measure *verb*
Measure is a word which describes a way of finding out how large something is. Each kind of measurement has its own **units**. Rulers measure **length** in **centimetres**. **Thermometers** measure **temperature** in **degrees**.
She measured the length of the piece of string in centimetres.

mechanical *adjective*
Mechanical is a word which describes **machines**. Engines, lifts, cranes and bicycles are all mechanical. They all contain moving parts which are connected together.
The mechanical digger made a hole in the road.

mechanical energy *noun*
Mechanical energy is energy which is released by **machines**. An **engine** changes a **fuel** into chemical energy. Mechanical energy does **work** by moving things.
Mechanical energy moved the motor car along the road.

medium waveband *noun*
The medium waveband is a group of radio **signals**. It is part of the **electromagnetic spectrum**. Radio **transmitters** using the medium waveband can send signals several hundred kilometres.
He tuned the radio to receive a music station in the medium waveband.

megabyte *noun*
A megabyte is a **unit** of measurement. It measures an amount of **data** or the size of the **memory** in a computer. A megabyte is the same as 1,000,000 **bytes** or 1,000 **kilobytes**.
The computer could store 2 megabytes of data.

melt *verb*
Melt is a word which describes how a **solid** changes when it is heated. A solid melts to form a liquid when the **temperature** of the solid reaches its **melting point**.
The strip of aluminium melted into a silvery liquid in the roaring fire.

melting point *noun*
Melting point is a term which describes the **temperature** of a melting solid. Different solids have different melting points. The melting point can change if the solid is not **pure**.
The melting point of pure ice is 0 degrees Celsius.

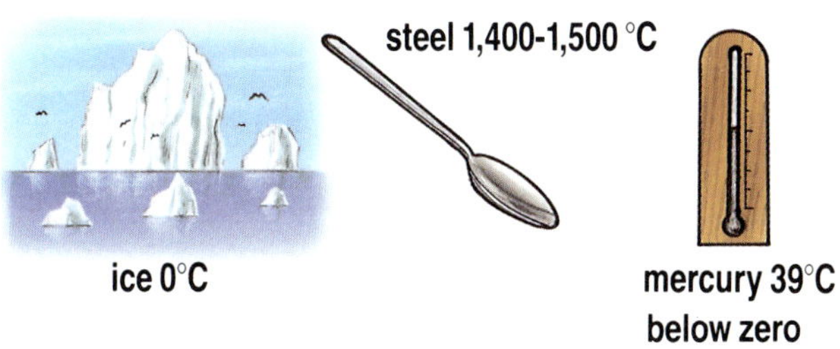

memory *noun*
Memory is a part of a **computer**. The two kinds of memory are **random access memory** and **read-only memory**. These memories store **data** or **programs**. The size of the memory is measured in **bytes**.
A pocket calculator stores numbers in its memory.

meniscus *noun*
A meniscus is the curved shape of the surface of a **liquid**. It is where the liquid touches the sides of its container. **Surface tension** causes the shape of the meniscus.
The meniscus curved upwards where the water met the sides of the bowl.

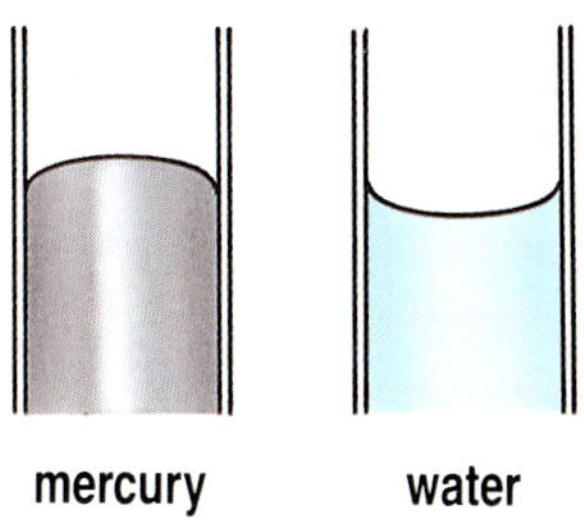

mercury *noun*
Mercury is a chemical **element**. It is a silvery **metal** which has a high **density**. Mercury is the only metal which is a liquid when it is kept at room **temperature**. Mercury helps to make fillings for teeth and it is also found in **thermometers.**
A small bottle of mercury weighs over 2 kilograms.

metabolism *noun*
Metabolism is a word which describes all the changes that happen inside a living thing. **Chemical reactions** cause these changes and **enzymes** control them. Metabolism breaks down food and uses it to build new **cells**.
The metabolism of a tortoise is very slow during the cold months of the year.

metal *noun*
A metal is a kind of **element**. All metals except **mercury** are solids. Metals are **malleable** and **ductile** and they shine when polished. They are also good **conductors** of heat and electricity.
Bridges, ships, aeroplanes, skyscrapers and vehicles are built from metals.
metallic *adjective*

metamorphosis *noun*
Metamorphosis is a word which describes a change in an **animal**. Metamorphosis happens during the **life cycle** of animals such as flies and moths.
Metamorphosis changed the larva into a butterfly.

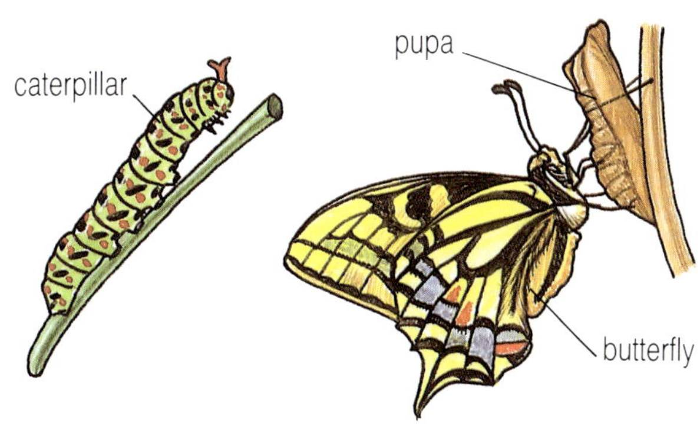

meter *noun*
A meter is a measuring instrument. **Analogue** meters have a **scale** with a pointer. **Digital** meters have a display of numbers. **Voltmeters** and **ammeters** make electrical measurements.
He carefully read the meter to see how much electricity they had used.

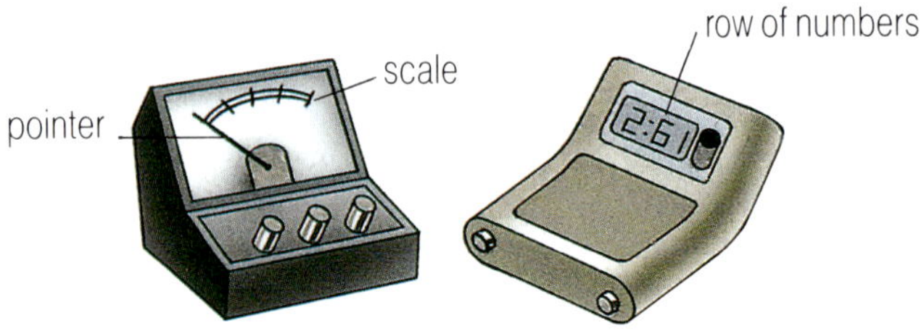

methane *noun*
Methane is a colourless **gas**. It is a **hydrocarbon** and is **flammable**. Methane does not smell or **dissolve** in water. **Natural gas** contains almost pure methane.
Methane burns with a hot, blue flame.

method *noun*
A method is a set of instructions which helps a scientist to carry out an **experiment**. A method contains several steps or stages. There is something to see or **measure** at the end of each step.
The scientists followed the method which was written down in the book.

metre *noun*
A metre, or m for short, is a **unit** of measurement. It measures **length**. There are 100 **centimetres** or 1,000 **millimetres** in a metre. There are 1,000 metres in a **kilometre**.
My desk is one metre wide.

metric system ► page 88

micro-organism *noun*
A micro-organism is a kind of living thing. You would need a **microscope** to see micro-organisms. They include **bacteria**, **viruses** and some **fungi**.
One drop of sea water contains thousands of micro-organisms.

microbe ► micro-organism

microchip ► integrated circuit

microcomputer *noun*
A microcomputer is the smallest **computer**. It can be found in homes, schools and small businesses. Microcomputers have less than 2 **megabytes** of **memory**. Many kinds of microcomputer use a language called **BASIC**.
The microcomputer helped them to solve the problem.

microprocessor *noun*
A microprocessor is a small part of a **computer**. It is made up of **integrated circuits** which have only a few thousand **gates**. Microprocessors control the **programs** and the **data** which flow in a microcomputer.
The microprocessor is fitted inside the computer's keyboard.

microscope ► page 90

microwave *noun*
A microwave is a kind of **electromagnetic radiation**. Microwaves have a very short **wavelength**. They are used as radio signals, which can beam messages to **satellites**.
The egg took 1 minute to cook in the microwave oven.

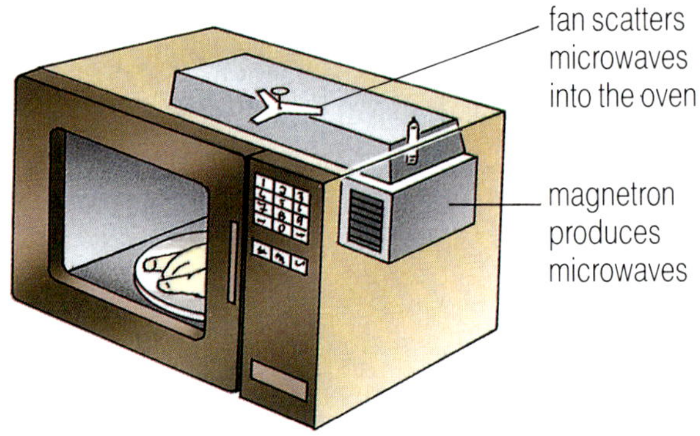

milli- *prefix*
Milli-, or m for short, is placed in front of a **unit** of measurement. It divides the unit by 1,000. A millimetre is one-thousandth of a **metre**.
The explosion happened in a millisecond.

milligram *noun*
A milligram, or mg for short, is a **unit** of measurement. Milligrams measure small amounts of **mass**. One milligram is one-thousandth of a **gram**. There are 1,000 milligrams in 1 gram.
A human hair weighs less than 1 milligram.

millilitre *noun*
A millilitre, or ml for short, is a **unit** of measurement. Millilitres measure small **volumes**. One millilitre is one-thousandth of a **litre**. There are 1,000 millilitres in 1 litre.
A small spoon can hold about 5 millilitres of a liquid.

millimetre *noun*
A millimetre, or mm for short, is a **unit** of measurement. Millimetres measure small **lengths**. One millimetre is one-thousandth of a **metre**. There are 1,000 millimetres in 1 metre.
Her thumb-nail is 8 millimetres wide.

mineral *noun*
A mineral is a kind of **solid**. It is an **inorganic** substance. Minerals are usually found in the ground and are usually made up from **crystals**. **Ores** and different kinds of rock are minerals.
The mineral looked like many small cubes of gold stuck together.

mixture *noun*
A mixture can be a **solid**, a **liquid** or a **gas**. A mixture is made when two or more substances are added together. The substances in a mixture do not change each other. The **atmosphere**, sea water and **alloys** are different kinds of mixture.
Toothpaste is a mixture of special soap and fine grit.

model *noun*
A model is a small copy of something which is large or complicated. Models are built to behave like larger things and help us to understand how they work.
They sailed a model of the ship to find out how a real ship would behave in a storm.

modem *noun*
A modem is a part of some **computers**. A modem connects a computer to a telephone line. Two computers with modems can send **data** to each other.
Modems help computers in different places to communicate with each other.

moderator *noun*
A moderator is a part of a **nuclear reactor**. Moderators are made from **graphite**, some kinds of light metal, or water which contains **deuterium**. They help to produce nuclear energy in a nuclear power station.
The moderator weighed over 150 tonnes.

molecule *noun*
A molecule is a small **particle**. Molecules contain two or more **atoms** which are joined together. A molecule of **oxygen** contains two atoms of oxygen. A molecule of water has two atoms of **hydrogen** and one atom of oxygen.
One drop from a tap contains millions of molecules of water.

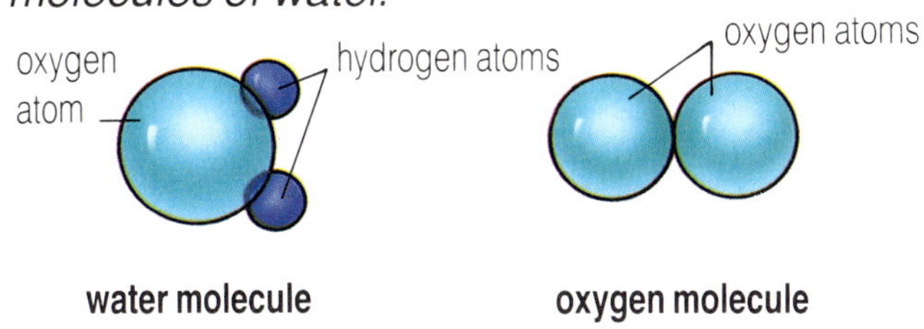

metric system *noun*

The metric system is a list of measuring **units**. The units in the metric system measure length, weight and **capacity.** The metric system makes units larger by multiplying them by 10, 100, 1,000 or 1,000,000.

The three basic units of the metric system are the metre, the gram and the litre.

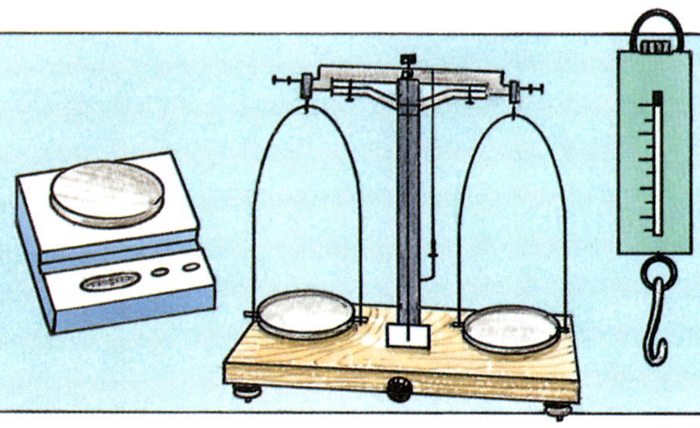

Mass

kilogram

1,000 grams = 1 kilogram

1,000 milligrams = 1 gram

1,000 kilograms = 1 tonne

Length

metre

1,000 millimetres = 1 metre

100 centimetres = 1 metre

1,000 metres = 1 kilometre

Time

second

1,000 milliseconds = 1 second

1,000,000 microseconds = 1 second

60 seconds = 1 minute

Prefixes

kilo- = × 1,000

centi- = ÷ 100

milli- = ÷ 1,000

micro- = ÷ 1,000,000

Abbreviations

milligram	mg	millimetre	mm	microsecond	μs
gram	g	centimetre	cm	millisecond	ms
kilogram	kg	metre	m	second	s
tonne	t	kilometre	km	minute	min

molten *adjective*
Molten describes a solid substance that has **melted**. A molten substance is a liquid which has been melted by **heat**.
A stream of molten rock pours out of the volcano.

momentum *noun*
Momentum is a word which describes a moving object. The amount of momentum depends on the **mass** of the object, plus how fast it is moving. Scientists use momentum to calculate how one moving object will affect another.
They worked out the momentum of the rocket to find out when it would reach Mars.

monera *noun*
Monera are a group of living things. They have a simple form and usually contain only one **cell**. **Bacteria** and plants called blue-green algae are different kinds of monera.
Most kinds of monera live in water.

blue-green alga

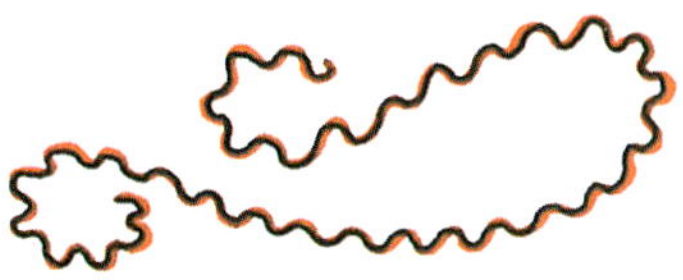
bacterium

monomer *noun*
A monomer can be a kind of **liquid** or **gas**. Monomers are **organic** chemicals which are used to make plastics. Monomers are often made from ethene. When thousands of molecules of a monomer are joined end to end, they make a long chain called a **polymer**.
The monomer he made was a sticky liquid.

motor *noun*
A motor is a kind of **machine**. Motors use other kinds of energy to release **mechanical energy**. Most motors have a shaft which spins around quickly so that it can do **work**. Clockwork motors, electric motors and engines are different kinds of motor.
The motor powered the toy motor car across the floor.

mouse *noun*
A mouse is a part of some **computers**. It is a small box with buttons on the top and a ball underneath. When you move the mouse, the ball rolls. This moves a marker on the **visual display unit**. By pressing the buttons, you can control the computer.
He selected a new program by pressing the buttons on the mouse.

mouse

multiplication *noun*
Multiplication is a kind of **arithmetic**. It is a way of working out problems with numbers. The sign for multiplication is ×. Multiplication is a quick way of adding numbers which are all the same. **Addition** shows that $3 + 3 + 3 + 3 = 12$. Multiplication shows that $4 \times 3 = 12$.
Multiplication helped her to find out the cost of six packets of biscuits.
multiply *verb*

microscope *noun*
A microscope is an **instrument** which can help us to see tiny things more clearly. An ordinary microscope has glass **lenses** which can **magnify** an object by up to 500 times.
He could see the hairs on the beetle's legs clearly under the microscope.

microscope

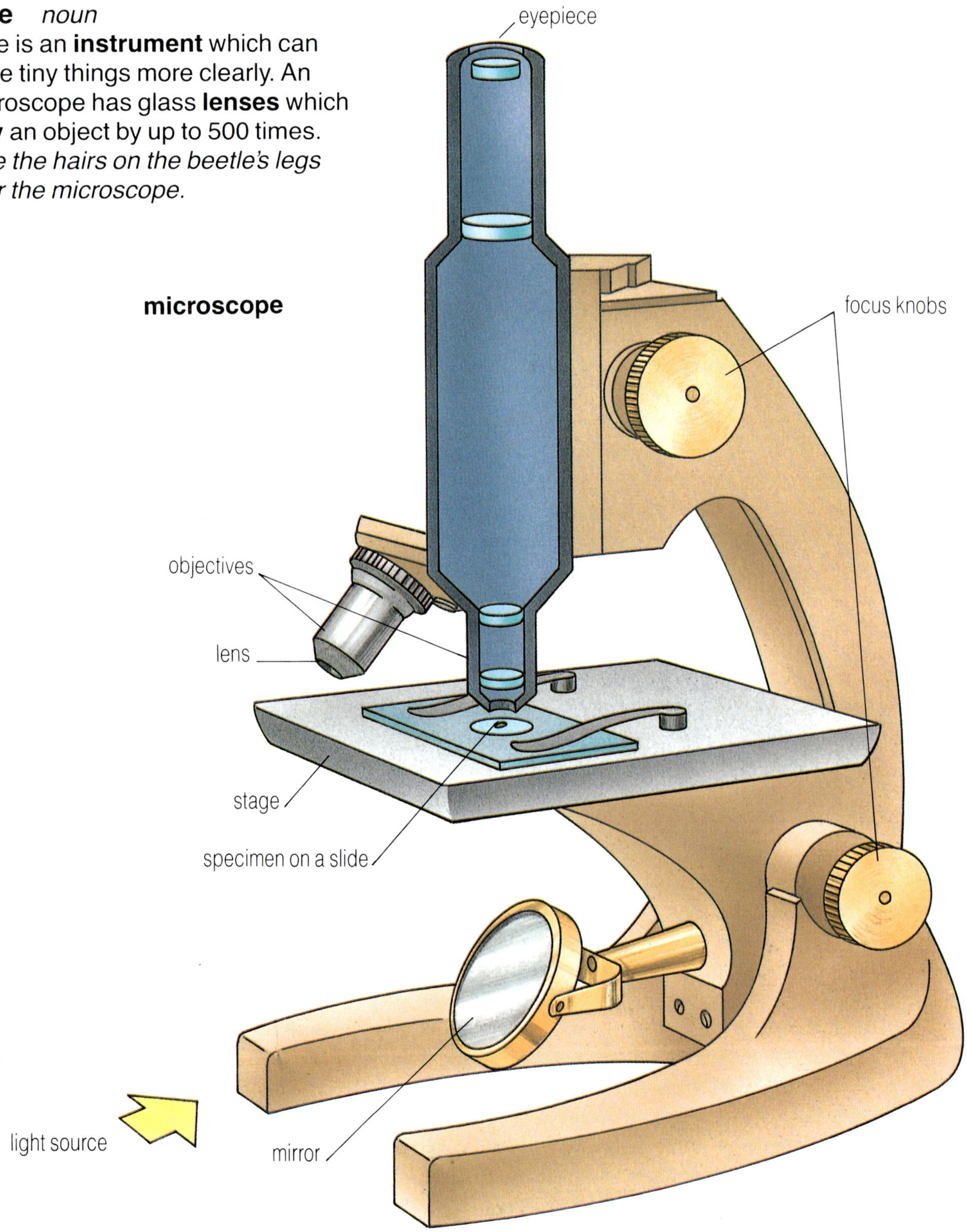

magnified things

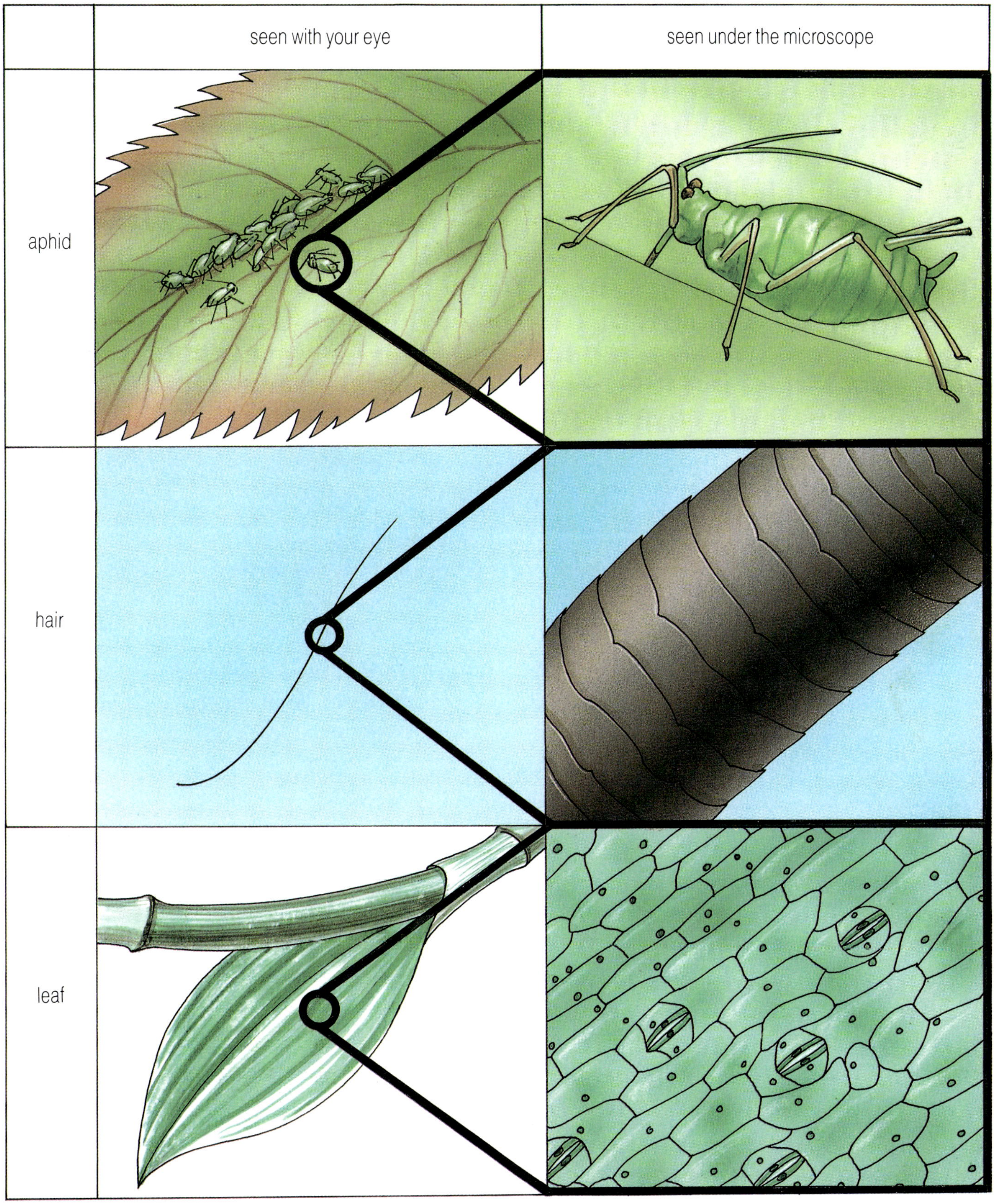

N

natural gas *noun*
Natural gas is a kind of **fossil fuel**. It is a mixture of **hydrocarbon** gases. It contains mostly **methane** with some ethane, **propane** and **butane**. Natural gas is burned as a fuel and helps in the manufacture of chemicals.
Natural gas heats the rooms and the water in many homes.

nautical mile *noun*
A nautical mile is a **unit** of measurement. It measures distances across seas and oceans. A nautical mile is 1,852 **metres** long.
The ship sailed 400 nautical miles each day.

negative *adjective*
Negative describes a kind of **electric charge**. **Electrons** and some **ions** have negative charges. Two negative charges repel each other. A negative charge attracts a **positive** charge.
He rubbed the strip of plastic with a cloth to give it a negative charge.

neon *noun*
Neon is a chemical **element**. It is a colourless **gas** which does not dissolve in water. It does not burn and does not allow things to burn in it. Some kinds of electric lamp contain neon.
There are tiny amounts of neon in the air which we breathe.

network *noun*
A network describes two or more **computers** that work together. The computers in a network share information and **data**.
The clothing company used a network to control the supply of clothes to its shops.

neutral *adjective*
1. Neutral describes something that has no **electric charge**. Substances are usually neutral because they contain equal numbers of **negative** electrons and **positive** protons.
A balloon is neutral until you rub it and give it a charge.
2. Neutral describes some kinds of **solution**. A neutral solution is neither an **acid** nor an **alkali**. It has a **pH** number of 7.
Pure water is a neutral liquid.

neutralize *verb*
Neutralize is a word which describes a kind of **chemical reaction**. An acid neutralizes a **base** to make a **neutral** solution. The new solution is a mixture of water and a **salt**.
She neutralized the vinegar in the bottle with bicarbonate of soda.
neutralization *noun*

neutron *noun*
A neutron is a tiny particle of **matter**. Neutrons are found in the nucleus of an **atom**. All matter except hydrogen contains neutrons. A neutron has the same mass as a **proton**, but it has no **electric charge**.
A speck of dust contains thousands of millions of neutrons.

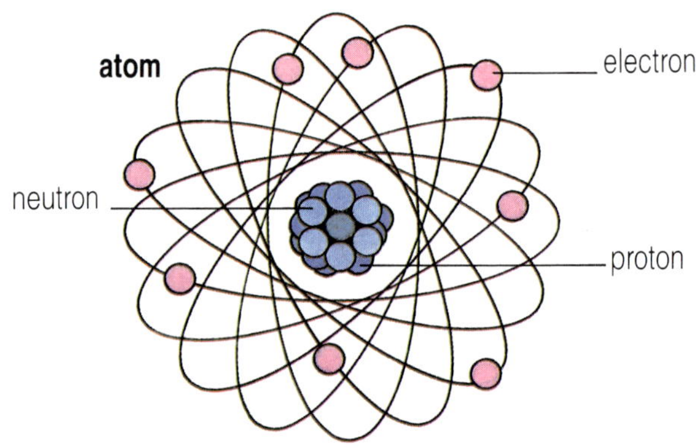

newton *noun*
A newton, or N for short, is a **unit** of measurement. Newtons measure **force**. **Gravity** pulls on a **mass** of 1 kilogram with a force of about 10 newtons.
The engine pushed the motor car with a force of 5,000 newtons.

nickel *noun*
Nickel is a chemical **element**. It is a hard, silvery **metal** which does not **corrode** easily. Nickel is mixed with iron and **chromium** to make stainless **steel**.
Many knives, forks and spoons contain nickel.

nitric acid *noun*
Nitric acid is a colourless and poisonous liquid. It is made from **ammonia** and it **corrodes** metals. Nitric acid helps to make dyes, explosives and **fertilizers.**
Nitric acid has a very strong smell.

nitrogen *noun*
Nitrogen is a chemical **element**. It is a colourless **gas** and a **non-metal**. Nitrogen makes up two-thirds of the **atmosphere**. Millions of tonnes of nitrogen are used each year to make **ammonia.**
A lighted match goes out when it is put into a jar of nitrogen.

nitrogen cycle ► page 94

non-metal *noun*
A non-metal can be a **solid**, a **liquid** or a **gas**. Non-metals are **elements** and include carbon, sulphur and oxygen. They are poor **conductors** of heat. All non-metals except carbon are electrical **insulators**.
Most non-metals are gases.

north pole *noun*
A north pole is a part of a **magnet**. It is one of the two **magnetic poles** which are found on every magnet. A magnet's north pole seeks, or is attracted towards, the magnetic north pole of the Earth. The opposite of north pole is **south pole**.
The full name for the north pole of a magnet is the north-seeking pole.

nuclear energy ► page 96

nuclear fission *noun*
Nuclear fission describes how some **atoms** break into pieces. Nuclear fission takes place when the nucleus of the atom splits. Heavy **radioactive elements**, such as uranium, split into new elements and release **nuclear energy**.
Nuclear fission helps scientists to find out how old some bones are.

nuclear fusion *noun*
Nuclear fusion describes how some **atoms** join together. Nuclear fusion takes place when the nuclei of two atoms join, or fuse, together at very high temperatures. Light **elements**, such as hydrogen, fuse to make a new element and release **nuclear energy**.
Nuclear fusion creates the intense heat inside the Sun.

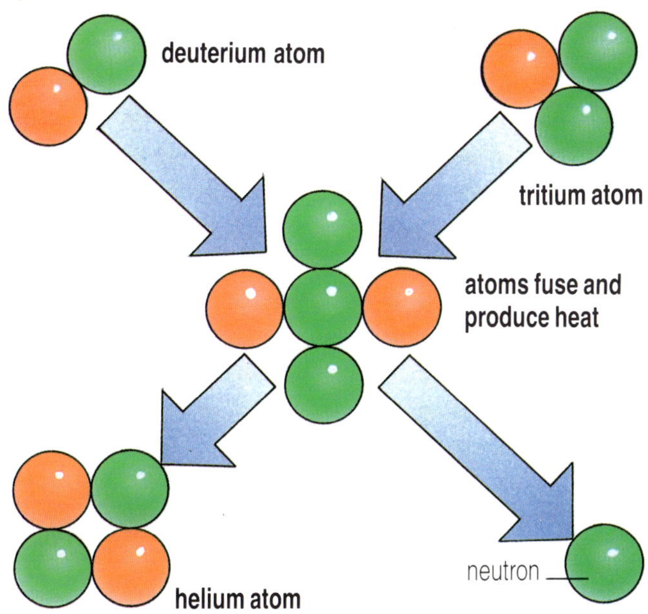

nitrogen cycle *noun*
The nitrogen cycle is a term which describes how **nitrogen** moves from living things to the **atmosphere** and back again. It shows how nitrogen from the atmosphere passes into the soil and is then used by plants and animals.
In the nitrogen cycle, rotting animals and plants put nitrogen back into the soil.

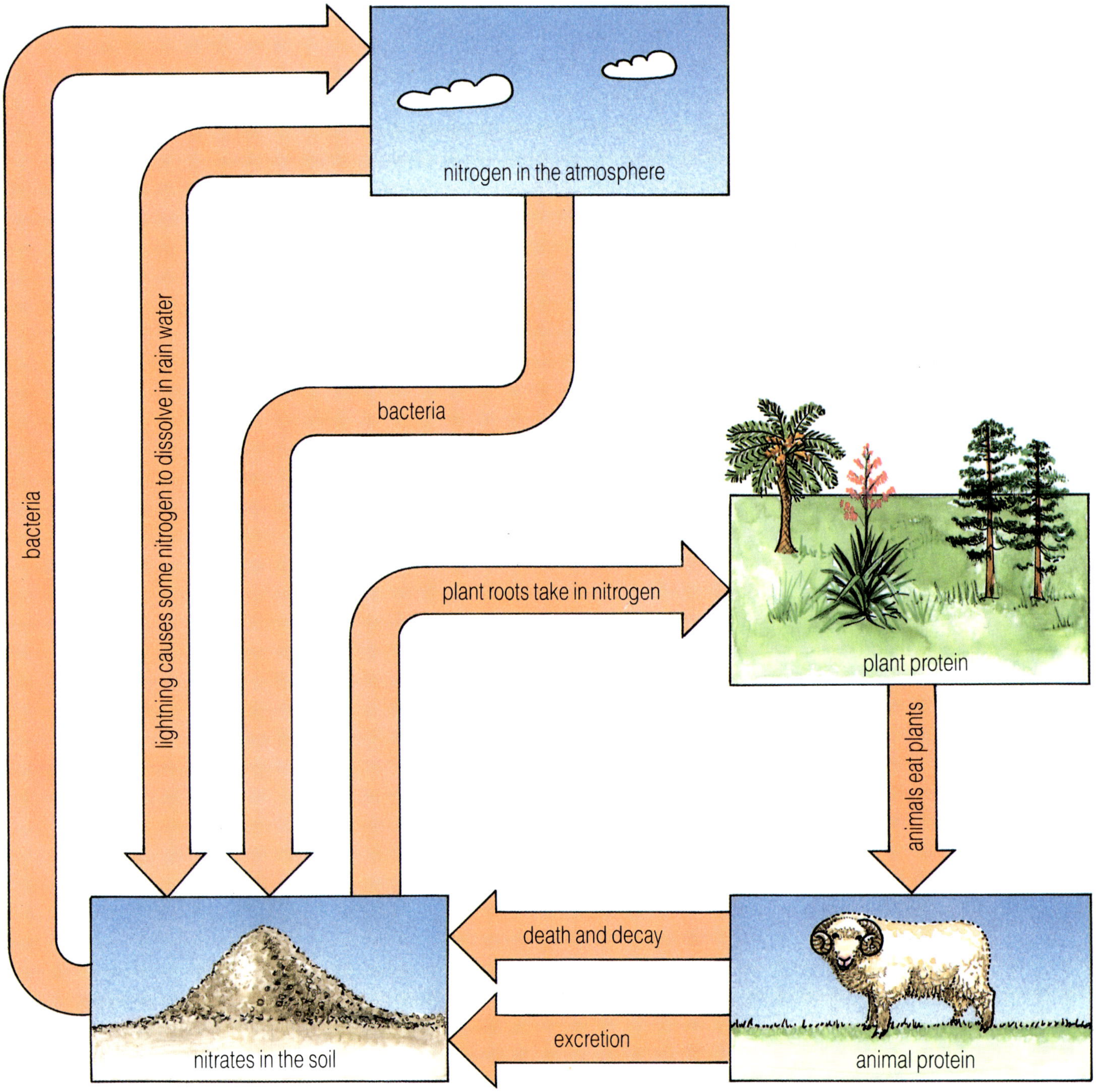

nuclear power station noun
A nuclear power station generates electricity. Heat from a **nuclear reactor** boils water to make steam. The steam drives a **turbine** which spins the shaft of a **generator**.
Many nuclear power stations are built beside the sea.

nuclear radiation *noun*
Nuclear radiation is a group of different **rays** and moving **particles**. These are **gamma rays**, **alpha particles**, **beta particles** and **neutrons**. Nuclear radiation is given off by the **nuclei** of atoms during nuclear fission and nuclear fusion.
Nuclear radiation is dangerous to living things.

nuclear reactor *noun*
A nuclear reactor is a device which releases **nuclear energy**. The reactor in a nuclear power station contains **uranium** fuel, a **moderator, control rods** and a **coolant**.
A thick, concrete wall surrounds a nuclear reactor.

nucleus (plural **nuclei**) *noun*
1. The nucleus is the centre of an **atom**. It contains **protons** and **neutrons**. Nuclei do not take part in a chemical reaction. They are changed only by **nuclear fission** and **nuclear fusion**.
The nucleus of an atom is extremely small.
2. The nucleus is the centre part of most living **cells**. The nucleus controls how the cell behaves. The nuclei of different kinds of cell contain different **genes**.
The nucleus of a cell looks like a small spot.

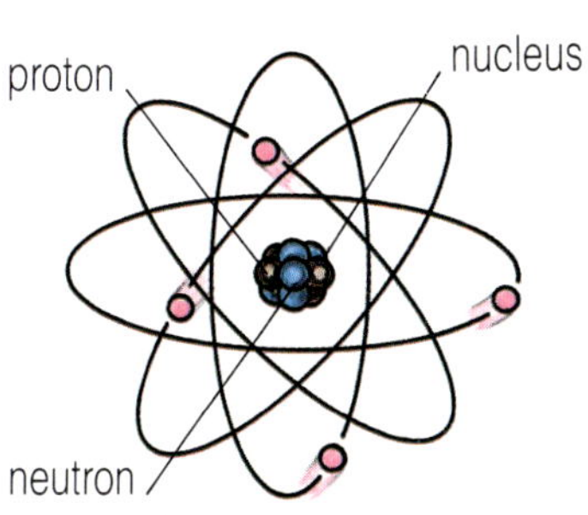

carbon atom

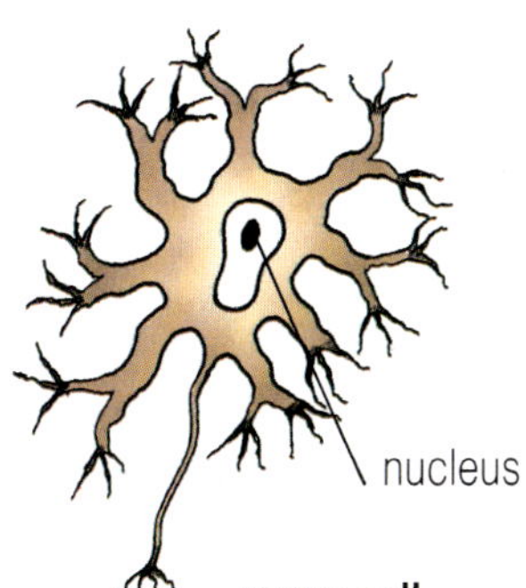

nerve cell

nut *noun*
A nut is a flat piece of **metal**. It has four or six sides and a hole in the middle. Inside the hole is a spiral groove called the thread. This fits with the thread on a **bolt**, so that the two can be screwed together.
He turned the nut to tighten it around the bolt.

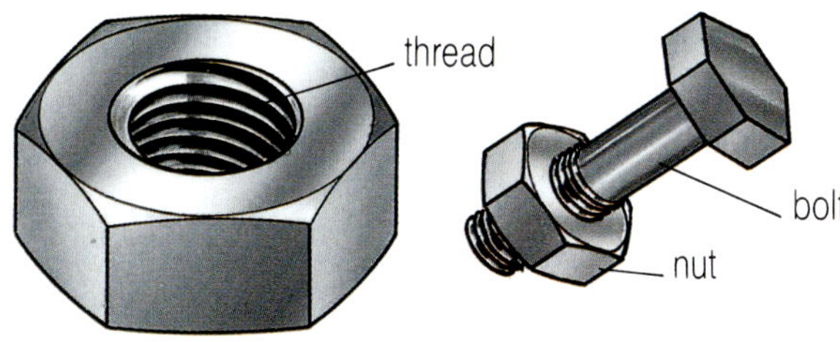

nylon *noun*
Nylon is a kind of **plastic**. It is a **polymer** which is made from chemicals. These chemicals come from **petroleum**. Machines spin nylon **fibres** to make cloth and ropes.
His socks were made from a mixture of nylon and cotton.

nuclear energy *noun*
Nuclear energy is energy which is released when the **nucleus** of an **atom** changes. The nucleus of a **radioactive** fuel, such as **uranium**, may be split into two to release nuclear energy. Nuclear energy is also called atomic energy.
Some power stations use nuclear energy to produce electricity.

nuclear fission

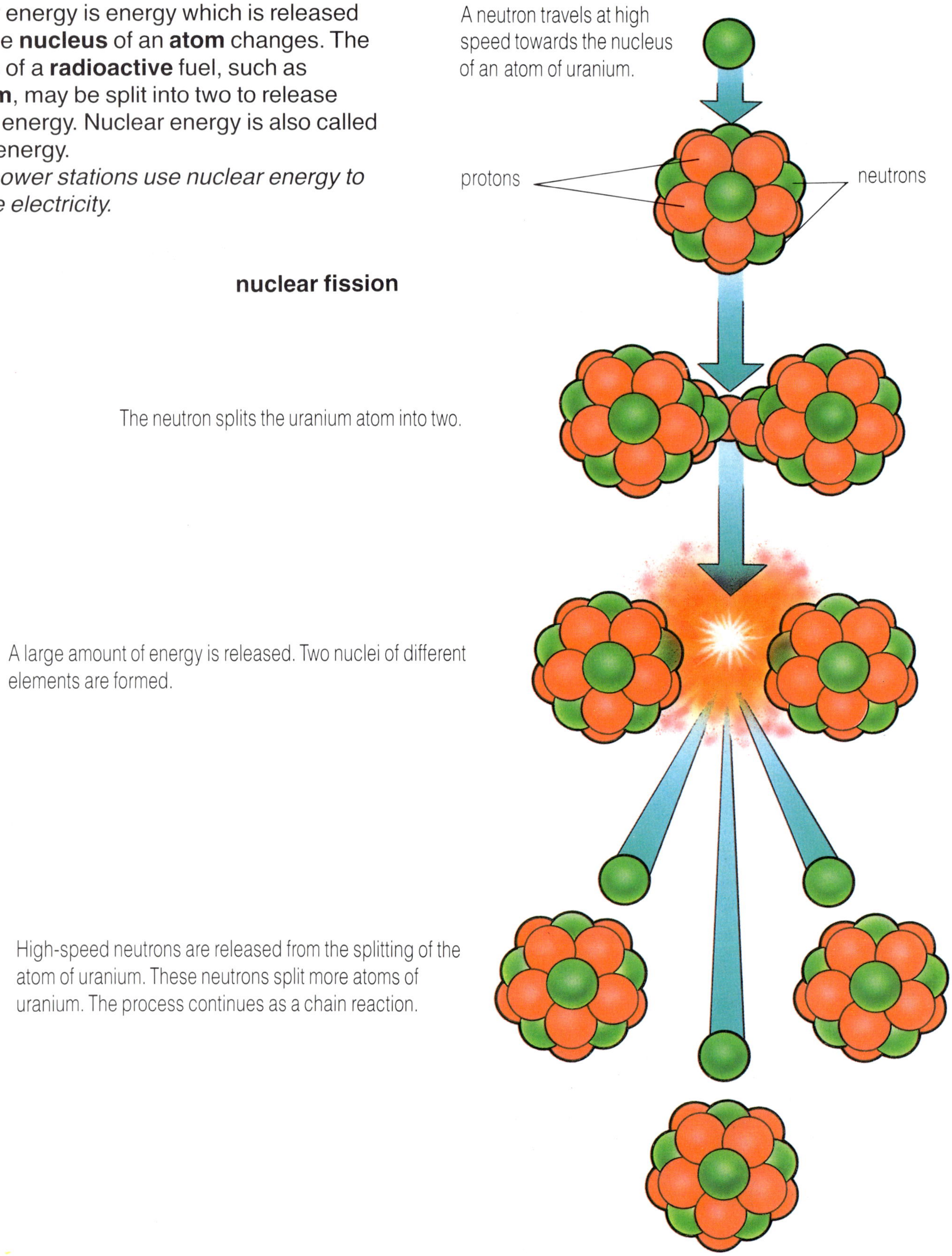

nuclear reactor

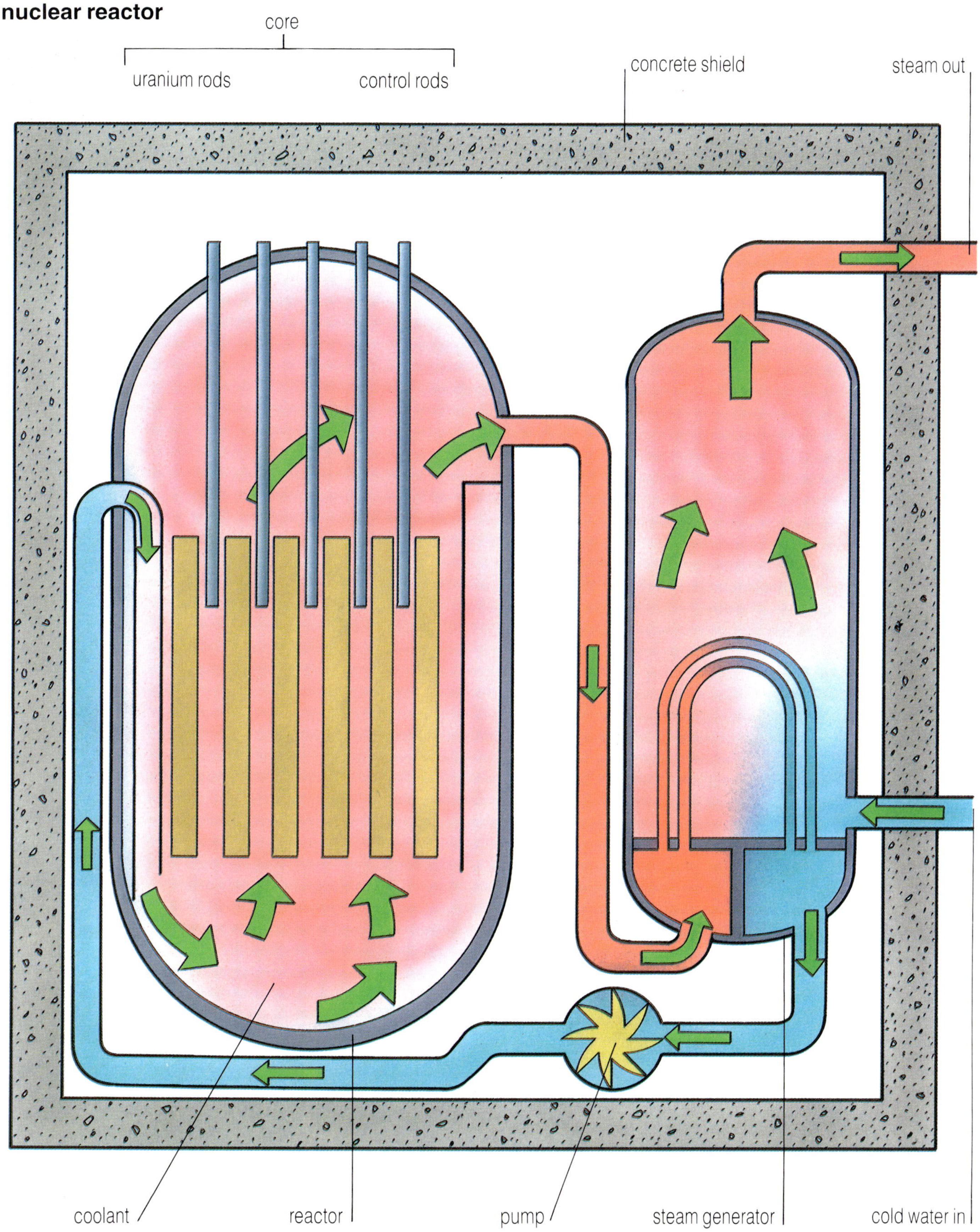

O

objective *noun*
An objective is a kind of **lens**. It forms part of a **microscope** or a **telescope**. The objective is the lens which is closest to the object being looked at. It is the lens which is farthest from the person's eye.
She moved the objective of the telescope to get a clearer view of the stars.

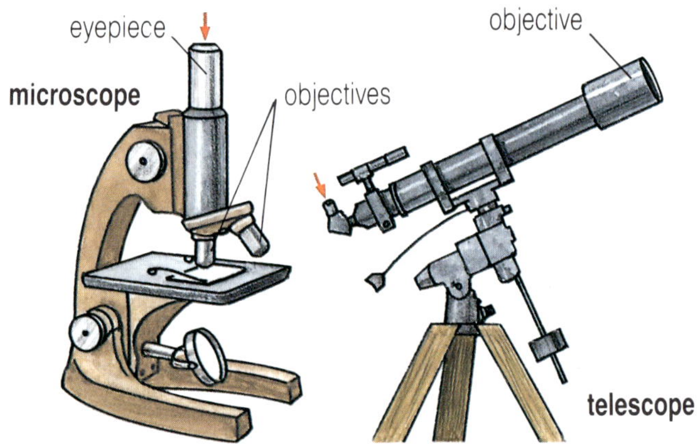

oil *noun*
Oil is a thick, slippery **liquid**. It does not mix with water. Oil is usually made from **petroleum** by **fractional distillation**.
Oil **lubricates** engines and other machines.
He poured a drop of oil on to the hinge to stop it from squeaking.

oil refinery ▶ page 100

opaque *adjective*
Opaque describes a substance which does not allow light to pass through it. The opposite of opaque is **translucent**.
Her hand makes a shadow because it is opaque.

optical fibre *noun*
An optical fibre is a long thread which is made from **glass**. Optical fibres carry light **signals** from **lasers** over long distances.
Optical fibres in the ground carry telephone, radio and television signals.

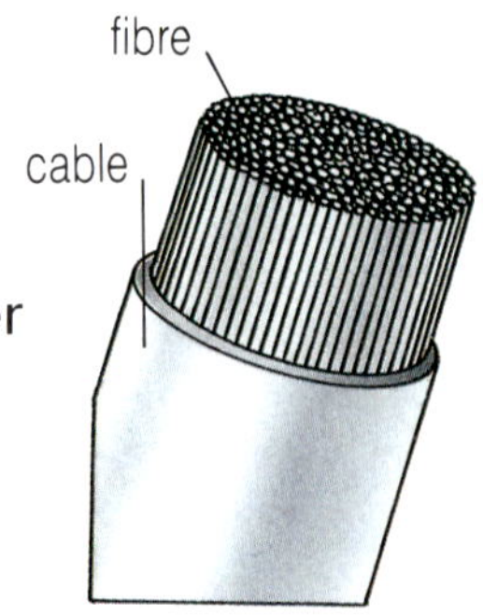

orbit *verb*
Orbit is a word which describes how one object moves around another object. The pathway of an object which is orbiting is usually shaped like an **ellipse**. Planets orbit around the Sun. **Electrons** orbit around the **nucleus** of an atom.
It takes the Earth one year to orbit around the Sun.
orbit *noun*

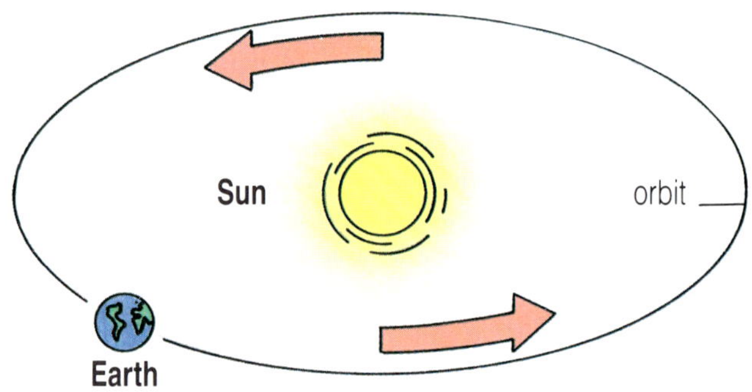

order *noun*
An order is a group of living things. All the living things in the same order have special **characteristics**. Orders are part of the system of **classification** which **biologists** have worked out.
Dogs, bears and seals are grouped together in an order called carnivores.

ore *noun*
An ore is a kind of **mineral** which is found in the ground. Different ores are used to make different metals, such as copper, iron and aluminium. **Smelting** or **electrolysis** releases the metal from the ore.
They dug out the ore from an enormous hole in the ground.

organic *adjective*
Organic describes substances which always contain atoms of **carbon**. The opposite of organic is **inorganic**.
All living things are made up of organic substances.

organism *noun*
An organism is a living thing. The five main kinds of organism are plants, **animals**, **monera**, **protists** and **fungi**. All organisms reproduce, can sense their environment and take in nourishment.
A whale, a tree, a sponge and a germ are different kinds of organism.

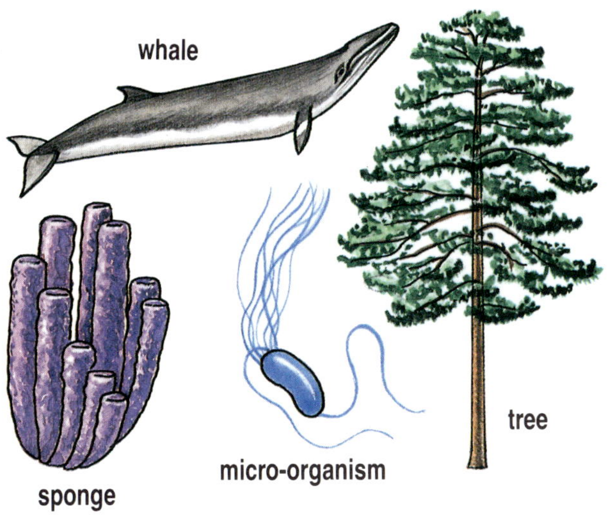

oscillate *verb*
Oscillate is a word which describes a kind of movement. Things oscillate when they **vibrate** or move steadily backwards and forwards. An **alternating current** oscillates as it becomes stronger and weaker in an electric circuit.
The strings of a guitar oscillate and make a sound.

output *noun*
Output describes what is produced from a **machine** or some other **device**. The output from a computer appears on a **screen** or on paper. The output from an engine is **mechanical energy**.
The output from a radio is sound.

oxidation *noun*
Oxidation is a kind of **chemical reaction**. A substance combines with oxygen during oxidation. During oxidation, **carbon** burns in air to make **carbon dioxide**.
Oxidation can give out large amounts of heat.

oxide *noun*
An oxide is a kind of chemical **compound**. It contains a metal or a **non-metal** which has combined with oxygen. **Carbon dioxide**, water and rust are all oxides. Oxides are the result of **oxidation**.
Copper oxide is a black powder.

oxygen *noun*
Oxygen is a chemical **element**. It is a colourless **gas** which is found in the **atmosphere**. Living things need oxygen for **respiration**. Fuels need oxygen to burn. **Compounds**, such as water, contain oxygen which has joined with other elements.
Almost half the substances in the Earth's crust contain oxygen.

ozone *noun*
Ozone is a colourless **gas** which has a strong smell. It is made when a **molecule** of oxygen joins with an extra atom of oxygen. Ozone is found in a layer high up in the **atmosphere**. It absorbs harmful **ultraviolet rays** from the Sun.
Scientists say that pollution is destroying the layer of ozone around the Earth.

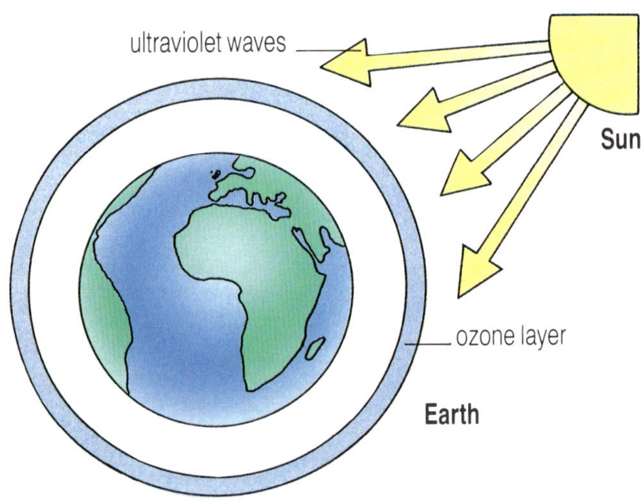

oil refinery *noun*
An oil refinery is a place where **crude oil** is processed into useful substances. The oil is heated in a furnace. A huge machine called a **fractionating column** separates the oil into many different liquids and gases.
Gases, waxes and fuel for cars and aeroplanes are all made at an oil refinery.

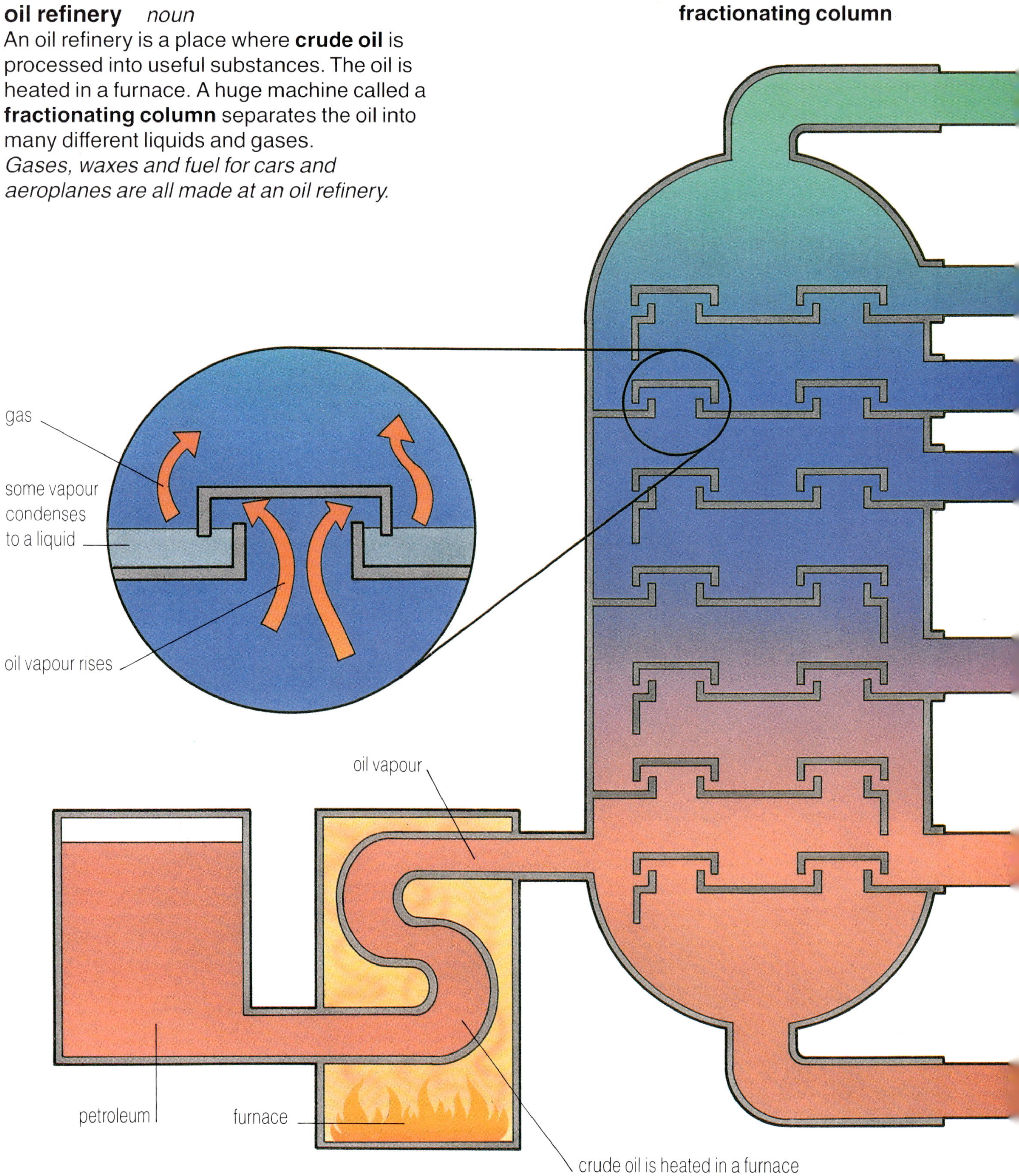

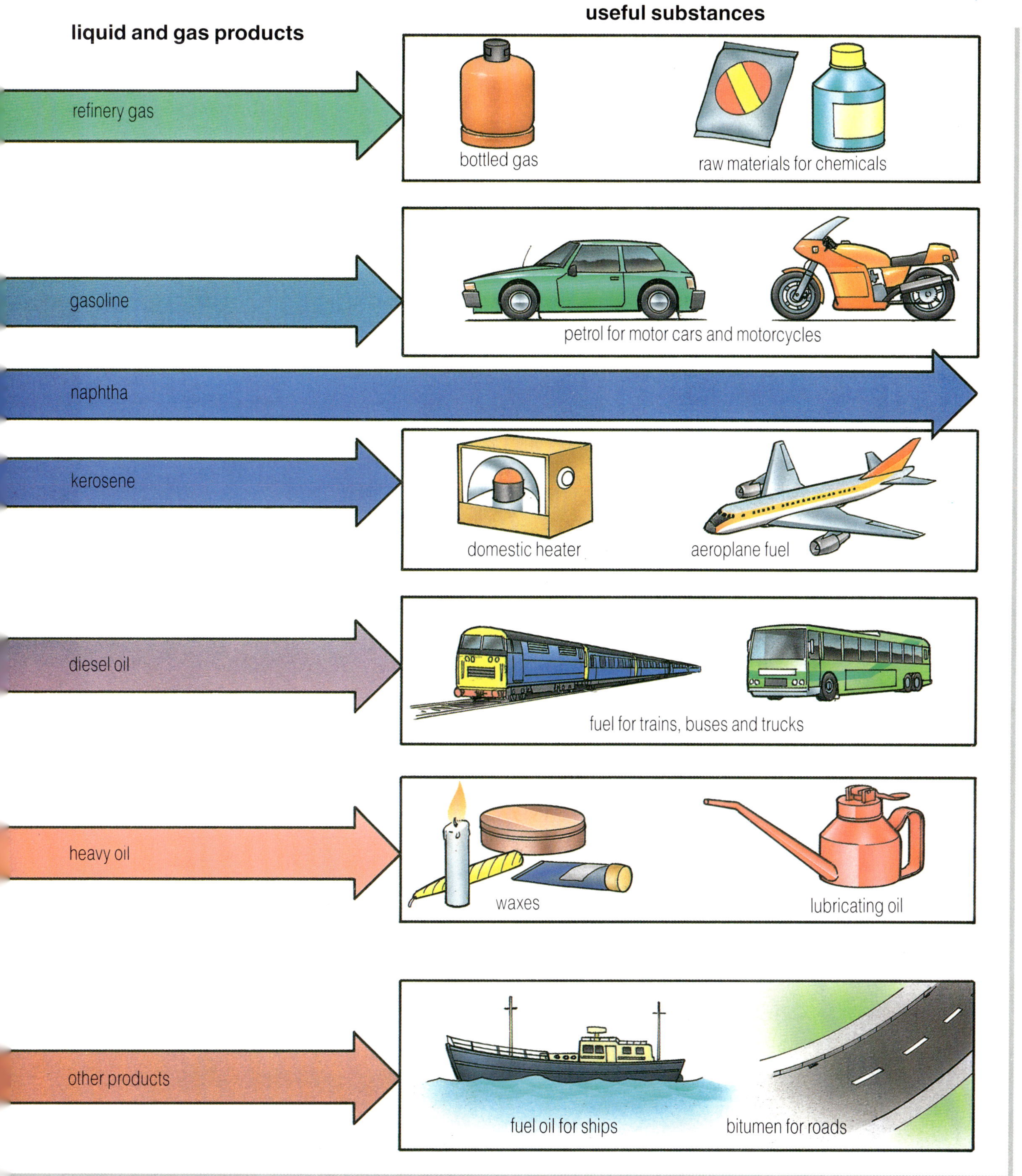
useful substances
liquid and gas products
refinery gas
bottled gas
raw materials for chemicals
gasoline
petrol for motor cars and motorcycles
naphtha
kerosene
domestic heater
aeroplane fuel
diesel oil
fuel for trains, buses and trucks
heavy oil
waxes
lubricating oil
other products
fuel oil for ships
bitumen for roads

P

paraffin *noun*
Paraffin is an oily **liquid**. It burns easily and does not mix with water. Paraffin is a **hydrocarbon** which is made from petroleum. It is burned as a fuel for heating and for powering **jet engines**.
The heater burned 3 litres of paraffin each day.

parallel circuit *noun*
A parallel circuit is a way of connecting together electrical **components**. The **electric current** in a parallel circuit splits into two or more different paths. Currents flow through the different paths and then join up again.
If one bulb in the parallel circuit breaks, the other bulb stays lit up.

particle *noun*
A particle is a very small part of a **substance**. Atoms, molecules, **ions** and **electrons** are different kinds of particle.
Everything in the universe is made up of particles which are too small to see.

periscope *noun*
A periscope is a **device** which helps us to see things over walls, around corners or in places where we would not usually see them. It contains two mirrors or **prisms**, which are fixed inside a tube. The crews of submarines use periscopes to see above the surface of the sea.
She looked through a periscope to see over the heads of the people in front of her.

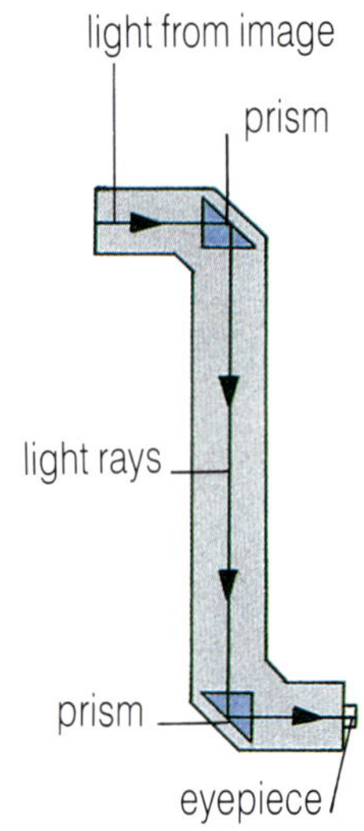

permanent magnet *noun*
A permanent magnet is an object which is always **magnetic**. Permanent magnets are made from iron or from special **alloys** which contain iron. Permanent magnets are used in electric motors, **compasses** and loudspeakers.
Permanent magnets held the door of the freezer shut.

petrochemical *noun*
A petrochemical is a substance which is made up from **organic** chemicals. These chemicals come from petroleum or from natural gas. Ethene, **methane**, diesel oil and **monomers** are different kinds of petrochemical.
Petrochemicals help to make all the plastics which we use every day.

petrol engine ► page 104

petroleum *noun*
Petroleum is a dark, oily **liquid** which is found beneath the Earth's surface. It is sometimes called crude oil and is a mixture of **hydrocarbons**. Petroleum is refined to make fuels and other **petrochemicals**.
Engineers drill deep into the ground to look for petroleum.

pH *noun*
pH is a **unit** of measurement. It measures the strength of an **acid** or an **alkali**. A pH of 7 is **neutral**. A very strong acid has a pH of 1. A very strong alkali has a pH of 14.
The pH of vinegar is about 3.

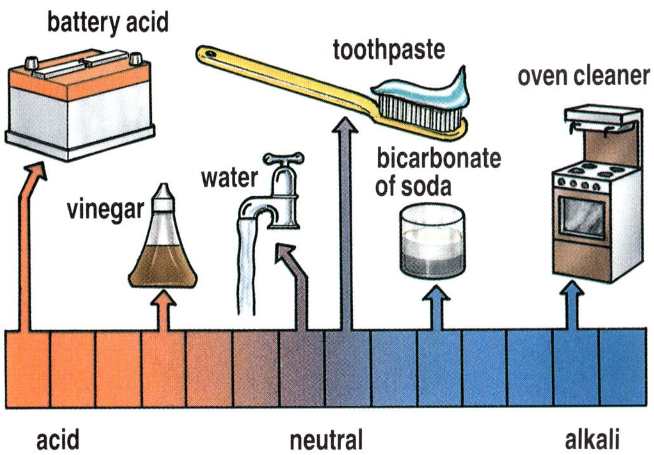

phase *noun*
Phase is a word which describes the shape of the Moon as we see it from the Earth. The main phases of the Moon are called quarter moon, half moon and full moon. The phase depends on how much sunlight is blocked by the Earth.
The phases of the Moon are repeated once every month.

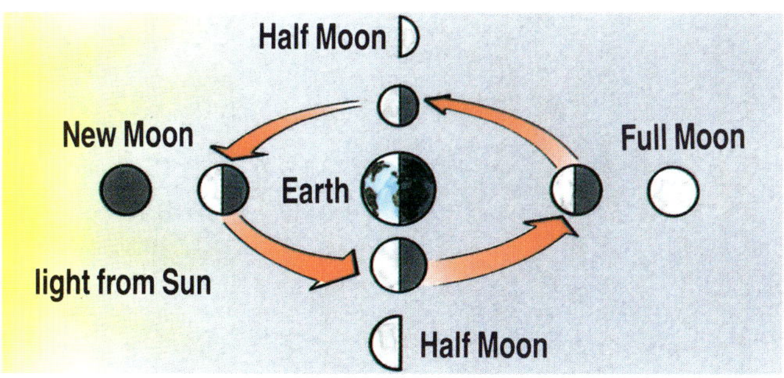

phosphate *noun*
A phosphate is a kind of **chemical**. Farmers add phosphates to the soil to help the crops grow well. Phosphates are also added to cleaners, such as soap powder and detergents, to make them more powerful. These phosphates can pollute rivers.
Rain washed the phosphate from the field into the stream.

phosphor *noun*
Phosphor is a kind of **solid**. Many thousands of phosphors are used to coat the inside of a **cathode ray tube**. A phosphor gives out light when hit by **electrons** from an **electron gun**.
Phosphors glow with light and make the picture we see on the television.

photon *noun*
A photon is a **particle** which has been invented by scientists to explain how light behaves. Light usually behaves like **waves** of energy. But sometimes, light behaves like a stream of **particles**. These particles are called photons.
Photons of red light have less energy than photons of violet light.

phylum (plural **phyla**) *noun*
A phylum is a group of living things. All the living things in the same phylum have special **characteristics**. Phyla are part of the system of **classification** which **biologists** have worked out.
Snails, slugs and octopuses are grouped together in a phylum called molluscs.

physics *noun*
Physics is a **scientific** subject. It is the study of how **matter** and **energy** affect each other. Physics includes heat, light, sound, electricity, magnetism and nuclear energy.
Physics helps us to understand how the Earth moves around the Sun.

pig iron *noun*
Pig iron is a grey **metal** which is **brittle**. It is **impure** iron which comes out of a **blast furnace**. Most pig iron is used to make **steel**.
The blast furnace made 1,000 tonnes of pig iron every day.

pigment *noun*
A pigment is a kind of coloured powder. Pigments are mixed with liquids to make paint.
He stirred the green pigment into the glue to make paint.

petrol engine *noun*
A petrol engine is a kind of **internal combustion engine.** It produces power by burning petrol and air in a **cylinder.** Most petrol engines are **four-stroke engines,** which means that the cylinders go through a series of four movements, or strokes.
Petrol engines usually have 4, 6 or 8 cylinders.

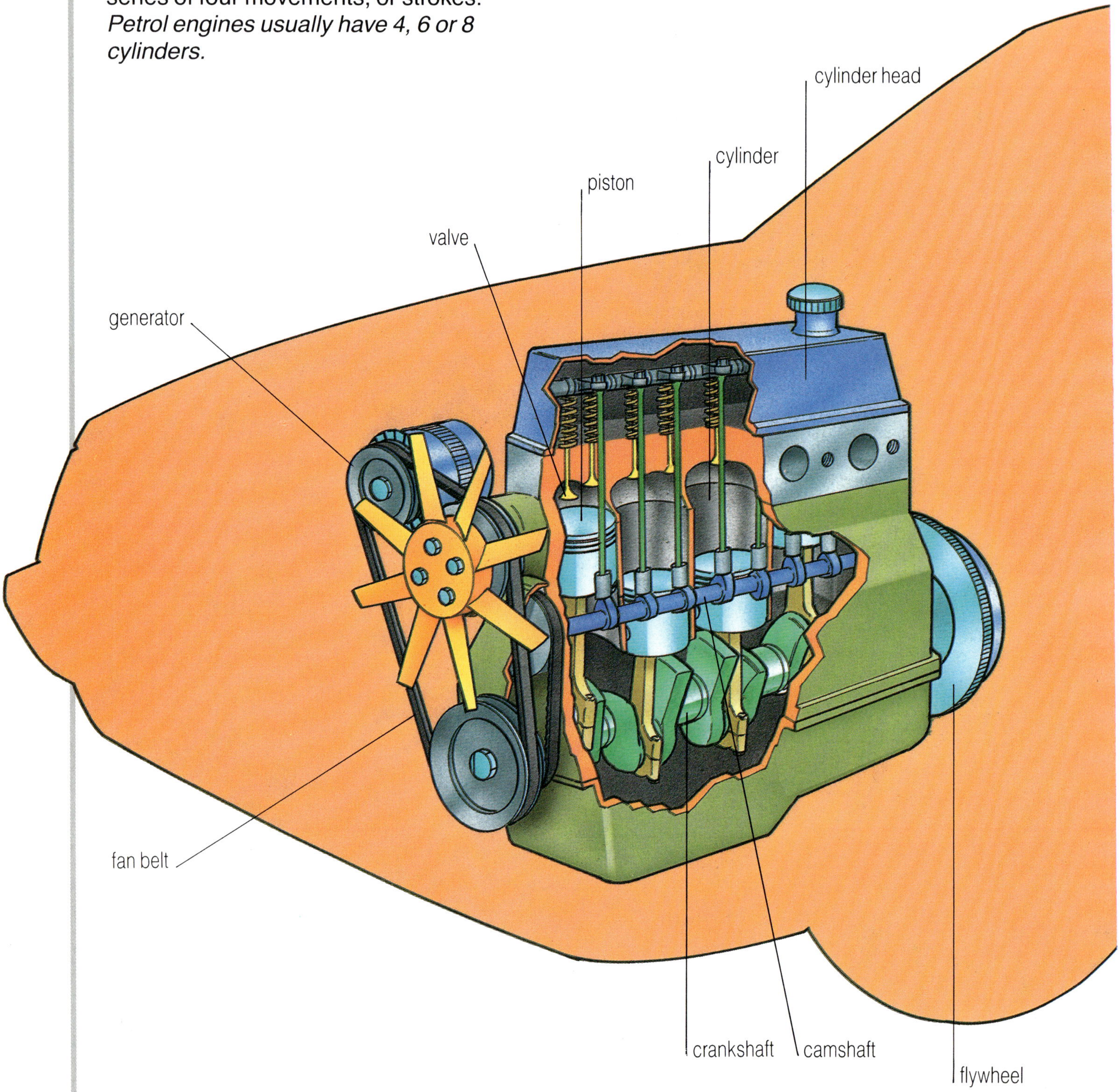

1st stroke

The piston moves down, and fuel and air are sucked in.

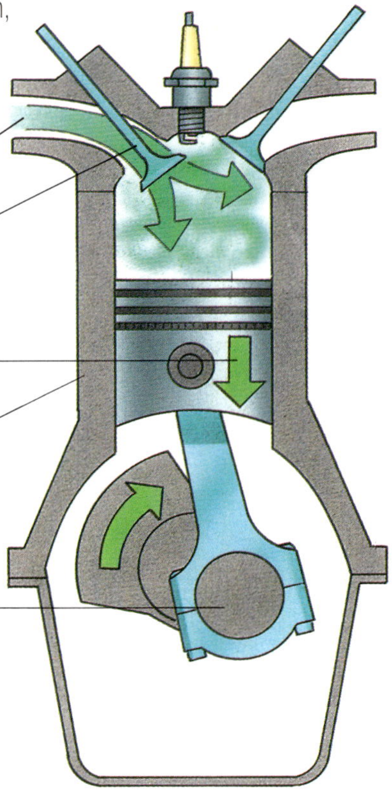

2nd stroke

The piston is pushed up, squeezing the fuel mixture into a small space.

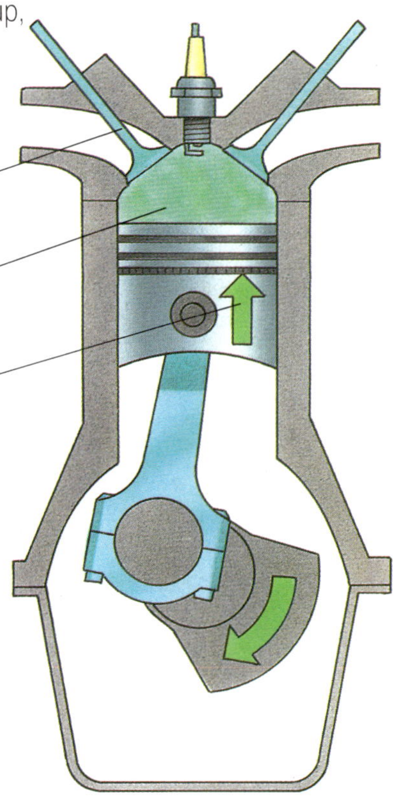

3rd stroke

A spark from a spark plug makes the mixture explode. The piston is pushed down.

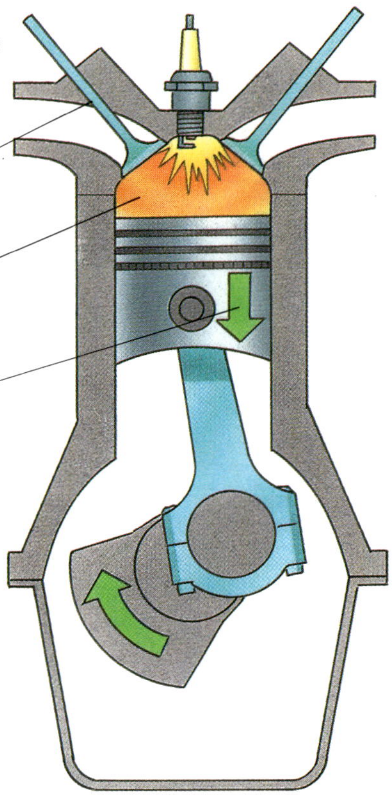

4th stroke

The piston comes up again, pushing burned gases out through the open valve.

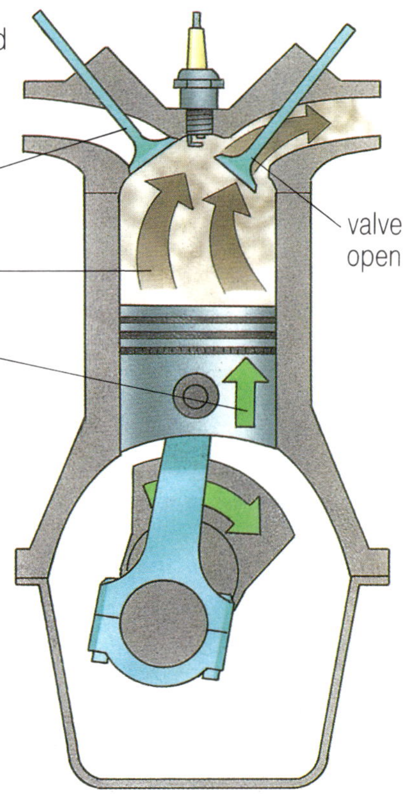

piston *noun*
A piston is a part of a **machine**. It fits inside a **cylinder** and moves backwards and forwards. Pistons are used in internal combustion engines, pumps and **hydraulic** machines.
The piston in a bicycle pump pushes air into the tyre.

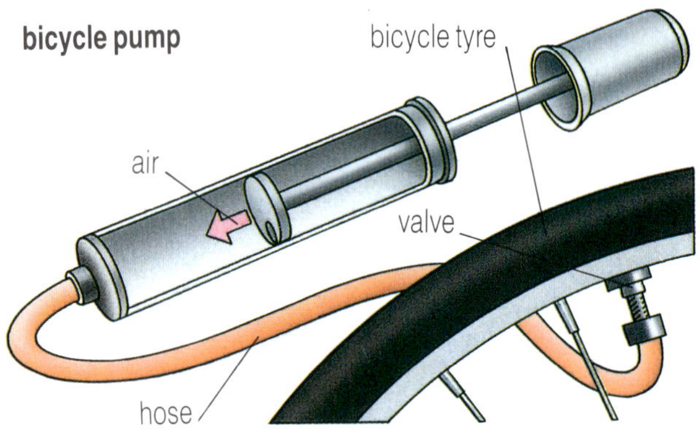

pitch *noun*
Pitch is a soft, black **solid**. It is the substance which is left behind when **coal tar** boils away. Pitch is like **bitumen** and melts when it is heated. Pitch helps to make **asphalt** for roads and waterproof coverings for roofs.
They mixed together sand and pitch, and rolled the mixture onto the road.

pivot *noun*
A pivot is a kind of short **shaft** or rod. It is fixed to a part inside a machine. The part rotates or **oscillates** around the pivot. **Axles** and **fulcrums** are kinds of pivot.
A wheel spins on its axle which acts as a pivot.

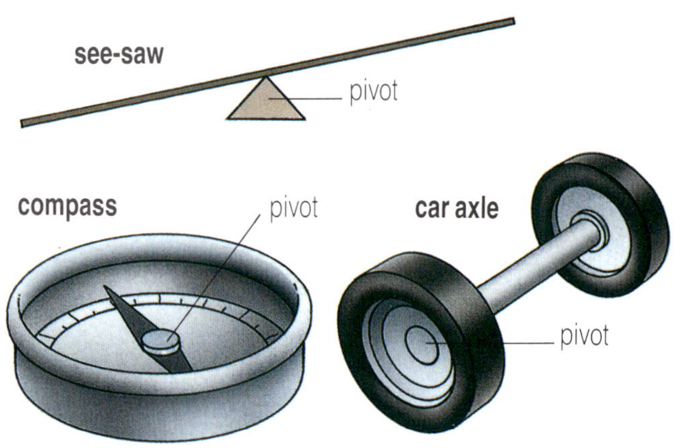

plasma *noun*
1. Plasma is the liquid part of **blood**. It is a clear liquid which is made up of water with substances dissolved in it. These substances include **glucose**, hormones and waste materials.
The body of an adult person contains about 3 litres of plasma.
2. Plasma is a very hot **gas**. The temperature of the particles in plasma is above 50,000 degrees **kelvin**. The atoms in plasma break up into individual **electrons** and **nuclei**.
The outside of the Sun is made up of plasma.

plastic *noun*
A plastic is a kind of **solid**. It is a **polymer** which is artificial. Plastics can be shaped easily because they soften when heated. Waste plastic can cause pollution because it does not rot.
Plastic can be moulded into many different shapes.

platinum *noun*
Platinum is a chemical **element**. It is a **precious metal** which has a silvery colour. It does not **corrode** easily and is used to make jewellery.
Platinum is usually as expensive as gold.

plutonium *noun*
Plutonium is a chemical **element**. It is a silvery **metal** which is **radioactive**. Plutonium is not found naturally as an **ore**. It is made from uranium in **nuclear reactors**. It powers some other kinds of nuclear reactor and also atomic weapons.
Scientists first made plutonium in 1940.

pneumatic *adjective*
Pneumatic is a word which describes a **device** that works with the help of air. Pneumatic tyres on motor cars and bicycles are filled with air at low **pressure**. **Compressed** air from a pump at high pressure drives a pneumatic drill.
The workman dug a hole in the road with his pneumatic drill.

polar *adjective*
Polar is a word that describes anything found near the North Pole or the South Pole of the Earth. The areas are called the polar regions and the animals are called polar **species**.
Polar bears live in the polar regions near the North Pole.

pole noun
A pole is a part of a **magnet**. A magnet has a **north pole** and a **south pole**. The **magnetism** of a magnet is strongest at its poles.
A bar magnet is shaped like a rod and has a pole at each end.

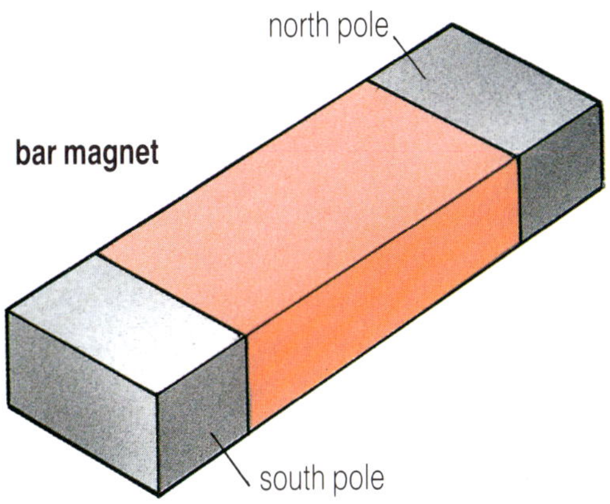

pollution *noun*
Pollution is a word which describes the spread of harmful or unwanted **substances** on to the land or into the air or water. Pollution is caused by substances such as **exhaust** fumes from motor cars and **smoke** from factory chimneys.
The smoke from the chimney caused pollution of the air around the factory.

polymer *noun*
A polymer is a very large **molecule**. Polymers are solid and are made up of thousands of **monomers**. These are joined in a chemical process to make long chains. Plastics are polymers which are made in this way. **Proteins** are natural polymers.
The polymer molecules are tangled together in the plastic.

polystyrene *noun*
Polystyrene is a kind of **plastic**. It is a **polymer** which is made from **petrochemicals**. Polystyrene is hard and **brittle**. Parts of toys and pens are made from polystyrene. Foam which is made from polystyrene is a good **insulator** of heat.
Polystyrene foam is made into cartons for keeping food hot.

polythene *noun*
Polythene is a kind of **plastic**. It is a **polymer** which is made from a **petrochemical** called ethene. Polythene is soft and flexible. It is used to make food storage bags and the coating on some kinds of electric cable.
The polythene bag kept his sandwiches fresh.

polyvinylchloride *noun*
Polyvinylchloride, or PVC for short, is a kind of **plastic**. It is a **polymer** which is made from **petrochemicals**. Polyvinylchloride is a tough solid. It can be made soft by adding chemicals called plasticizers.
Some plastic raincoats are made from shiny polyvinylchloride.

pore *noun*
A pore is a kind of hole. Pores are often found in the outer layer or skin of a living thing. **Liquids** or **gases** pass through pores. When you are hot, sweat flows out through pores in your skin.
The pore on the leaf was so small that he needed a microscope to see it.

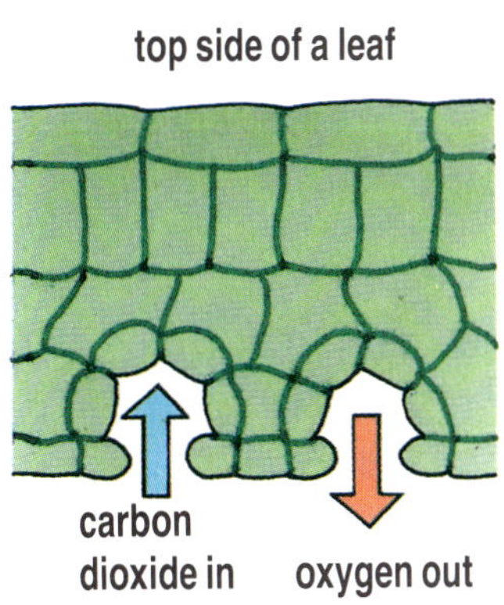

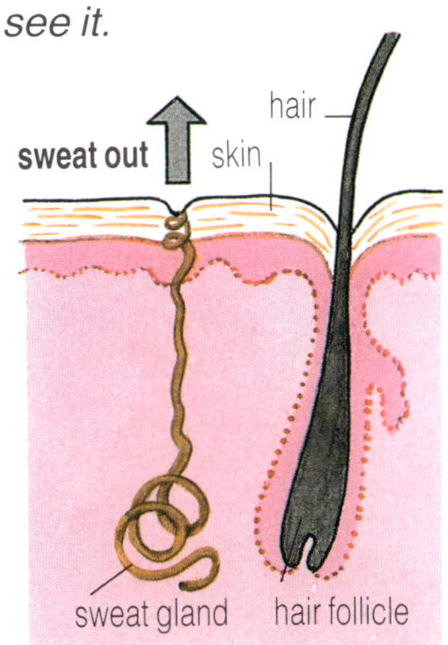

porous *adjective*
Porous describes a substance which is full of **pores**. A container which is made of a porous substance allows gases and liquids to enter and escape slowly.
A paper bag is porous so it cannot hold water.

positive *adjective*
Positive is a word which describes a kind of **electric charge**. **Protons** and some **ions** have a positive charge. Two positive charges repel each other. A positive charge attracts a **negative** charge.
If you comb your hair in dry weather, you will give it a positive charge.

potassium *noun*
Potassium is a chemical **element**. It is a **metal** which reacts violently with water and quickly **corrodes** in air. As a **pure** metal, potassium has almost no uses. **Salts** which contain potassium are important in the manufacture of fertilizers.
Potassium metal is so soft that it can be cut with a knife.

potential energy *noun*
Potential energy is stored **energy**. Electrical energy in a battery, nuclear energy and chemical energy are different kinds of potential energy. When an object is lifted above the ground, it stores potential energy. This energy is used when the object falls back to the ground.
Water loses potential energy as it flows down the side of a hill.

power *noun*
1. Power describes how much **work** is being done in a certain length of time. The power of an engine is the greatest amount of work it can do to drive a machine. It is usually measured in units called horsepower. The power of a light bulb describes the amount of light it emits and how much **energy** it uses. It is measured in **watts**.
A television set uses eight times more power than a light bulb.
2. Power describes how we can **multiply** numbers. We can write $2 \times 2 \times 2$ as 2^3. This is called 2 to the power of 3.
The number 10 to the power of 4 is written as 10^4*, which equals 10,000.*

power station *noun*
A power station is a place where electricity is generated. In a power station, fuel is burned to boil water and make steam. The pressure of the steam spins a **turbine** which drives a **generator**. Hydro-electric power stations and nuclear power stations are two kinds of power station.
The power station burned 1,000 tonnes of coal every day.

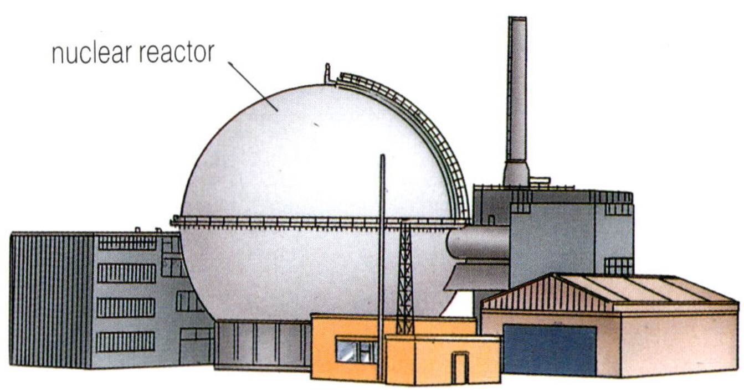

nuclear power station

precious metal *noun*
Precious metal is a term which describes metals such as **gold, silver** and **platinum**. All precious metals are rare and expensive. They do not **corrode** easily.
The jeweller made rings and bracelets from different precious metals.

precipitation *noun*
1. Precipitation describes a kind of **chemical reaction**. During the reaction, chemicals which are dissolved in **solutions** are mixed together. A new chemical is formed in the reaction. This chemical is a solid which can be seen as **particles** in a liquid.
He mixed the two clear liquids, and precipitation made a yellow solid.
2. Precipitation is a word which describes the liquid or solid water that comes from the **atmosphere**. Precipitation includes rain, drizzle, dew, hail, sleet, snow and hoar frost.
Precipitation can happen when clouds meet

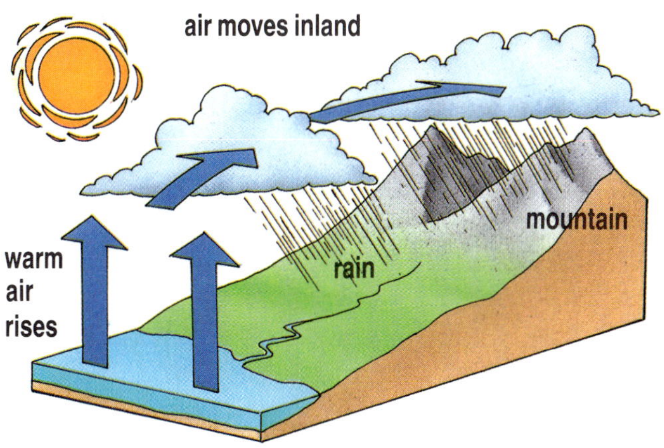

pressure *noun*
Pressure is a word which describes how much **force** is pressing on the surface of an object. It is measured in **newtons** per square metre. A large force which presses on a small **area** of an object produces a large pressure.
The pressure of the air inside a bicycle tyre makes the tyre hard.

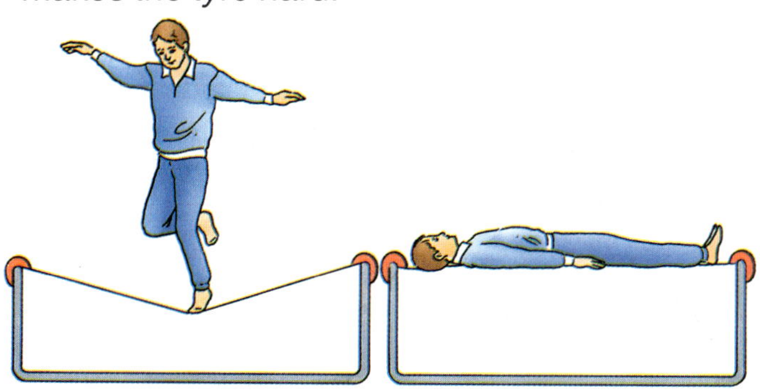

primary colour *noun*
A primary colour is one of three different colours of **light**. Red, green and blue are primary colours. When they are mixed together in equal amounts, they make white light. The three primary colours used in art are red, blue and yellow.
You can make any colour by mixing different amounts of the three primary colours.

principle *noun*
A principle is a kind of rule or **law**. Principles help to decide what will happen in a particular situation. **Archimedes' principle** tells us which substances will float in water and which ones will sink.
The principle that hot air rises explains why smoke goes up the chimney.

printer *noun*
A printer is a **machine** which is connected to a computer. It prints the **output** from the computer on sheets of paper. Some printers can draw pictures. The main kinds of printer are daisy wheel printers, dot matrix printers and **laser printers**.
Some printers type in three different colours.

prism *noun*
A prism is a piece of glass or clear plastic. A prism is usually **triangular** in shape. It **refracts** any light **ray** that passes through it. Prisms can split white light into a **spectrum** of colours.
Binoculars and cameras both contain prisms.

processor *noun*
A processor is a part of a **computer**. It is a kind of **integrated circuit** which is found in the **central processing unit**.
The computer's processor makes the printer type out the letter.

product *noun*
1. A product is something which has been made. **Chemical reactions** make products that include solids, liquids, gases and **energy**. Some machines can make very complicated products such as **integrated circuits**.
When substances containing carbon burn in the air, the product is carbon dioxide.
2. A product is the result of **multiplying** two or more numbers. The product of 3 and 4 is 12 ($3 \times 4 = 12$). The product of 2, 3 and 5 is 30 ($2 \times 3 \times 5 = 30$).
She wrote down the product of the four numbers.

program *noun*
A program is a set of instructions which tells a **computer** how to work. Programs are stored on **floppy disks** or **magnetic tape**, or in **integrated circuits**. Different programs help the computer to do different tasks.
He loaded a new program into the computer.

propane *noun*
Propane is a colourless **gas**. It is a **hydrocarbon** which is made from **petroleum**. Propane burns easily and is used as a fuel for heating and cooking. When propane is **compressed**, it changes into a liquid. Liquid propane is stored in thick, metal bottles.
They cooked their food in an oven which was heated by propane gas.

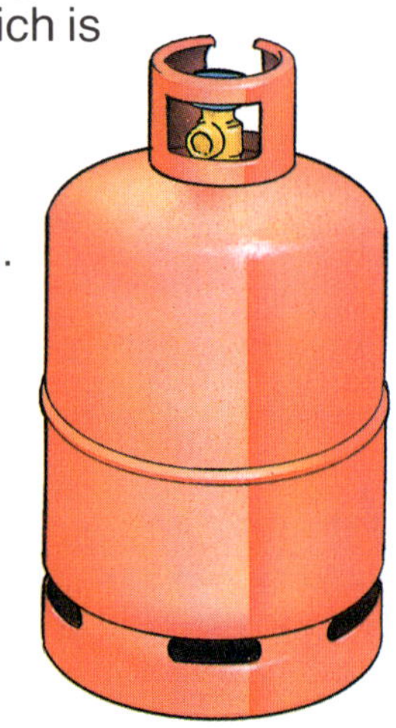
cylinder of propane

propeller *noun*
A propeller is a part of a ship and of some aeroplanes. It has two or more curved plates called blades. The blades join onto a **shaft**. An engine turns the shaft of the propeller which generates a **force**. This pushes the ship or aeroplane along.
Some aeroplanes have four propellers.

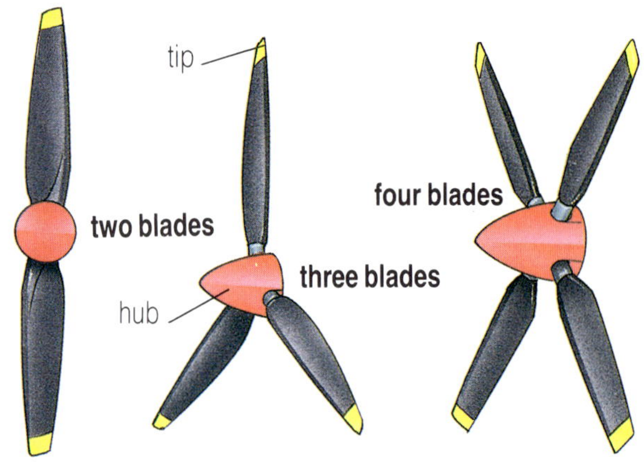

property *noun*
The property of something is a special feature which belongs to it and helps us to recognize it. The properties of water include its appearance, its **density**, its **freezing point** and its **boiling point**.
A property of glue is its stickiness.

protein *noun*
A protein is a kind of **organic chemical**. Proteins are natural **polymers** which make up living things. An **enzyme** is a protein. Muscles, blood, eggs, skin and bones all contain proteins.
Some of our food contains proteins which help us to stay healthy.

protist (plural **protista**) *noun*
A protist is a kind of living thing. It has a simple form. The **cells** in protista are more complicated than the cells in **monera**. Protista include simple plants called algae and some other **micro-organisms** called protozoa.
Most protista, such as amoebas, are made up of a single cell.

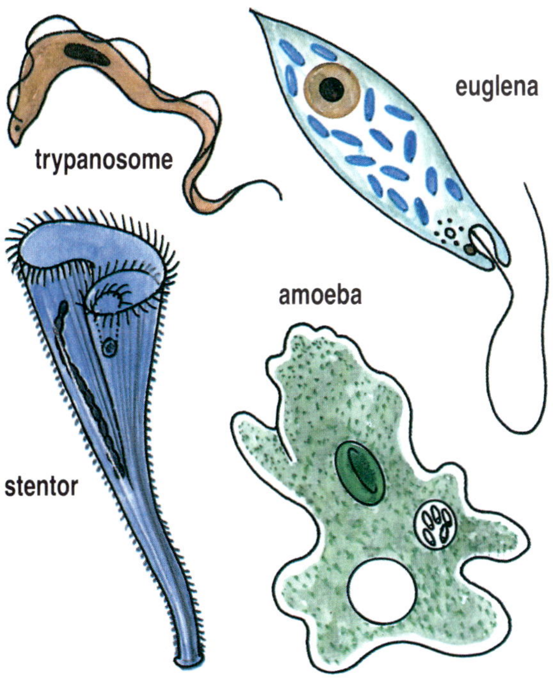

proton *noun*
A proton is a tiny **particle** of matter. All matter contains protons. They have the same **mass** as **neutrons** and they have a **positive** electric charge. Protons, neutrons and **electrons** are all known as **subatomic** particles. Protons are found in the **nucleus** of an atom. The nucleus of a **hydrogen** atom is made up of only one proton.
The Sun gives out streams of protons.

protoplasm *noun*
Protoplasm is the main part of all living things. It includes the **cytoplasm** and the **nucleus** in a cell. The protoplasm includes everything inside the **cell membrane**.
Our bodies are made up almost completely of protoplasm.

pulley *noun*
A pulley is a simple **machine**. It has a wheel with a groove around its outside edge. A rope or a chain fits into this groove. When you pull on one end of the rope, a weight on the other end can be moved. By using more than one pulley wheel on the same rope, heavier loads can be lifted.
The pulley helped him to lift the heavy box off the ground.

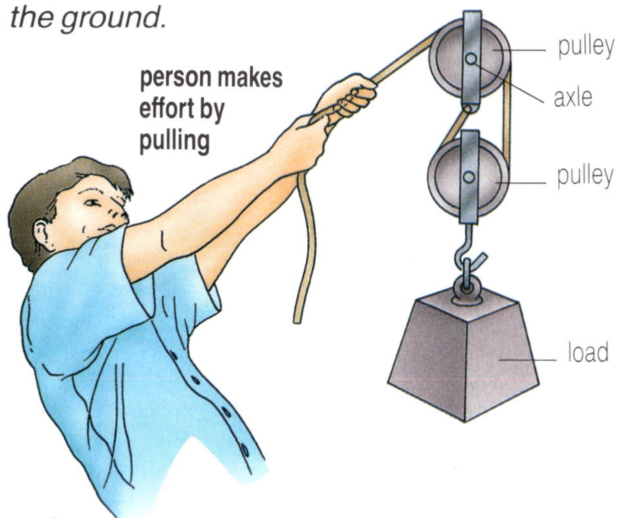

pulse *noun*
1. A pulse is a short, sharp spurt. A pulse describes how electricity, liquids and gases can flow. When an **electric current** is switched on and off quickly, pulses are sent through an electric circuit.
The sound from a siren is made up of pulses of air.
2. A pulse is the way in which **blood** flows. Every time the heart beats, it pumps out a surge of blood through tubes called arteries. This surge makes the arteries **expand** and **contract** slightly. A person's pulse can be felt in any artery which is near the surface of their skin.
The doctor placed her fingers on the patient's wrist to feel his pulse.

pure *adjective*
Pure describes a substance which does not have any other substances mixed in with it. The opposite of pure is **impure**.
Electric wires are made from copper which is almost completely pure.
purify *verb*

pylon *noun*
A pylon is a kind of tower which is made from **steel** or wood. Pylons support electricity **cables**, which run from power stations to towns and cities. The cables hang from **insulators** which are fixed to the pylons.
Huge pylons carry cables across the countryside.

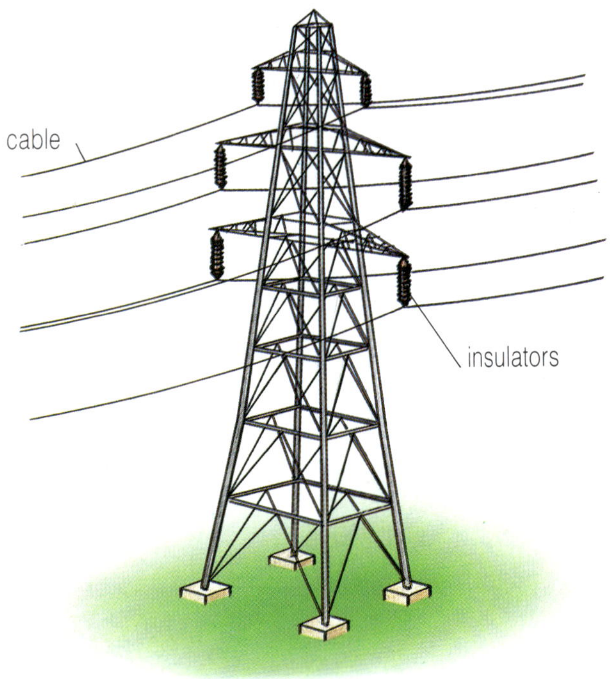

quantity *noun*
Quantity is a word which describes the amount of something. Quantities can be **measured**. They include length, mass, volume, speed, force and electric current. Each kind of quantity has its own **unit**.
The quantity of petrol in the car was 55 litres.

quantum mechanics *noun*
Quantum mechanics is a **scientific** subject. It is the part of **physics** that deals with radiation and the movement of atomic particles. The quantum theory, on which quantum mechanics is based, states that energy is made up of little bursts of light. Each burst is called a quantum.
By using quantum mechanics, the scientist showed that each quantum has a particular wavelength.

R

radar *noun*
Radar is a way of finding out where objects are when they cannot be seen. A radar set is an **electronic** device. It sends out **pulses** of radio waves. Ships and aircraft, for example, **reflect** some pulses which return to the radar set. A picture on a **cathode ray tube** shows where the ships and aircraft are.
Radar helped them to spot the aeroplanes 100 kilometres away.

radiant heat *noun*
Radiant heat is a kind of **energy**. It is the same as **infra-red radiation**, which is given off by hot objects. Radiant heat can travel through empty space.
He held out his hands to feel the radiant heat coming from the stove.

Sun

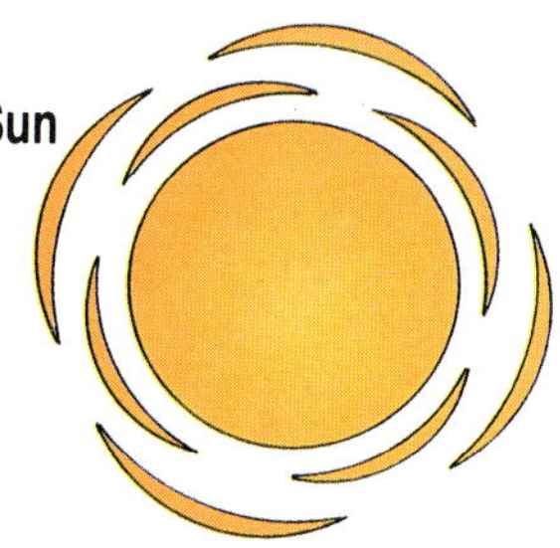

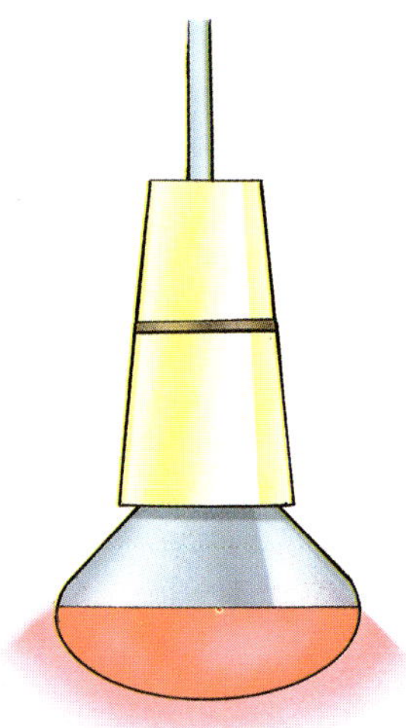

infra-red lamp

fire

radiation *noun*
Radiation is a kind of energy which is moving. Radiation includes **electromagnetic waves**, **photons** and the streams of particles which come from **radioactive** substances.
The radiation from the Sun includes heat and light.
radiate *verb*

radio *noun*
A radio is an **electronic device**. A radio **transmitter** sends electric signals to an **aerial**. The aerial gives out radio waves which carry information to a radio **receiver**.
The pilot in the aeroplane speaks on his radio to the people in the control tower.

radio-pager *noun*
A radio-pager is a small radio **receiver**. People who are away from their place of work may carry a radio-pager. It makes a bleeping sound when it receives a radio **signal** from the caller.
The radio-pager told the doctor that she must telephone the hospital.

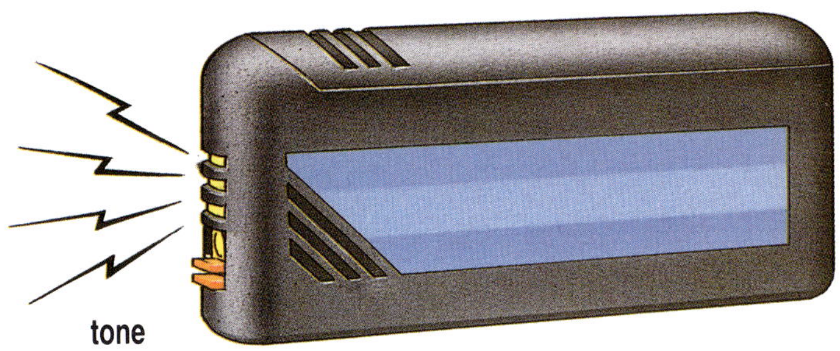

tone

radio-pager

radio wave *noun*
A radio wave is a kind of **electromagnetic radiation**. Aerials that are connected to **transmitters** give out radio waves. The waves are picked up by other aerials which are attached to **receivers**. Radio waves carry information.
Radio waves travel at a speed of 300,000 kilometres per second.

radioactive *adjective*
Radioactive is a word which describes some **elements**. Radioactive elements break down and give out **alpha particles**, **beta particles** or **gamma rays**. During nuclear fission, part of the **mass** of a radioactive element disappears and changes into energy.
Some radioactive elements help doctors to cure diseases.
radioactivity *noun*

radiography *noun*
Radiography describes how **radiation** helps to make pictures. These pictures show the inside of an **opaque** object. The radiation passes through the object and onto a photographic film or a special **screen**.
Radiography showed the doctor what was wrong with the girl's back.

radiotherapy *noun*
Radiotherapy is used by doctors to help some of their patients. These patients have a disease called cancer. **Cells** in their bodies grow dangerously fast. Radiotherapy beams **radiation** at these cells and kills them.
The doctor used radiotherapy to treat the patient.

RAM ▶ random access memory

random access memory *noun*
A random access memory, or RAM for short, is a part of a **computer**. It is made up of special kinds of **integrated circuit**. These circuits contain the **program** and the **data**.
When you switch off a computer, its random access memory will become empty.

rate *noun*
Rate is a word which describes how fast something is happening. The speed of a motor car is the rate at which it travels. **Frequency** measures the rate at which a **wave** vibrates.
The water poured out of the pipe at a rate of 10 litres per minute.

ratio *noun*
A ratio is a way of comparing two numbers or amounts. A comparison of two lengths, such as 4 centimetres and 6 centimetres, can be written as the ratio 4 : 6.
If the speed of the bicycle is 10 kilometres per hour and the speed of the car is 50 kilometres per hour, the ratio of their speeds is 1 : 5.

raw material *noun*
A raw material is a natural **substance**. Raw materials can be made into many useful **products**. **Ores** are raw materials that are made into metals. **Petroleum** is the raw material from which **petrochemicals** and fuels are made.
Sea water is the raw material from which salt is made.

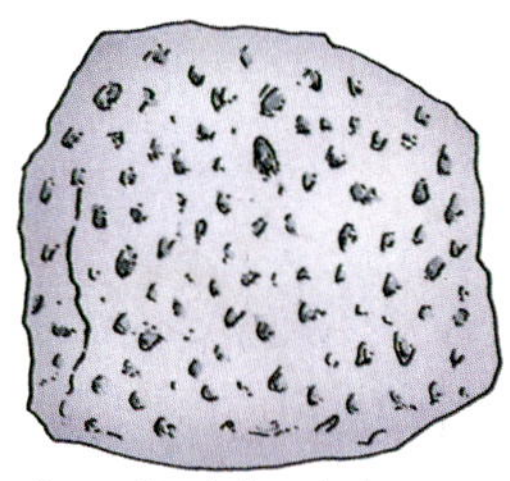
bauxite (aluminium ore)

sugar cane

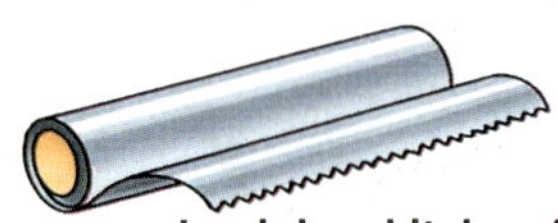
aluminium kitchen foil

sugar crystals

ray *noun*
A ray is a narrow beam of **radiation**. It shows the direction in which the radiation travels. The edges of a ray are straight.
A ray of sunlight entered the room through a small hole in the window blind.

reaction *noun*
1. A reaction is a kind of **force**. It pushes against another force. When you stand on the floor, the force of gravity pulls you down. You do not move because the reaction of the floor pushes up against your feet.
The upward reaction of the ground pushes against the downward weight of a car.
2. ▶ chemical reaction

reactor ► **nuclear reactor**

read-only memory *noun*
A read-only memory, or ROM for short, is a part of a **computer**. It is made up of special kinds of **integrated circuit.** These memory circuits contain instructions which the computer needs in order to work properly.
The instructions stay in the read-only memory, even when a computer is switched off.

receiver *noun*
1. A receiver is an **electronic device**. Radios, televisions and parts of **radar** sets are receivers. An **aerial** picks up **radio waves**. Electric **signals** from the aerial flow through the receiver, which changes them into sound or pictures.
He switched on the receiver and listened to the news programme.
2. A receiver is the part of a telephone that you hold against your ear. **Vibrating** electric **signals** flow in an **electromagnet** inside the receiver. This makes a steel **diaphragm** vibrate and give off sound.
He held the receiver against his ear and listened to his friend's story.

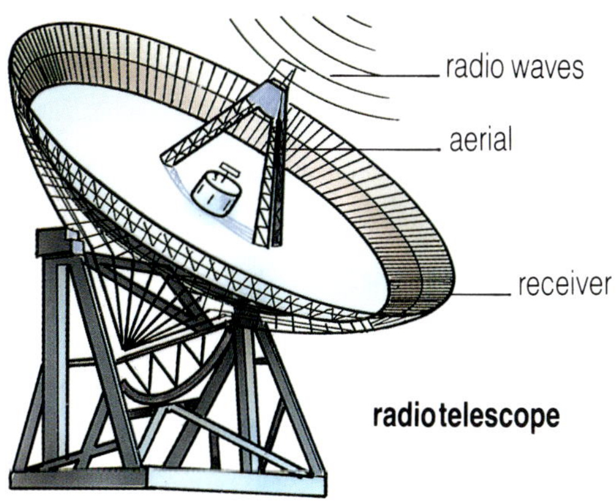

radiotelescope

receptor *noun*
A receptor is a special kind of **cell**. Your eyes, ears, nose, tongue and skin all contain receptors. They send messages to your brain. These messages tell you what is happening around you.
Receptors in the lining of your nose help you to smell food.

refine *verb*
Refine is a word which describes how something is made more **pure**. Substances are refined in a **refinery**. During refining, **mixtures** are separated and **impure** substances are removed.
Brown sugar is refined to make pure and colourless sugar crystals.

refinery *noun*
A refinery is a factory where substances are refined. Refineries make useful products from **raw materials**. An **oil refinery** refines petroleum into fuels and **lubricants**.
The sugar refinery changes a sticky juice from plants into pure sugar.

reflect *verb*
Reflect is a word which describes the way some **waves** change direction. Sound waves can be reflected back from a wall and we hear an **echo**. Light waves are reflected from a mirror and we see an **image**.
The lamp shade reflected light into the room.

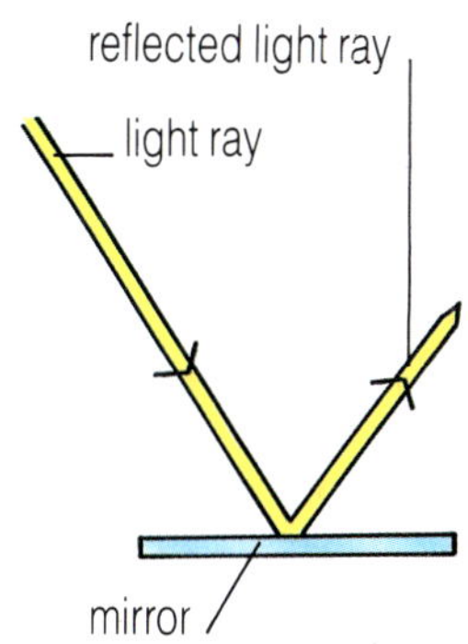

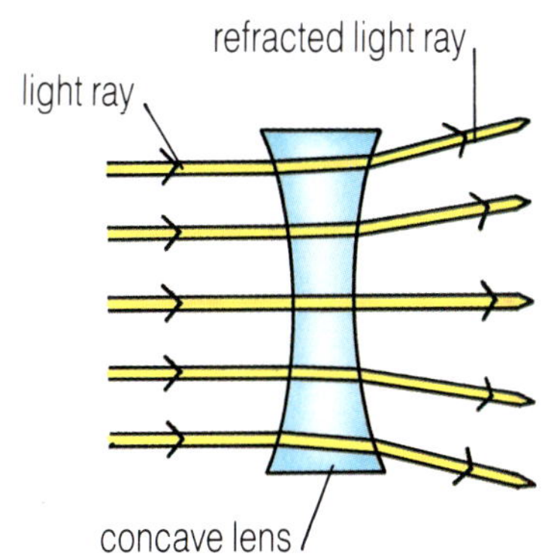

refract *verb*
Refract is a word which describes the way a **ray** of light changes direction. When a ray enters or leaves a **transparent** object, such as a **prism** or a **lens**, it is refracted.
The lenses in a telescope refract the light from the stars.

refrigeration ► page 116

refrigeration *noun*
Refrigeration is a way of cooling things. Refrigeration moves heat from one place to another. A special cold liquid is pumped along pipes in a refrigerator. The liquid takes heat from inside the refrigerator, and **evaporates** to become a gas. A pump **compresses** the gas, which gives off heat into the room outside. The gas **condenses** into a liquid again.
In refrigeration, very cold gas makes water turn to ice in the freezer.

inside a refrigerator

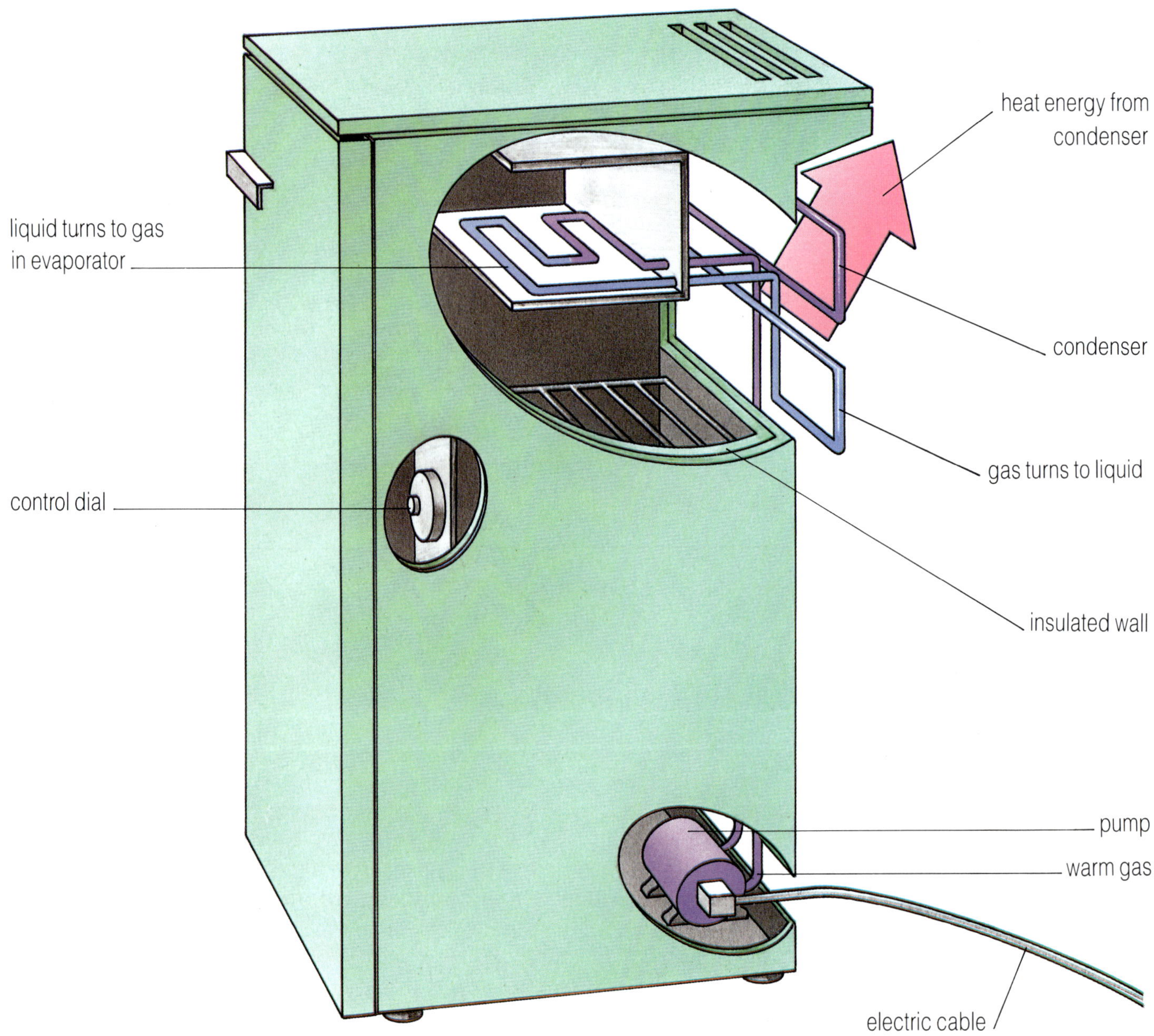

relay *noun*
A relay is a kind of **switch**. A small electric current in an electric circuit flows through an **electromagnet**. This **attracts** a steel bar which works a switch. The switch turns on a large electric current in another circuit.
A large relay controls the electricity which flows to a city.

repel *verb*
Repel is a word which describes how some objects push other objects away from them. The north pole of a magnet, for example, repels the north pole of another magnet. **Particles** which have the same **electric charge** repel and move away from each other. Some animals give out chemicals which repel other animals.
The ants sprayed out a liquid which repelled the wasps.

reprocessing *noun*
Reprocessing describes how a factory changes **impure** substances into **pure** ones. Reprocessing changes the used fuel from a nuclear reactor into pure plutonium.
Reprocessing changes dirty oil from motor car engines into clean oil.

reproduction *noun*
Reproduction describes how living things make copies of themselves. Reproduction means a **species** of a plant or an animal can continue from one generation to the next.
Kittens, calves, seedlings and babies are all the result of reproduction.
reproduce *verb*

cow

bean

calf

bean seedling

research *noun*
Research is the work scientists do to discover new ideas. During research, scientists use **data** and the results of **experiments** to make up new **theories**.
The scientists hoped that their research would find a cure for colds.

reservoir *noun*
A reservoir is a container which holds a liquid or a gas. A small reservoir in a car stores the oil that works the brakes. River water is collected behind a **dam** to form a large reservoir.
Water from the reservoir in the valley helped the crops to grow.

resin *noun*
A resin is a kind of **polymer**. Resins are **brittle** solids or sticky liquids. **Synthetic** resins are chemicals which are used to make some kinds of **plastic**. Trees and other plants make natural resins which often have a pleasant smell.
They mixed the two liquid chemicals to make a hard resin.

resistance *noun*
Resistance causes a wire to heat up when an **electric current** passes through it. Thin wires have a higher resistance than thick wires. This means that thin wires become hot more quickly.
The thin wire glows red-hot because it has a high resistance.
resist *verb*

respiration ► page 118

respiration *noun*
1. Respiration is a word which describes the process of breathing air through the lungs. During respiration, oxygen is taken out of the air and **carbon dioxide** is passed into the air.
In respiration you breathe in fresh air and get rid of the stale air from your lungs.
2. Respiration is a word which describes how living things make **energy** in order to stay alive. During respiration, living things take in **oxygen** from the air or water. The oxygen helps to release energy from the food inside the living things.
Respiration makes the gas called carbon dioxide which we breathe out.
respire *verb*

respiration in a fish

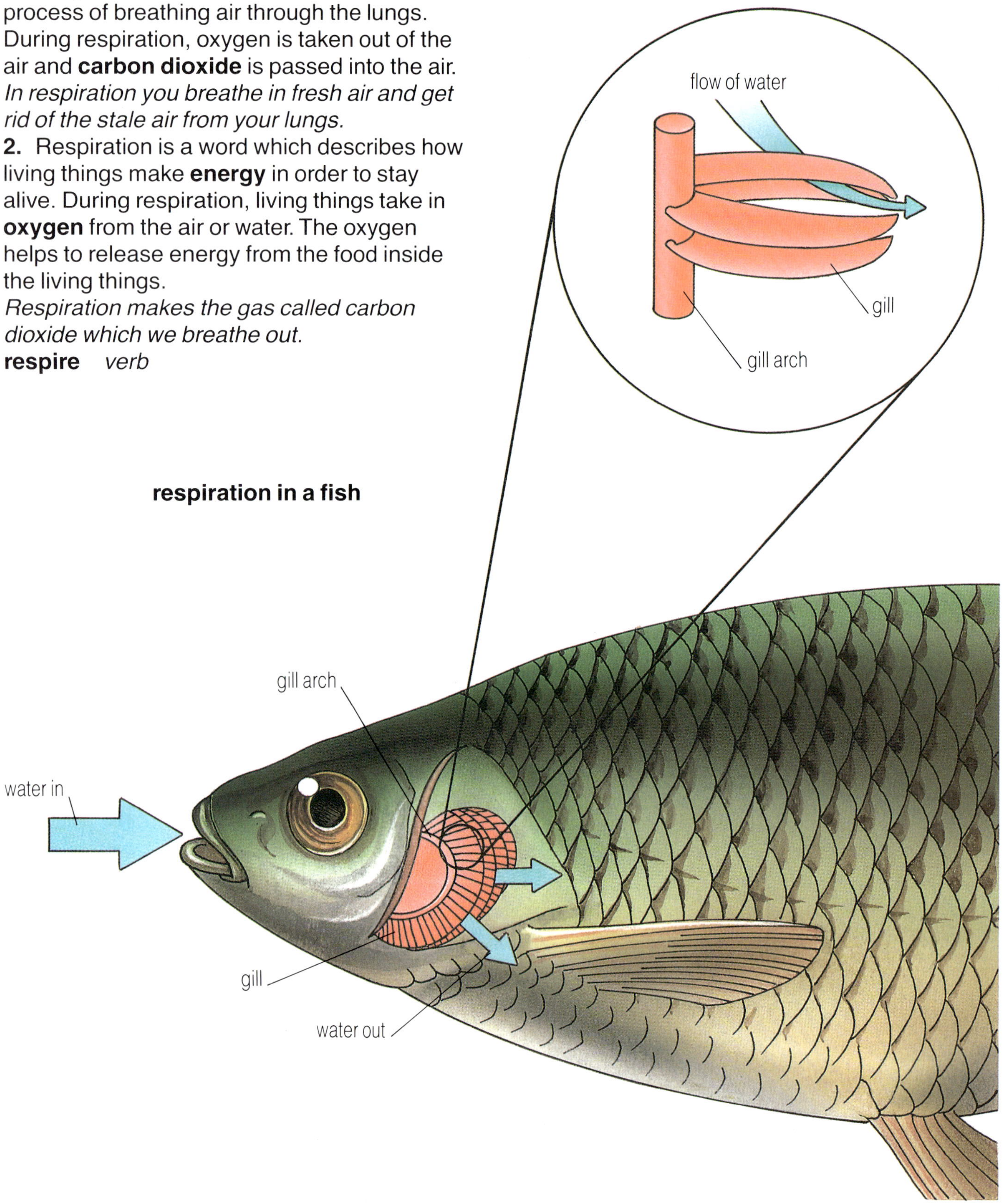

respiration in a human being

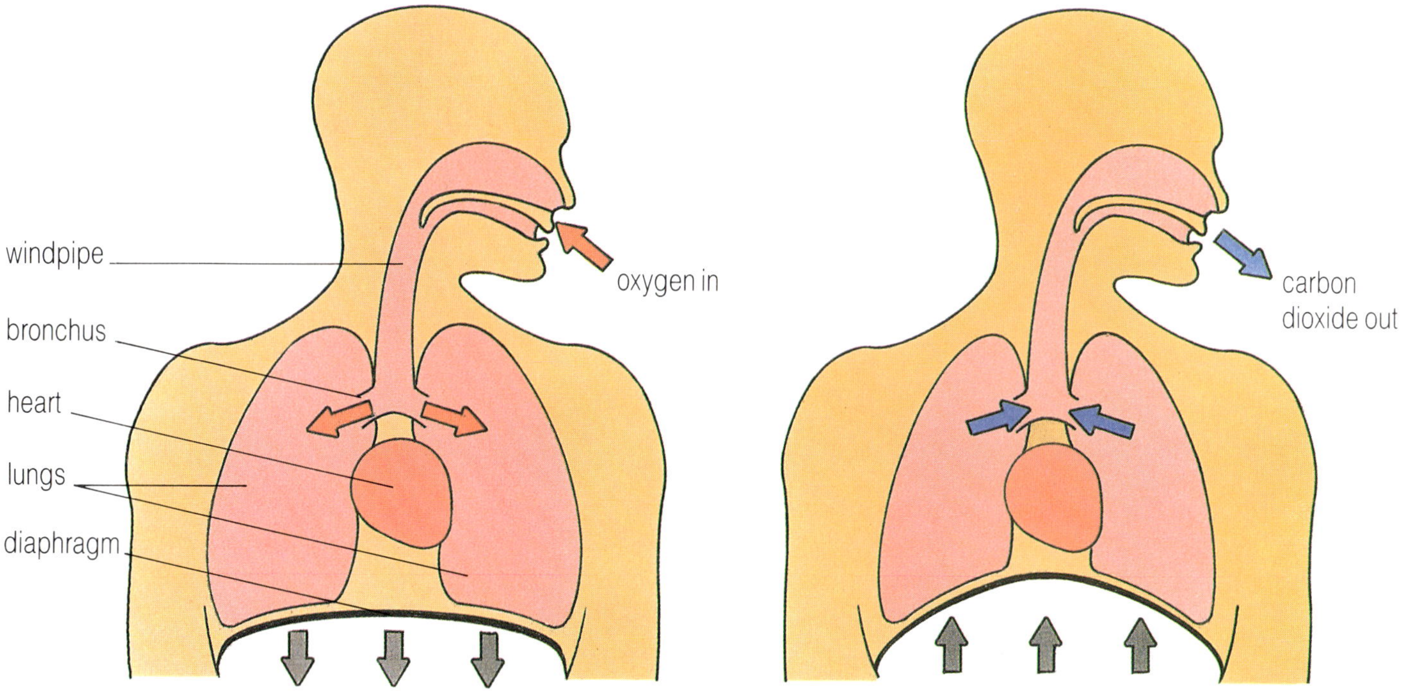

breathing in **breathing out**

respiration in a leaf

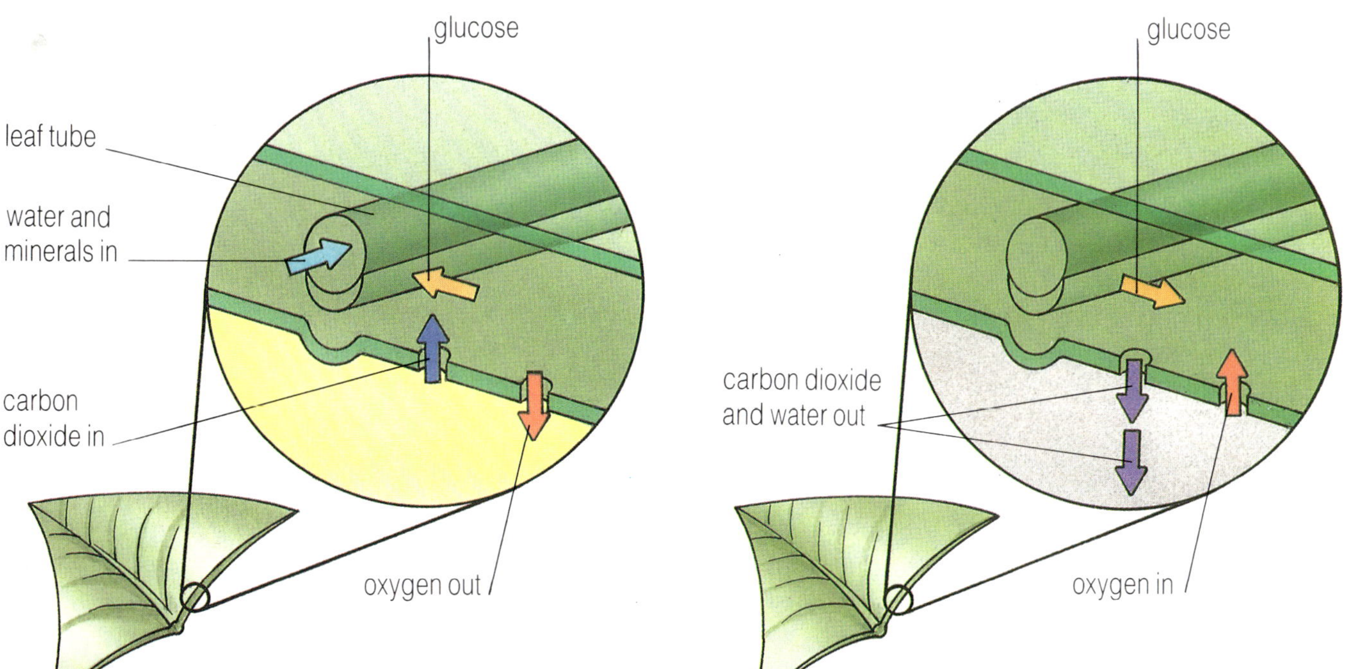

during the day **at night**

robot *noun*
A robot is a kind of **machine** that can do jobs without human help. Robots can be programmed to do boring or dangerous jobs. Some robots **weld** together steel panels to help make cars. Other robots do dangerous jobs inside **nuclear reactors**.
The robot repeated the same task all through the day and the night.

ROM ► read-only memory

rot *verb*
Rot is a word which describes how natural materials **decay**. Dead plants and animals rot. **Micro-organisms** feed on the rotting materials and break them down into simple substances.
Dead leaves rot and slowly disappear into the soil.

rotate *verb*
Rotate is a word which describes a spinning movement. An object rotates when it spins around its **axis**. **Gears** rotate inside a car engine. The **propeller** on a ship or an aeroplane rotates.
The wheels on a bicycle rotate as it travels down a road.

ruler *noun*
A ruler is an instrument which **measures** length. It is a thin, flat bar which is made from metal, wood or stiff plastic. A **scale** is marked on each side of the ruler.
She held the ruler against the book to measure the width of the page.

S

sac *noun*
A sac is a bag-shaped part found inside some living things. It has a skin-like membrane on the outside and contains liquids, gases or organs.
The sac inside a hen's egg contains the yolk.

safety valve *noun*
A safety valve is a kind of **valve** which opens automatically. It is fitted to a container or a pipe, which is filled with a liquid or a gas at high **pressure**. When the pressure is too high, the safety valve opens.
Steam escapes from the pressure cooker through the safety valve.

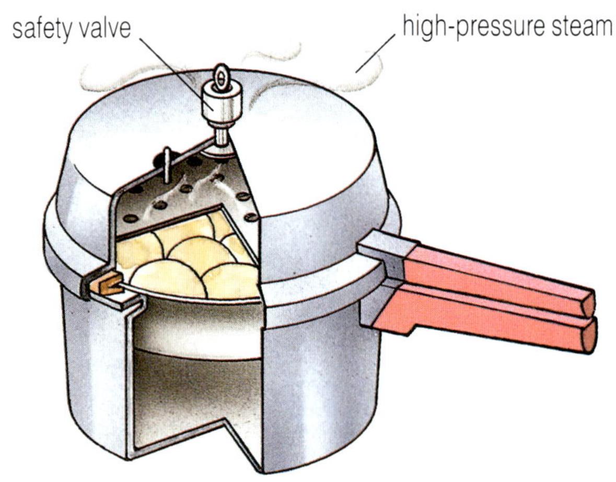

pressure cooker

saline *adjective*
Saline describes water that contains **salt**. The salt has **dissolved** in the water to make it saline.
Sea water is saline and tastes salty.

salt *noun*
1. A salt is a kind of **chemical substance**. It is formed when different metals and non-metals join together.
Chalk comes from a salt called calcium carbonate.
2. Salt is the name of a chemical **compound** which is made when **sodium** and **chlorine** join together. Salt is a solid which is made up of **crystals**. Salt **dissolves** easily in water to make a solution called brine. It is also known as 'common salt'.
Sodium chloride is the scientific name for the salt we put on our food.

salt crystals

satellite *noun*
A satellite is a kind of spacecraft. It is launched into space by a rocket. Satellites **orbit** around the Earth, the Sun and the Moon. Satellites help to forecast the weather, to transmit telephone calls and to take measurements.
The satellite took photographs of the Earth.

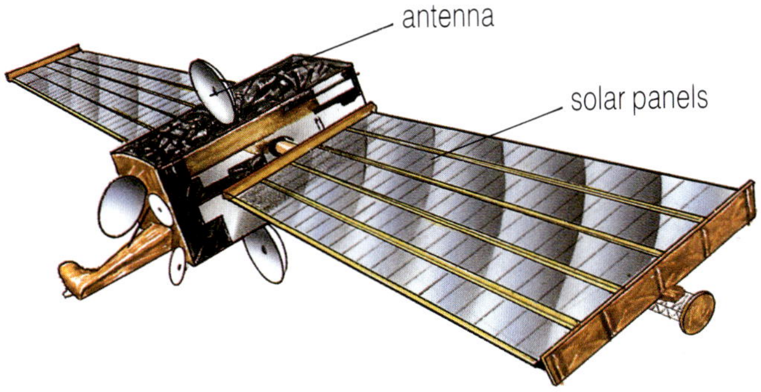

satellite dish *noun*
A satellite dish is a kind of **aerial**. The dish collects **signals** sent from satellites.
The satellite dish received signals from the satellite in orbit around the Moon.

saturated *adjective*
Saturated describes a substance which has taken in as much as possible of another substance.
A saturated sponge cannot hold any more water.

scale *noun*
A scale is a row of marks and numbers which is used to **measure** something. A scale is often marked on the side of an item of measuring equipment, such as a **beaker**.
The scale on this ruler is marked from 1 to 20 centimetres.

scale drawing *noun*
A scale drawing of an object is a special kind of drawing. It is marked with a **scale**. The lines in a scale drawing are usually much shorter than those on the real object.
The scale drawing of the bridge was 500 times smaller than the actual bridge.

scanner *noun*
A scanner is a **machine** which examines objects. Part of the scanner moves backwards and forwards, and collects information about the object. This information can be used to make a picture.
A body scanner in a hospital can look at all parts of your body.
scan *verb*

colour scanner

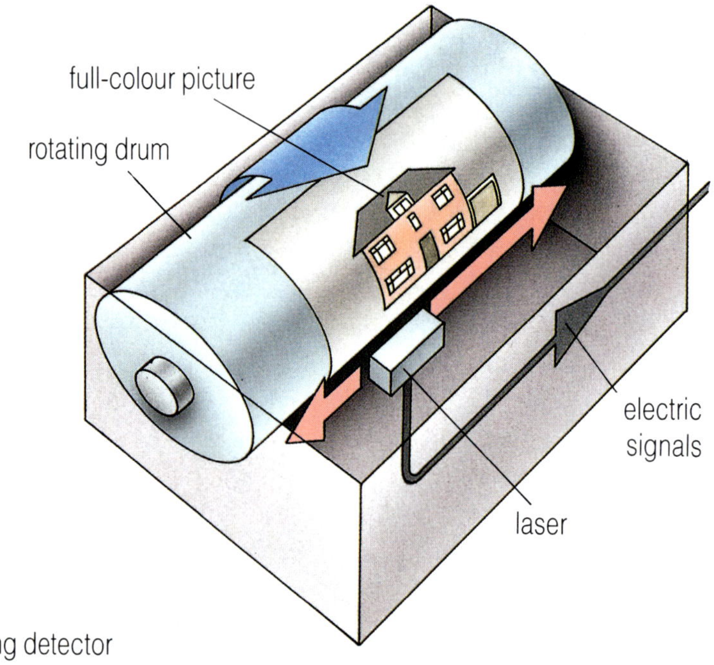

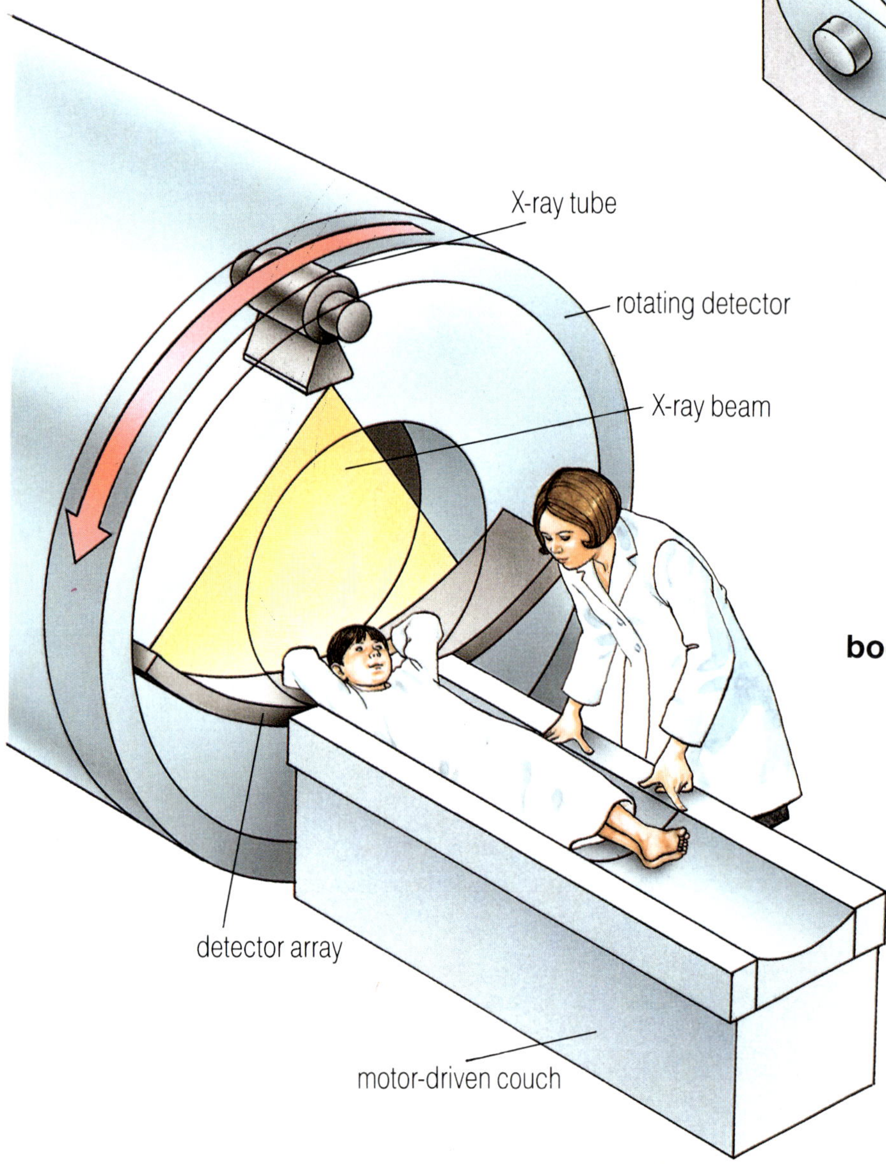

body scanner

science *noun*
Science is the study of all the things around us. It helps to answer questions, prove facts and solve problems. Students of science carry out **experiments** and look carefully at the results.
Science can help farmers to discover ways of growing healthy crops.

scientific *adjective*
Scientific is a word which describes the way we think and work when using **science** to investigate things.
The chemist carried out scientific tests to try and solve the problem.

scientist *noun*
A scientist is a person who studies **science** and uses it to solve problems. Many kinds of scientist study the different areas of science.
Chemists, biologists and engineers are different kinds of scientist.

scramble *verb*
Scramble is a word which describes how information is mixed up so that it cannot be understood. Information is scrambled and then sent from one person to another, or from one **computer** to another.
The computer unscrambled the secret message and then printed it on paper.

screen *noun*
A screen is the curved surface on the front of a television set or a **visual display unit**. Pictures appear on a television screen. A computer screen shows us information from inside the computer.
Words and a coloured picture appeared on the computer's screen.

screw *verb*
Screw means to twist and push at the same time. It describes the movement you make when inserting a **screw** into a piece of wood or metal.
She screwed the stick into the ground to make a deep hole.

screw *noun*
A screw is a **metal** pin which fastens together two or more objects. It has a wide top, called the head, and a long body with a sharp, pointed end. A spiral groove, called the thread, runs around the body of the screw.
As he turned the screw, the threads disappeared into the wood.

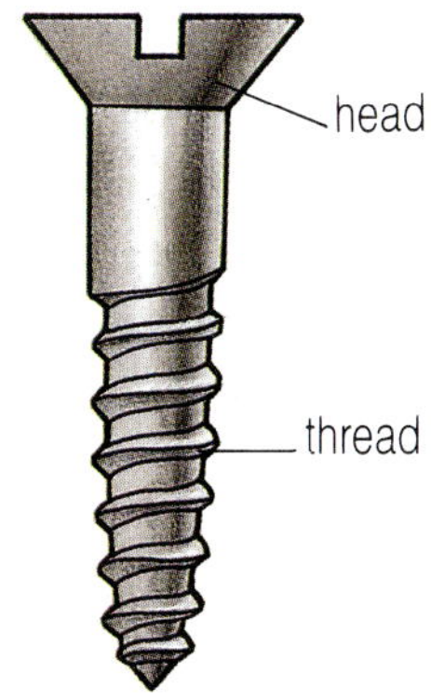

scrubber *noun*
A scrubber is a **device** which helps to clean gases. It sprays water down the inside of a pipe while gases pass up through the pipe.
The scrubber stopped the factory chimney from smoking.

second *noun*
A second, or sec for short, is a **unit** of measurement. Seconds measure time. There are 60 seconds in 1 minute, and 3,600 seconds in 1 hour.
It took about 1 second for the stone to fall 10 metres to the ground.

seed *noun*
A seed is something which many kinds of plant produce for **reproduction**. Seeds have a protective outer skin and contain a plant **embryo** and a store of food. Each seed can grow into a new plant.
The tiny seed sprouted and began to grow into a new plant.

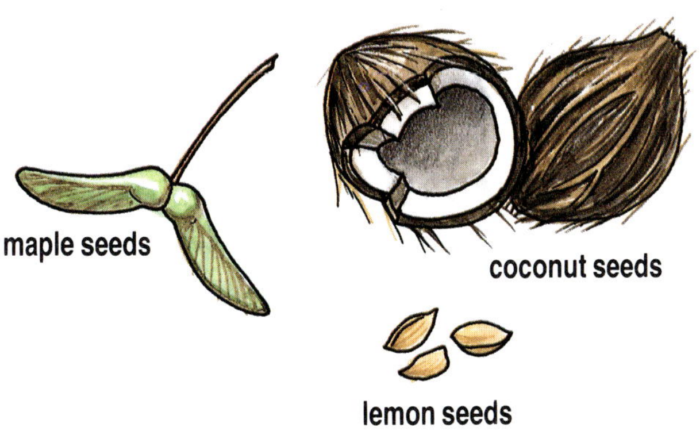

semiconductor *noun*
A semiconductor is a kind of **solid** material. A semiconductor does not allow electricity to pass easily. Semiconductors, such as **silicon**, are used to make **electronic** equipment.
Semiconductors inside a computer help it to work quickly.

sequence *noun*
A sequence is a list of numbers in a special order. Each number in a sequence is related to the numbers before it. A sequence of even numbers is 2, 4, 6, 8, 10.
Each number in the sequence 1, 2, 4, 8, 16, 32 is twice as large as the number before it.

series *noun*
A series is a list of **data** or information. All the things written in a series are similar. A series can be a list of lengths or any other measurements.
He measured the growing plant each day and wrote down a series of results.

series circuit *noun*
A series circuit is a way of connecting together electrical **components**. The components are connected end to end. This makes the **electric current** flow through each component in turn.
All the bulbs in a series circuit will go out if one of them breaks.

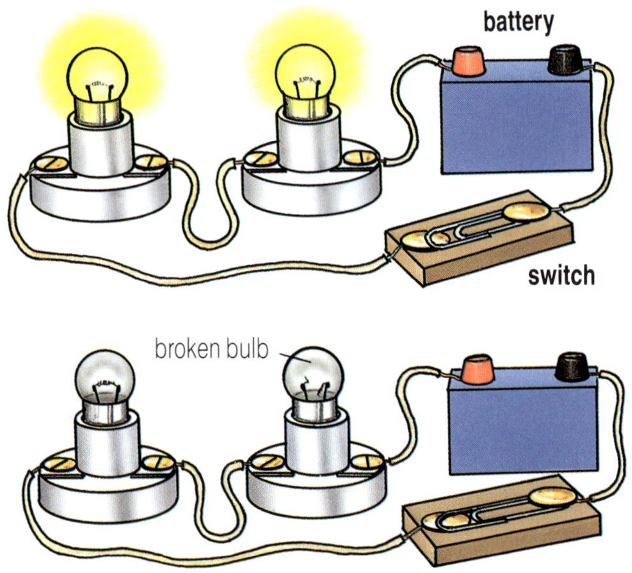

shaft *noun*
A shaft is a rod which **rotates**. It is connected to the **axis** of a wheel or a **gear**. When the shaft rotates, the wheel or the gear turns with it. Engines, motors, turbines and propellers have shafts.
The crankshaft inside a car engine turns round about 4,000 times each minute.

short circuit *noun*
A short circuit is a fault in an **electric circuit**. When there is a short circuit, the **electric current** does not flow through the circuit's **component**. The short circuit conducts the current around it. The short circuit has a low **resistance**.
A short circuit makes a dangerously large current flow in the wires.

short waveband *noun*
The short waveband is a group of radio **signals**. It is part of the **electromagnetic spectrum**. Short waveband radio **transmitters** can send signals right around the world. The part of the **atmosphere** called the ionosphere reflects these signals.
She tuned her radio to the short waveband.

shutter *noun*
A shutter is a part of a **camera**. It is a set of metal flaps which is fitted between the **lens** and the film. The shutter is normally closed and stops light from reaching the film. When the shutter is open, light falls on the film.
The shutter opens for a fraction of a second and the camera takes a photograph.

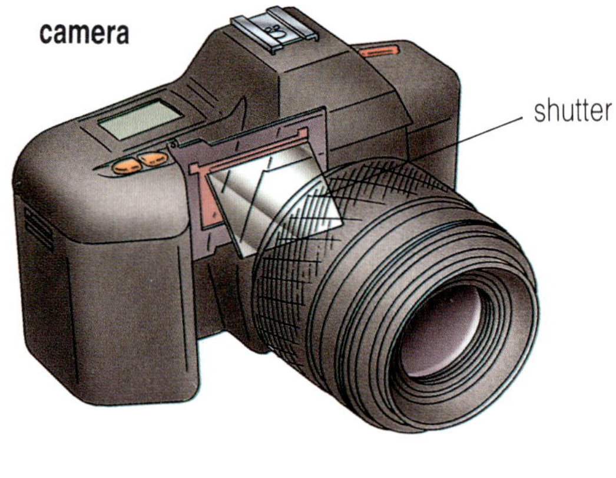

SI unit *noun*
SI unit is short for Système International unit. It is a **unit** of measurement which uses the **metric system**. All SI units are based on the **metre**, the **kilogram** and the **second**.
Scientists throughout the world use SI units to make measurements.

signal *noun*
A signal is a kind of message. It carries information from one place to another. Radio waves carry signals from **transmitters** to **receivers**. Electric currents can carry telephone signals. **Optical fibres** carry light signals.
The radio signal travels around the world at the same speed as light.

silicon *noun*
Silicon is a chemical **element**. It is grey. Silicon is especially useful to scientists, since it behaves as if it is a metal and a **non-metal**. It is used to make **semiconductors**, such as diodes, transistors and integrated circuits.
Sand and many kinds of rock contain silicon.

silicon chip *noun*
A silicon chip is a kind of **crystal**. The chip is made from **silicon** and is the main working part inside an **integrated circuit**. The silicon chip has microscopic **electric circuits** on its surface.
The sides of some silicon chips are only 2 millimetres long.

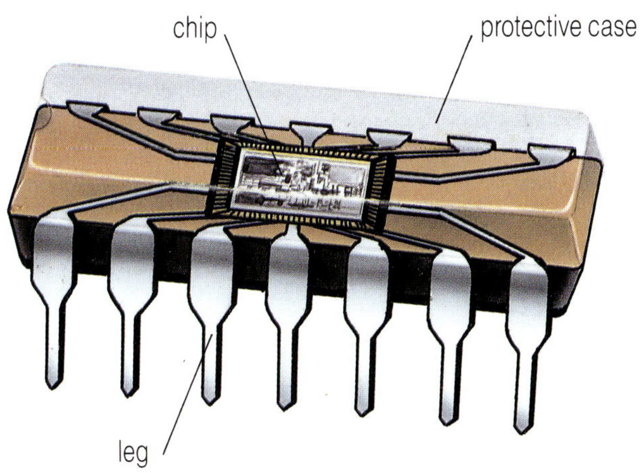

silver *noun*
Silver is a chemical **element**. It is a soft, greyish-white, **precious metal** which can be easily beaten into shapes. Silver is a very good **conductor** of electricity. A coat of silver can be put on cutlery and ornaments by a process called **electroplating**. Silver also helps to make photographic film.
He made a beautiful pair of earrings out of silver.

siphon *noun*
A siphon is a curved pipe or tube. Siphons are used to move **liquids** from one container to another. The liquid flows upwards from one container and then down into another container. The second container must be at a lower level than the first.
He used a siphon to empty the water out of the tank.

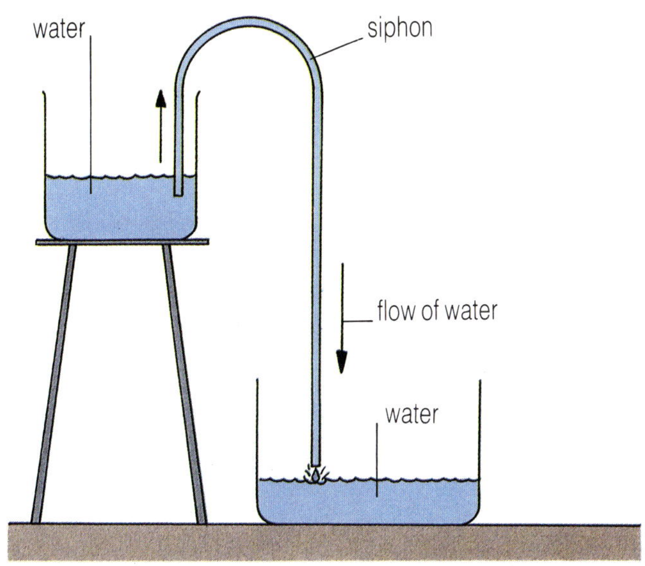

slag *noun*
Slag is a kind of waste material. It forms during **smelting** in a furnace. **Molten** slag collects in the furnace. It flows out, cools and turns into a hard, rocky solid. Some kinds of slag are used to make cement. Another kind can be made into **fertilizer**.
There was a huge mountain made of slag outside the steel factory.

smelting *noun*
Smelting is a word which explains how **ores** are changed into metals. During smelting, the ore is heated in a **furnace**. Coke and other substances are used to separate the ore into metal and **slag**.
At the factory, 1,000 tonnes of iron were made each day by smelting.

smoke *noun*
Smoke is a mixture of tiny, solid **particles** and gases. Wood and coal often give off smoke when they burn. Most smoke is made when something starts to burn and its **temperature** is low.
Thick smoke poured out of the chimney.

soap *noun*
Soap is a soft solid which is used for washing. It is made when **oil** from plants is heated and then mixed with a strong **alkali**.
He washed the dirt from his hands with soap.

socket *noun*
1. A socket is a kind of hole. An electric socket connects a plug or a bulb to the **electricity** supply.
She pushed the plug into the socket on the wall and turned on the appliance.
2. A socket is a part of some machines and other devices. The socket holds a **shaft** or an **axle**.
The drive shaft in the motor car's engine fitted into a socket.

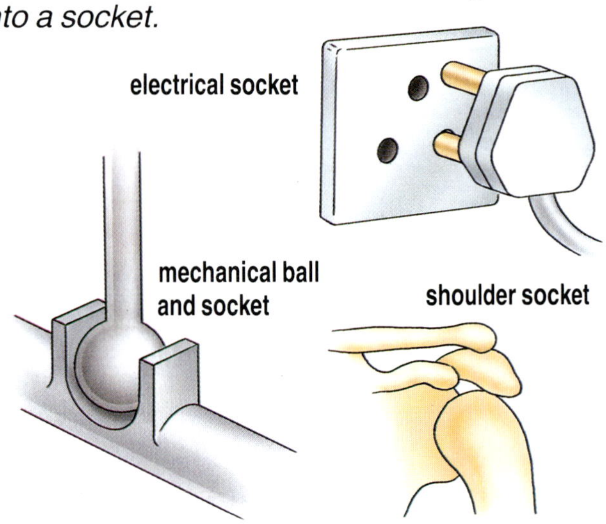

sodium *noun*
Sodium is a chemical **element**. It is a soft, grey **metal**. It reacts quickly with water and **corrodes** rapidly in air. Sodium is used in some kinds of **nuclear reactor**.
A piece of sodium floats on water and makes a fizzing sound.

sodium carbonate *noun*
Sodium carbonate is a white **solid**. It is a **compound** which is made from **sodium**. Sodium carbonate dissolves in water to form an **alkaline solution**. It is also known as washing soda. Sodium carbonate may be used to soften **hard water**. It is also used in the making of glass and **bicarbonate of soda**.
The scented bath crystals contained sodium carbonate.

sodium chloride ► salt

soft water *noun*
Soft water is water which does not contain calcium or magnesium **salts**. Soap in soft water lathers well and does not form scum. The opposite of soft water is **hard water**.
You only need a small amount of soap when washing your hands in soft water.

software *noun*
Software is **programs** and **data** that are used by computers. The software flows through the computer's **hardware**. **Hard disks**, **floppy disks** and magnetic tapes store software.
He bought some new software for his computer and tried out one of the programs.

solar energy ► page 128

solder *noun*
Solder is an **alloy**. It is a mixture of tin and lead. Solder melts easily when it is heated. It is used to join together wires and electronic **components**. Solder also helps to join together copper water pipes.
The parts inside a computer are held together by solder.

solenoid *noun*
A solenoid is a part of an **electromagnet**. An electric current flows in the solenoid and makes a magnetic **force** inside it. Solenoids are found in **relays** and electric door locks.
When he switched on the electricity, the steel bar moved towards the solenoid.

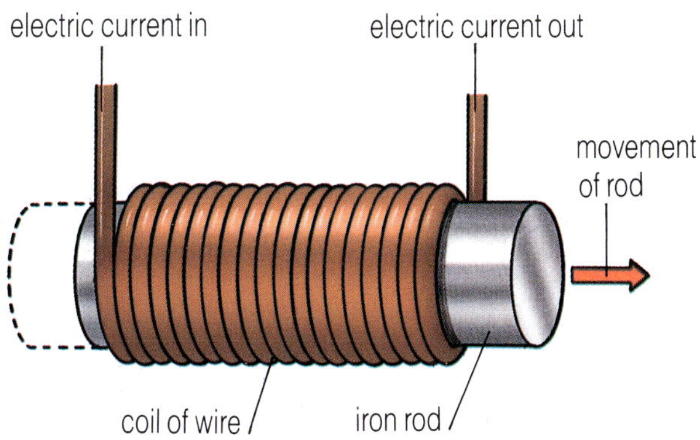

solid *noun*
A solid is a kind of **substance**. A solid has a fixed shape and does not flow like a liquid or a gas. The **particles** in a solid are firmly joined to each other.
She melted the solid by heating it.

solubility *noun*
Solubility describes how much **solute** dissolves in a certain amount of **solvent**, at a particular temperature. The solubility of a **solid** usually increases, and the solubility of a **gas** decreases, as the solvent is heated.
The solubility of sugar is greater in hot coffee than in cold milk.

soluble *adjective*
Soluble is a word which describes some **substances**. A soluble solid or gas can dissolve in a liquid to make a **solution**.
Salt is soluble in water.

solute *noun*
Solute is a word which describes some **solids** and **gases**. A solute dissolves in a liquid to form a **solution**. The solute in **brine** is salt.
Carbon dioxide gas is the solute in fizzy lemonade.

solution *noun*
A solution is a **mixture** which contains mostly a liquid. It is made up of a **solute** which has dissolved in a liquid **solvent**. **Brine** is a solution of salt in water.
Fizzy lemonade is a solution of a gas in sugary water.

solvent *noun*
A solvent is a **liquid**. It is the liquid part of a **solution**. Different solvents can dissolve different solids and gases.
Water is a solvent for salt and sugar.

sonar *noun*
Sonar is a **device** which is fitted to ships and submarines. It is used to find objects under water. Sonar gives out **pulses** of **ultrasound**. Objects under water reflect these pulses. Special equipment shows the reflections as a kind of picture.
Sonar helped the fishermen to find the shoals of fish.

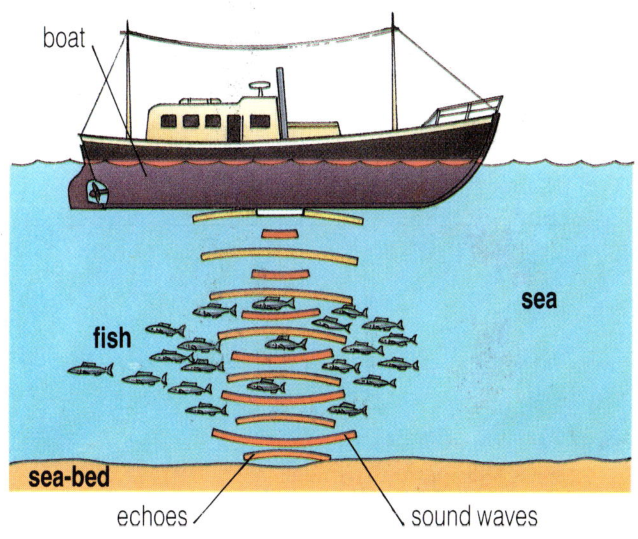

sound *noun*
Sound is a kind of **vibration** that animals can hear. It travels through solids, liquids and gases. Humans can hear sounds which have a **frequency** between 20 **hertz** and 16,000 hertz.
The jet aeroplane made a loud sound as it flew low above the houses.

solar energy *noun*

Solar energy is the kind of energy which comes from sunlight in the form of heat. It can be used to **generate** electricity. With the help of mirrors and **lenses**, solar energy can be made powerful enough to heat water or even melt metals.

Solar energy can power electric cars, telephones and pocket calculators.

solar energy powers a car

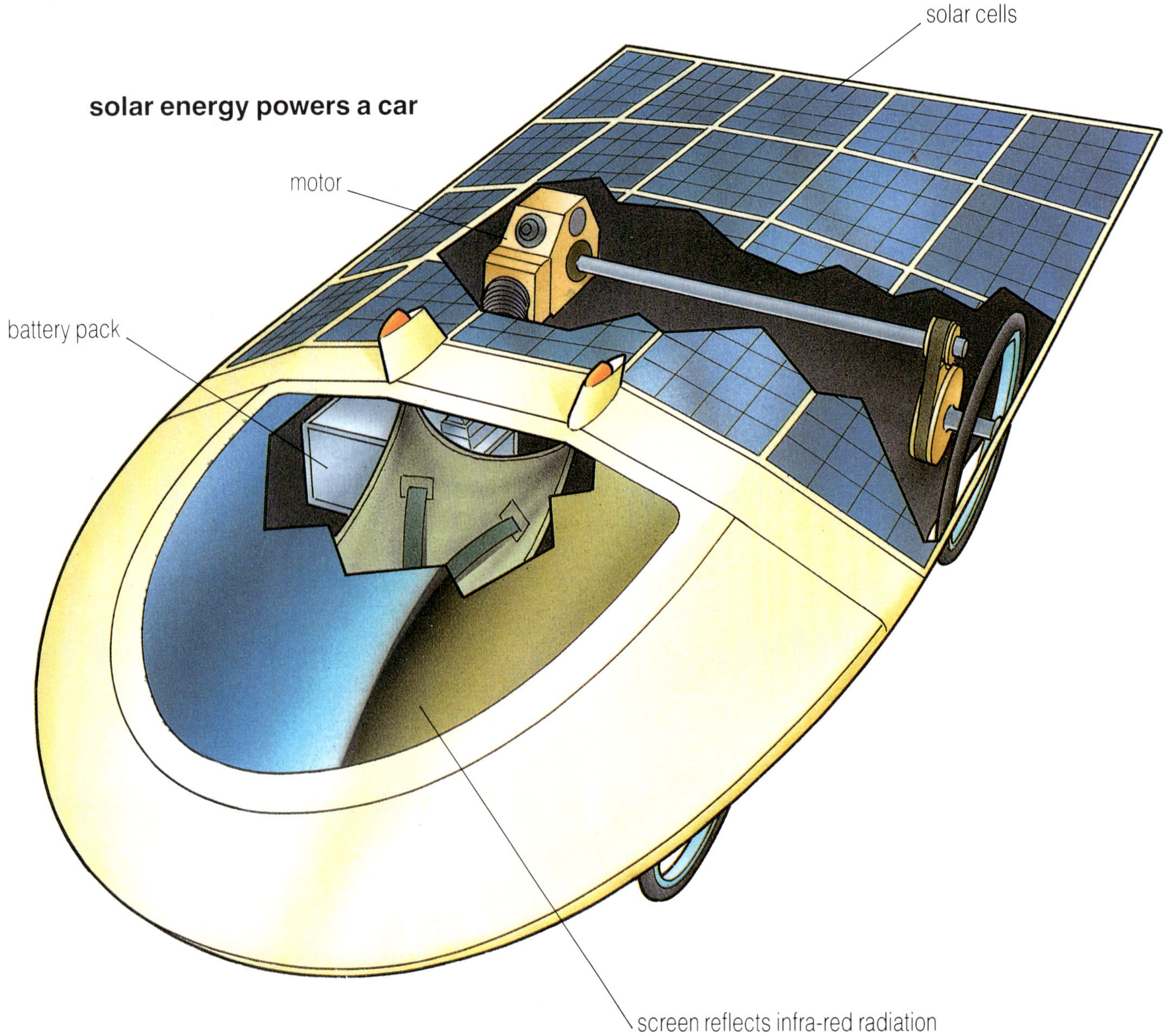

solar energy heats a house

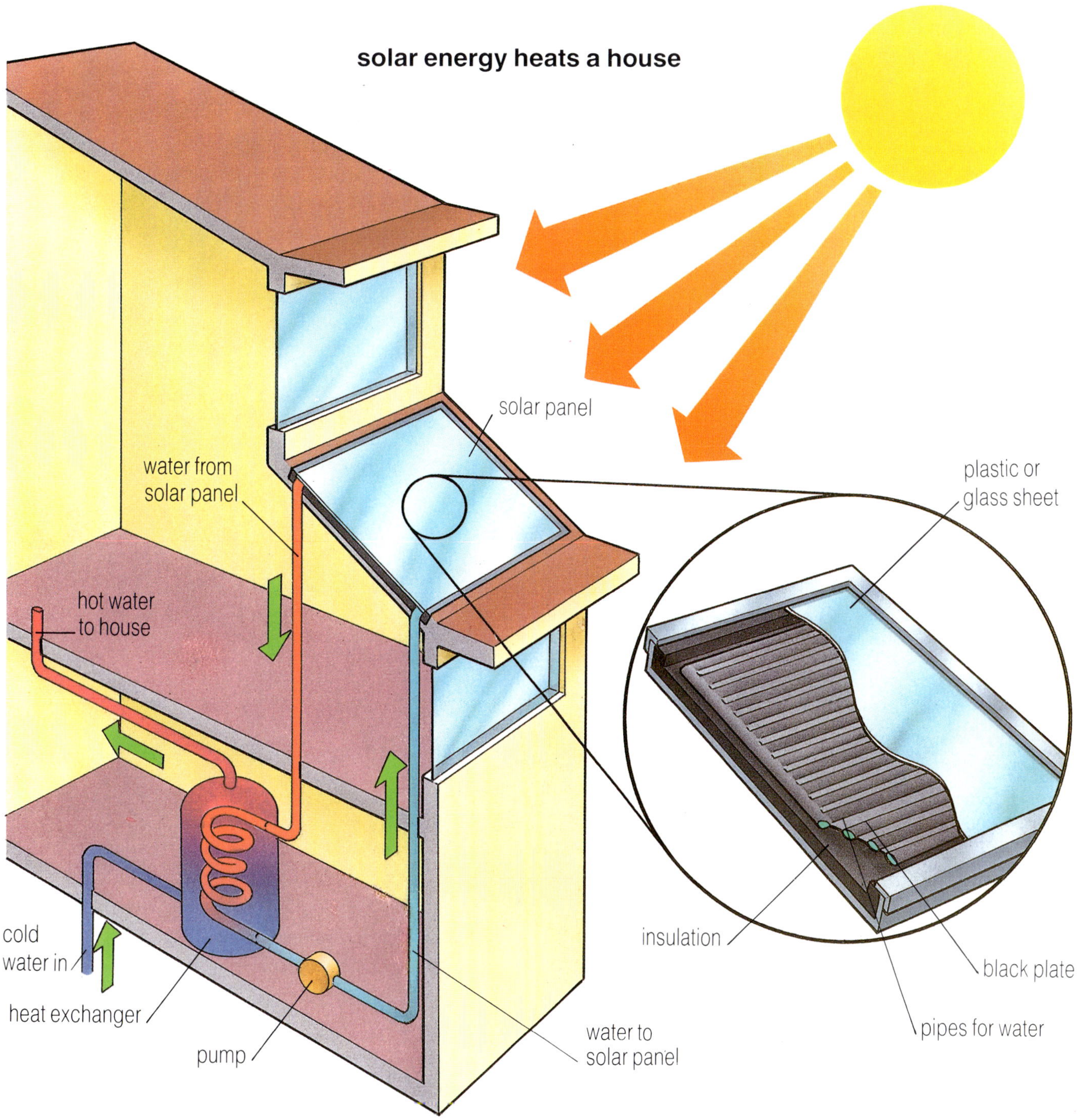

sound energy *noun*
Sound energy is a kind of **vibration** that we hear. Telephones change electrical energy into sound energy. When you clap your hands, **mechanical energy** changes into sound energy.
Sound energy travels through the air at a speed of 332 metres per second.

south pole *noun*
A south pole is one of the two **magnetic poles** on every **magnet**. A south pole is attracted towards the south pole of the Earth. The opposite of south pole is **north pole**.
The full name for the south pole of a magnet is the south-seeking pole.

space *noun*
1. Space is the room that **matter** takes up. The amount of space that an object takes up is the same as the object's **volume**. Three **dimensions** are needed to measure a space. Space is measured in cubic **units**.
There was enough space in the matchbox to hold 50 matches.
2. Space is an abbreviation for outer space. This includes all the parts of the Universe that are outside the Earth's **atmosphere**.
The Moon, Sun and stars are all in space.

span *verb*
Span is a word which describes how an object is fixed across the distance between two points. A bridge spans the distance between the two banks of a river. A spider's web spans the space between two stalks of grass.
A plank of wood spanned the hole in the ground.

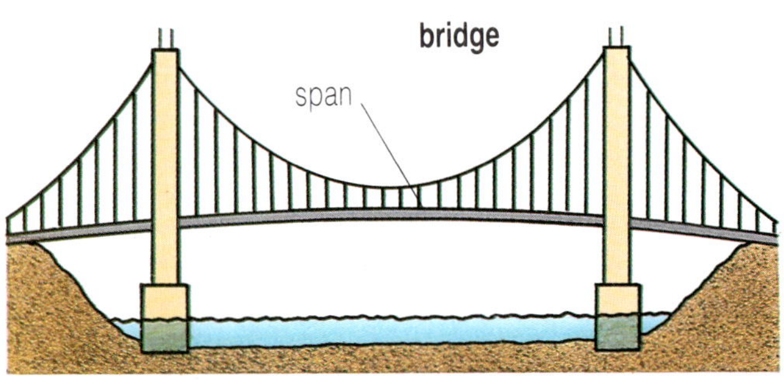

spatula *noun*
A spatula is a kind of **apparatus**. It has a handle and a wide, flat blade. Large spatulas are used for spreading or scraping materials such as paint, plaster and adhesives. Small spatulas are used to pick up small amounts of a **solid**.
The scientist collected a sample of soil with a spatula.

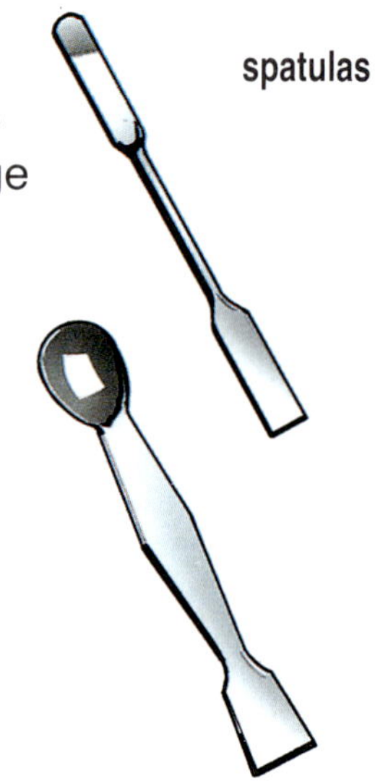

species (plural species) *noun*
A species is a group of living things. Males and females in the same species can breed with each other and reproduce young. The young can also breed and reproduce their own young. Species are part of the system of **classification** which biologists have worked out.
Horses and donkeys are members of different species.

spectrum *noun*
A spectrum is a range of things that are sorted into a **series**. A **prism** splits white light into a spectrum of colours. The **electromagnetic spectrum** is made up of the different kinds of **electromagnetic radiation**, from the lowest to the highest **frequency**.
The orchestra gave out a whole spectrum of different sounds.

speed *noun*
Speed is a kind of measurement which describes how fast something is moving. It measures how far an object travels during a fixed amount of time. **Units** of speed include **metres** per second and **kilometres** per hour.
The car travelled at a speed of 80 kilometres per hour.

sphere *noun*
A sphere is a perfectly round, solid shape. All the points on the **surface** of a sphere are the same distance from its centre.
The ball was a sphere made out of rubber.
spherical *adjective*

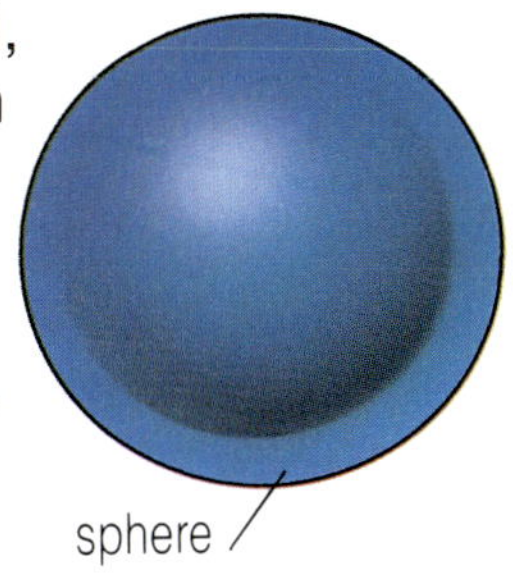

spring *noun*
1. A spring is a **device**, such as a coiled piece of steel wire or a flat, steel bar. Springs return to their original form after being forced out of shape. When a spring is out of shape, it has **potential energy**. It is said to be in **tension**.
The weight on the end of the spring bounced up and down.

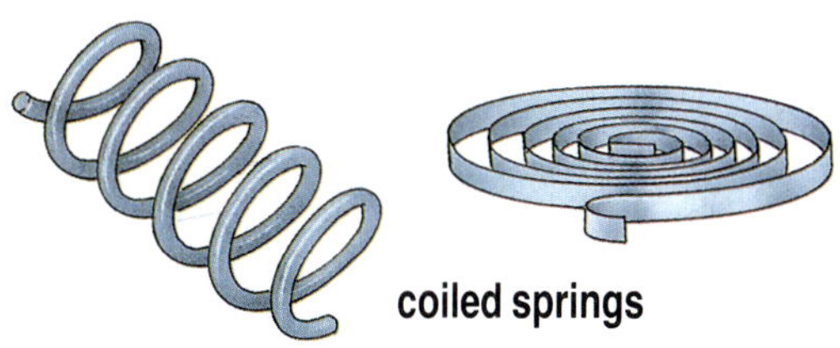
coiled springs

2. A spring is a place where water comes out of the ground. Rainwater soaks into **porous** rocks and flows under the ground. The water returns to the surface as a spring, usually where porous and non-porous rocks meet.
The water from some springs is hot and steamy.

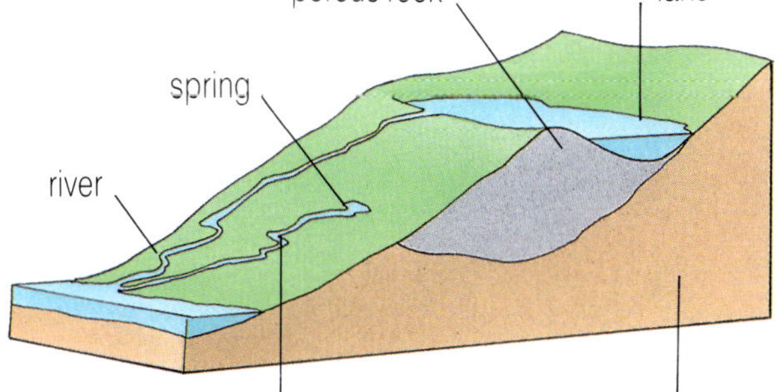

spring balance *noun*
A spring balance is a type of weighing instrument. It contains a coiled **spring**. The top end of the spring is fixed. When you hang a **mass** on the lower end of the spring balance, a pointer is pulled down along a **scale**.
She weighed the bags of apples on the spring balance.

sprocket *noun*
A sprocket is a part of a **machine**. Sprockets are pointed teeth which stick out around a wheel. They grip the links of a chain. Sprockets on one turning wheel move the chain, which moves another wheel with sprockets.
The pedals on a bicycle use a chain and sprockets to drive the rear wheel.

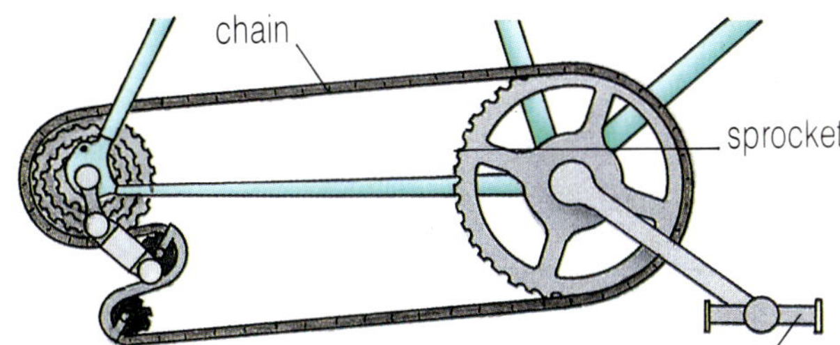

state *noun*
State is a word which describes whether a substance is a **solid**, a **liquid** or a **gas**. When a substance is heated, it melts or boils and changes its state. When a substance is cooled, it condenses or freezes and changes its state.
Water is in the liquid state when it flows out of a tap.

static electricity *noun*
Static electricity is a kind of **energy**. It builds up when **electrons** move from one object to another object. Static electricity does not flow steadily like an **electric current**. It stays still or leaps between objects.
Static electricity in the clouds leaped to the ground as a streak of lightning.

statistics *noun*
Statistics is a subject which is a part of **mathematics**. A statistician collects and sorts out long lists of **data**. Then the statistician usually works out the **average** from these lists.
From statistics, we know that the temperature of the planet Earth is slowly rising.

stator *noun*
A stator is a part of a **machine**. It is an **electromagnet** inside an electric motor or a **generator**. The stator stays still while the **armature** spins close to it.
Electricity flowed through the stator.

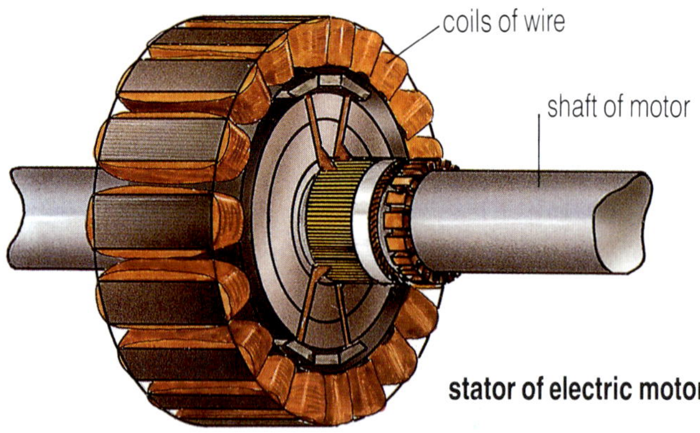

stator of electric motor

steam *noun*
Steam is a colourless **gas**. It is made when water is boiled. Steam at high **pressure** drives **turbines** in power stations. It also drives steam engines which pull trains. When the temperature is below 100 degrees **Celsius**, steam condenses back to water.
A boiling kettle gives off steam.

steam engine ► page 134

steel *noun*
Steel is a type of **alloy**. Steels are made from iron which is mixed with a small amount of **carbon**. Other elements, such as **silicon**, **nickel** and **chromium**, are also mixed in. Stainless steels contain chromium and do not **corrode**.
Tools, cars, engines and bridges are all made from different kinds of steel.

stereo- *prefix*
Stereo- describes things that are made to seem real or solid. Sound from a stereophonic record or **tape** comes from different loudspeakers. Animals with eyes pointing forward have stereoscopic vision.
Our stereoscopic vision helps us to gauge distances.

sterile *adjective*
1. Sterile is a word which describes something that is completely free from **bacteria** and other **micro-organisms**. Doctors use sterile instruments during operations so that their patients do not become infected.
The nurse gave him an injection with a sterile needle.
2. Sterile is a word which describes a female plant or animal that is not able to produce cells for **reproduction**.
The sterile cat was unable to have kittens.
sterility *noun*

streamlined *adjective*
Streamlined is a word which describes the shape of some objects. A streamlined object can move easily through the air or water. Streamlined shapes have low **drag**. They make little **turbulence** as they move.
Fish, submarines, birds, aeroplanes and arrows have a streamlined shape.

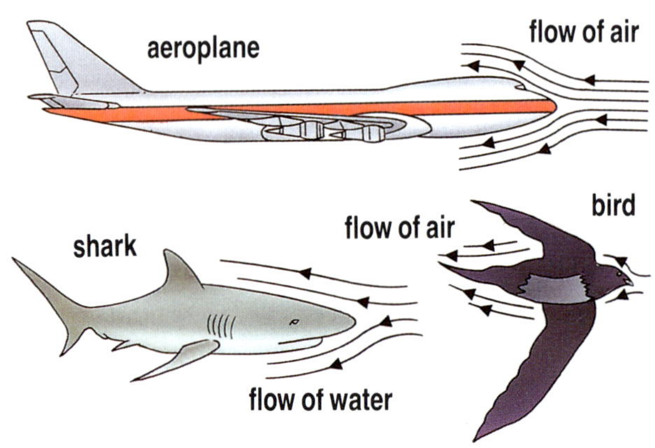

stress *noun*
A stress is a kind of **force**. It makes a body change its shape. Stress can **compress** or stretch a body. It can also make parts of a body slide over each other.
Stress squashed the rubber ball as it bounced on the ground.

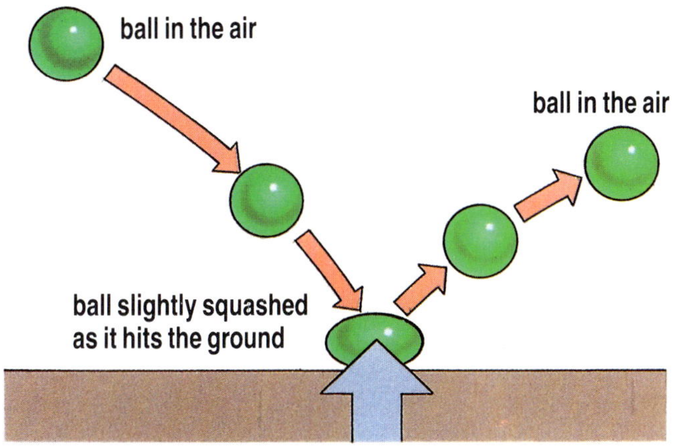

structure *noun*
1. A structure is a solid object. Structures enclose, support or **span** other things. Shells and tunnels are structures which enclose. Pillars and posts are structures which support. Bridges and spider's webs are structures which span.
Honeycomb is a structure which is found inside a bee's nest.
2. Structure is a word which describes the shape of an object. It also describes how the parts of an object fit together.
The structure of honeycomb is made up of hexagonal shapes which are joined together.

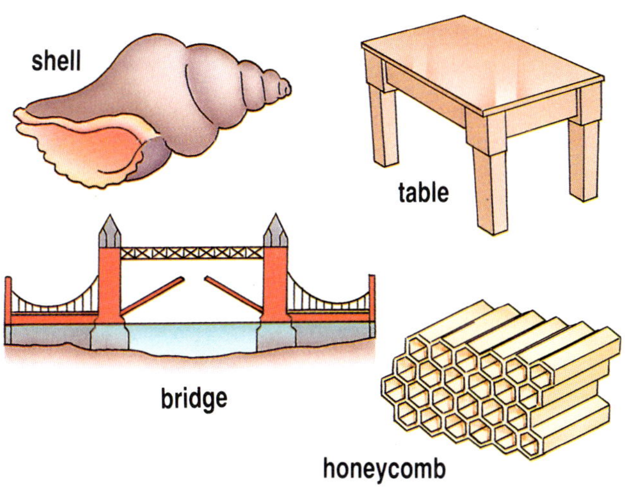

subatomic *adjective*
Subatomic is a word which describes the tiny **particles** that make up an **atom**. The three main kinds of subatomic particle are the **proton**, **neutron** and **electron**.
The nucleus of an atom is made up of subatomic particles called protons and neutrons.

submarine *noun*
A submarine is a type of boat. It floats with the help of tanks that are full of air. When the air in these tanks is replaced by water, the submarine sinks. **Batteries** or a **nuclear reactor** propel the submarine under water.
The submarine travelled at 100 metres below the surface of the sea.

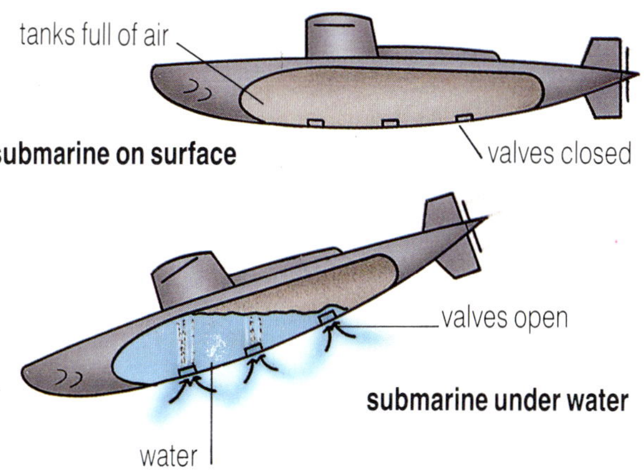

submersible *adjective*
Submersible is a word which describes something that can be covered with or plunged into water. It also describes something that can be kept under water.
A submersible object is not harmed by water.
A **submarine** is submersible.
She took photographs under water with a submersible camera.
submerge *verb*

substance *noun*
Substance is any kind of **matter**. A substance can be a solid, a liquid or a gas. It can be a pure **element,** a **compound** or a mixture.
Glue is a sticky substance which helps to fasten together pieces of paper.

steam engine *noun*
A steam engine is a kind of engine which boils water and produces **steam**. The **pressure** of the steam pushes against a **piston** inside the engine and makes it slide backwards and forwards. This produces **mechanical energy.**
In some countries of the world, railway locomotives are still powered by steam engines.

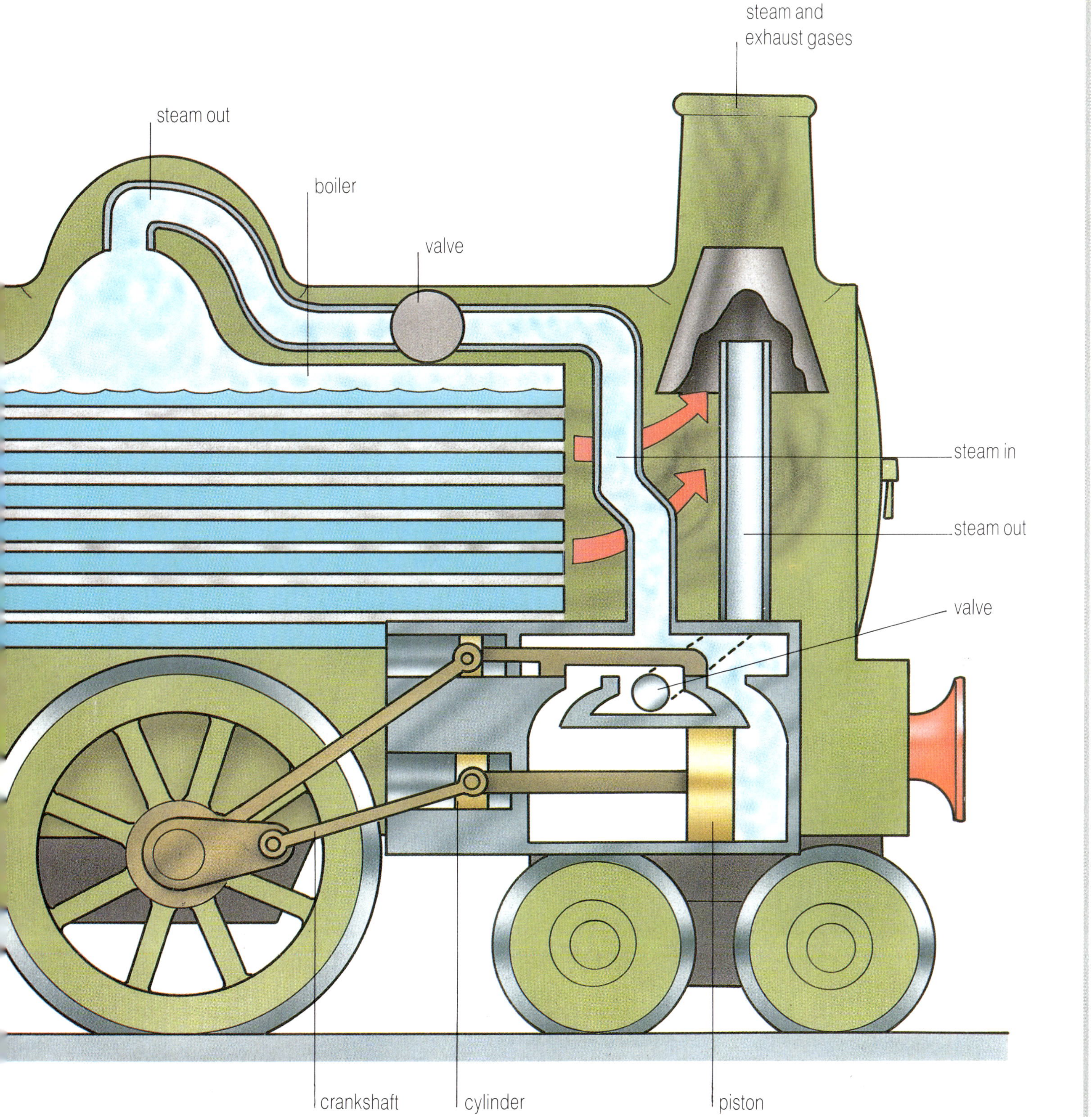
steam and exhaust gases
steam out
boiler
valve
steam in
steam out
valve
crankshaft
cylinder
piston

subtraction *noun*
Subtraction is a kind of **arithmetic**.
It describes how we take one number away from another number. The sign for subtraction is −. Subtraction can work out that if you have nine biscuits and you eat five of them, there will be four biscuits left. The sum is written $9 - 5 = 4$.
Subtraction helped them to work out how many days were left until the end of the month.

sucrose *noun*
Sucrose is a solid which is made up of colourless **crystals**. Sucrose is the **scientific** name for ordinary sugar. It dissolves easily in water and tastes sweet. Sucrose is made from a plant called sugar cane or a vegetable called sugar beet.
He added a spoonful of sucrose to his bowl of cereal.

sulphur *noun*
Sulphur is a chemical **element**. It is a yellow **non-metal**. Sulphur is found as a compound in **minerals**, petroleum and **ores**. It burns easily and is used to make **sulphuric acid**.
It is also used to make medicines.
Pure sulphur can be found in Italy and the United States of America.

sulphur dioxide *noun*
Sulphur dioxide is a colourless **gas** which can make people cough. When fossil fuels are burned, sulphur dioxide is released into the **atmosphere**. This causes a kind of pollution called **acid** rain. Sulphur dioxide is used to kill **microbes** in some food factories.
The bottle of wine contained a small amount of sulphur dioxide.

sulphuric acid *noun*
Sulphuric acid is a **liquid**. It is oily and it **corrodes** metals. When sulphuric acid is mixed with water, it is a strong **acid**. Millions of tonnes of sulphuric acid are made from **sulphur** every year.
Sulphuric acid helps to make detergents, paints, dyes, plastics and fertilizers.

supercharger *noun*
A supercharger is a **device** which is fitted to some **engines**. It is a kind of pump.
A supercharger gives engines more **power**.
It forces more air into the engine so that more fuel can burn.
They fitted a supercharger to the engine of the racing car.

superconductor *noun*
A superconductor is a substance which has no electrical **resistance**. An electric current can flow in a superconductor without getting weaker. Superconductors are special alloys which are kept at very low temperatures.
Superconductors help some types of train to float above the track.

superheated *adjective*
1. Superheated describes a **liquid** which is heated under **pressure**. It is heated to a temperature higher than its normal **boiling point**, without turning to **vapour**.
The superheated water from deep under ground burst out as a hot spring.
2. Superheated describes **steam** which is heated to a very high temperature until it contains no water droplets. It can then be kept at the right **pressure** to power an **engine**.
Superheated steam drives the train's engine.

supersonic *adjective*
Supersonic is a word which describes the **speed** of some objects. A supersonic speed is faster than the speed of **sound**, which is 1,080 kilometres per hour.
Concorde travels at supersonic speeds.

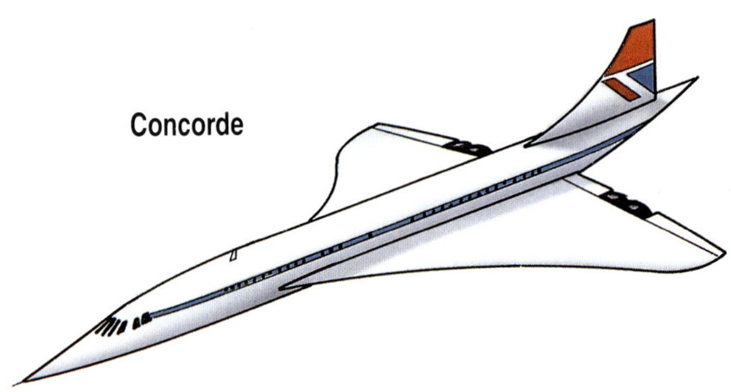

surface *noun*
The surface is a part of a **solid** or a **liquid**. It is where the outside air touches the solid or liquid. The surface of a liquid in a container is **horizontal**. It is the highest part of the liquid. A surface can be **vertical**, such as the side of a building.
The piece of wood floated on the surface of the water.

surface area *noun*
Surface area is a kind of measurement. It describes how much of a solid or a liquid touches the outside air. Surface area is measured in units of **area**, such as square **metres**. When a solid, such as a piece of paper, is folded or cut into tiny pieces, it has a large surface area.
The surface area inside his lungs was 120 square metres.

surface tension *noun*
Surface tension is a kind of **force**. It makes the **molecules** in the **surface** of a liquid cling together. This makes the liquid behave as if it has a skin. Surface tension means that some insects can walk on water. Surface tension also causes **capillary action**.
Surface tension gives drops of water a round shape.

suspension *noun*
1. The suspension is a part of motor cars and other vehicles. It joins the wheels to the body of a vehicle. Each wheel is joined to an **axle**. A **spring** joins each axle to the body.
The car's suspension gave them a smooth ride over the bumpy ground.
2. A suspension is a mixture of a liquid and an **insoluble** solid. It is made when an insoluble powder is shaken up with water. The powder does not **dissolve**, but sinks downwards after a while.
She made a suspension by stirring fine sand into water.

switch *noun*
A switch is an electric **device**. It can join or break a wire in an **electric circuit**. This turns the electric current on and off.
She pressed the switch to turn on the light.

symbol *noun*
A symbol is a mark or a shape which stands for something else. The alphabet contains 26 symbols which we use to write down words. **Mathematics** uses the symbols + and – to stand for **addition** and **subtraction.**
The symbol for percentage is %.

symmetrical *adjective*
Symmetrical is a word which describes the shape of some things. A symmetrical cube can be turned in any direction and still appears the same. A butterfly is symmetrical because each side of it is a perfect **image** of the other side. A hand is not symmetrical.
Two of the sides in a symmetrical triangle are the same length.

synthetic *adjective*
Synthetic is a word which describes an artificial **substance**. Synthetic substances are made in factories from **raw materials**. Many carpets and items of clothing are made from synthetic **fibres,** such as **nylon**, rather than from natural fibres, such as wool.
The synthetic orange juice did not taste the same as real orange juice.

system *noun*
1. A system is a collection of parts which work together. Your digestive system helps your body to break down and **absorb** food. A computer system includes both the **hardware** and the **software**.
The telephone system helps us to talk to friends in far-away countries.
2. A system is a collection of planets or stars. The solar system includes the Sun, the planets and their moons. A star system is a group of stars which forms a pattern in the sky.
The star system looked like a cross made from five stars.

T

table *noun*
A table is a kind of list. A table of results lists data from an **experiment**. The data are written down in rows and columns. **Multiplication** tables list the **products** of numbers.
Sailors look in tables to find out the times of the sea's tides.

tape ► **magnetic tape**

tape recorder *noun*
A tape recorder is a **machine**. It can store electric signals on a **magnetic tape**. These signals can be played back as sounds, pictures or computer **programs**.
The tape recorder was small enough to fit in her pocket.

portable cassette tape recorder

telecommunications ► page 140

telegraph *noun*
A telegraph is a **machine** which sends messages over long distances. The messages are sent as a code of long or short electrical **pulses** along a wire, or by pulsed radio waves. The code is called Morse Code.
She listened to the telegraph and changed the code back into letters and words.

teleprinter *noun*
A teleprinter is a machine which is used for **communications.** It has a **keyboard.**
A teleprinter sends signals in **code** through telephone wires or by **radio waves**. Another teleprinter changes the code back into numbers and letters.
The teleprinter automatically printed the message on a piece of paper.

telescope *noun*
A telescope is an instrument which makes far-away objects seem closer and larger.
A telescope in which **lenses** and mirrors are used to **magnify** objects is called an optical telescope.
Astronomers watch the stars at night through telescopes.

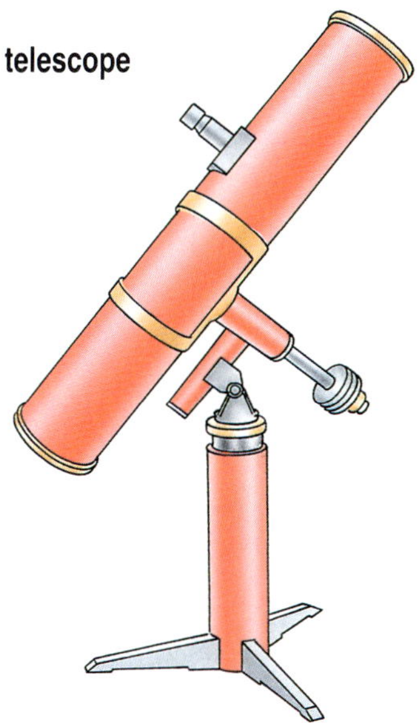

teletext *noun*
Teletext is information which appears on some kinds of television. The information is hidden at the top and bottom of the ordinary picture which appears on the **screen**.
A special **electric circuit** called a decoder shows the information on the screen when it is needed.
He read the latest news from the teletext on his television.

telex *noun*
Telex is a kind of **telecommunications**. It is a **system** which is used to send messages. Telex is made up from **teleprinters** which are linked together by ordinary telephone lines.
He sent the message by telex from London to his friend in Hong Kong.

temperature *noun*
Temperature is a kind of measurement.
It describes how hot or cold something is. Temperature is measured in **degrees** by thermometers. The main temperature **scales** are the **Fahrenheit** scale, the **Celsius** scale and the **kelvin** scale.
The temperature of boiling water is 100 degrees Celsius.

tension *noun*
Tension is a kind of **force**. It is a pull which tries to stretch an object. There is tension in a string which holds up a weight. The opposite of tension is compression.
They pulled hard on the rope and the tension snapped it tight.

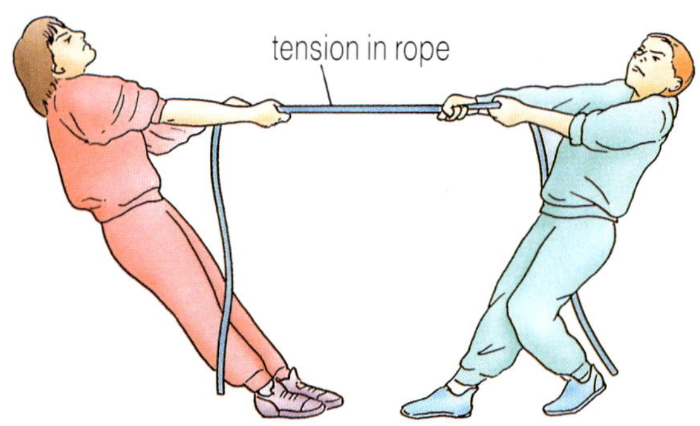

terminal *noun*
A terminal is a part of an electric **component**. It connects the component to the wires in an **electric circuit**. A battery has a **negative** and a **positive** terminal. Bulb holders and most **switches** have two terminals.
He connected the wires to the terminals on the battery.

telecommunications *noun*
Telecommunications is a word which describes the different ways that people send information to each other. **Radio waves** or **electric currents** in wires carry the information.
Telecommunications includes radio, television, fax machines and telephones.

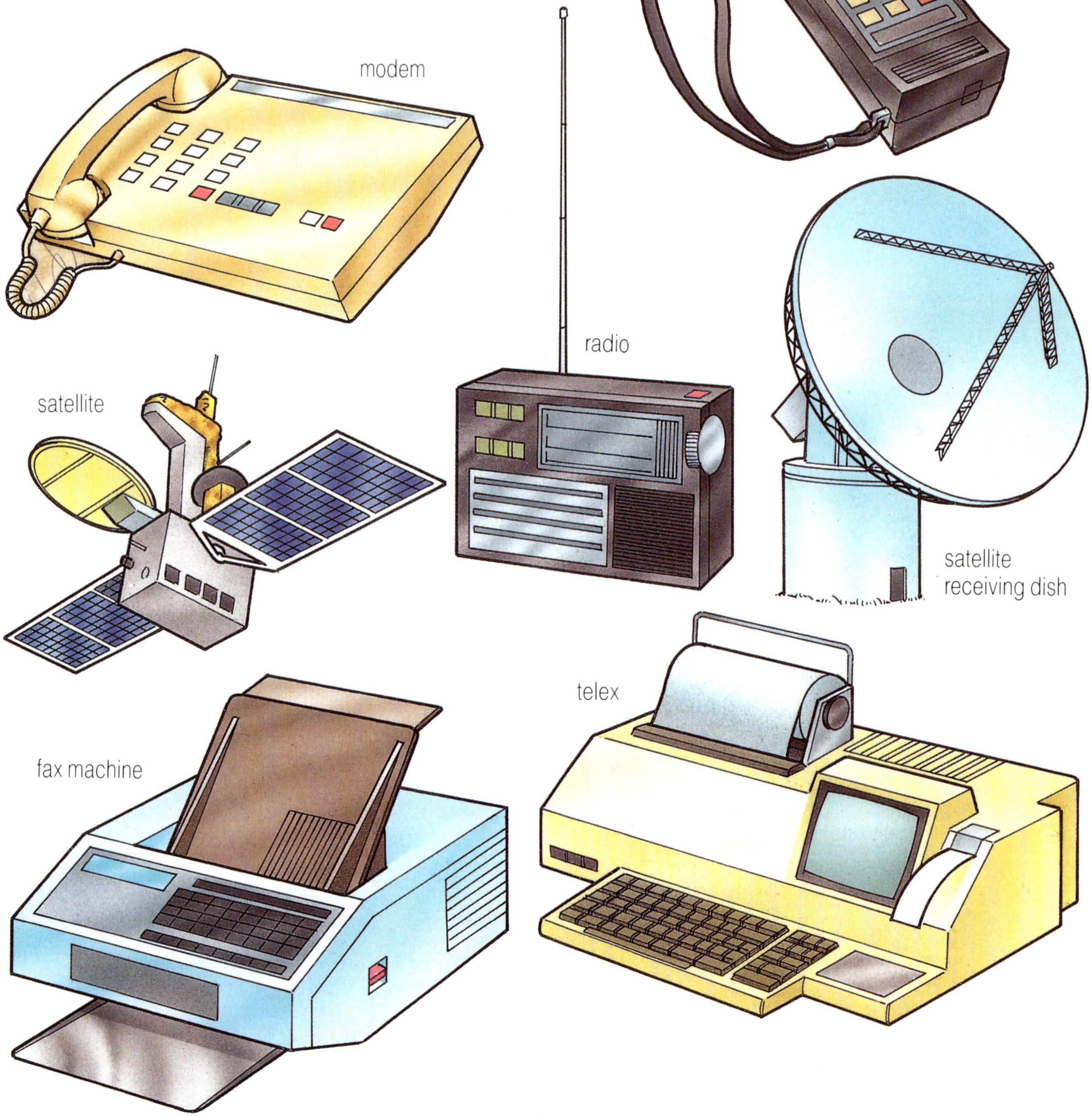

telephone

The mouthpiece of a telephone turns sound waves into electric signals. The earpiece turns the signals back into sound.

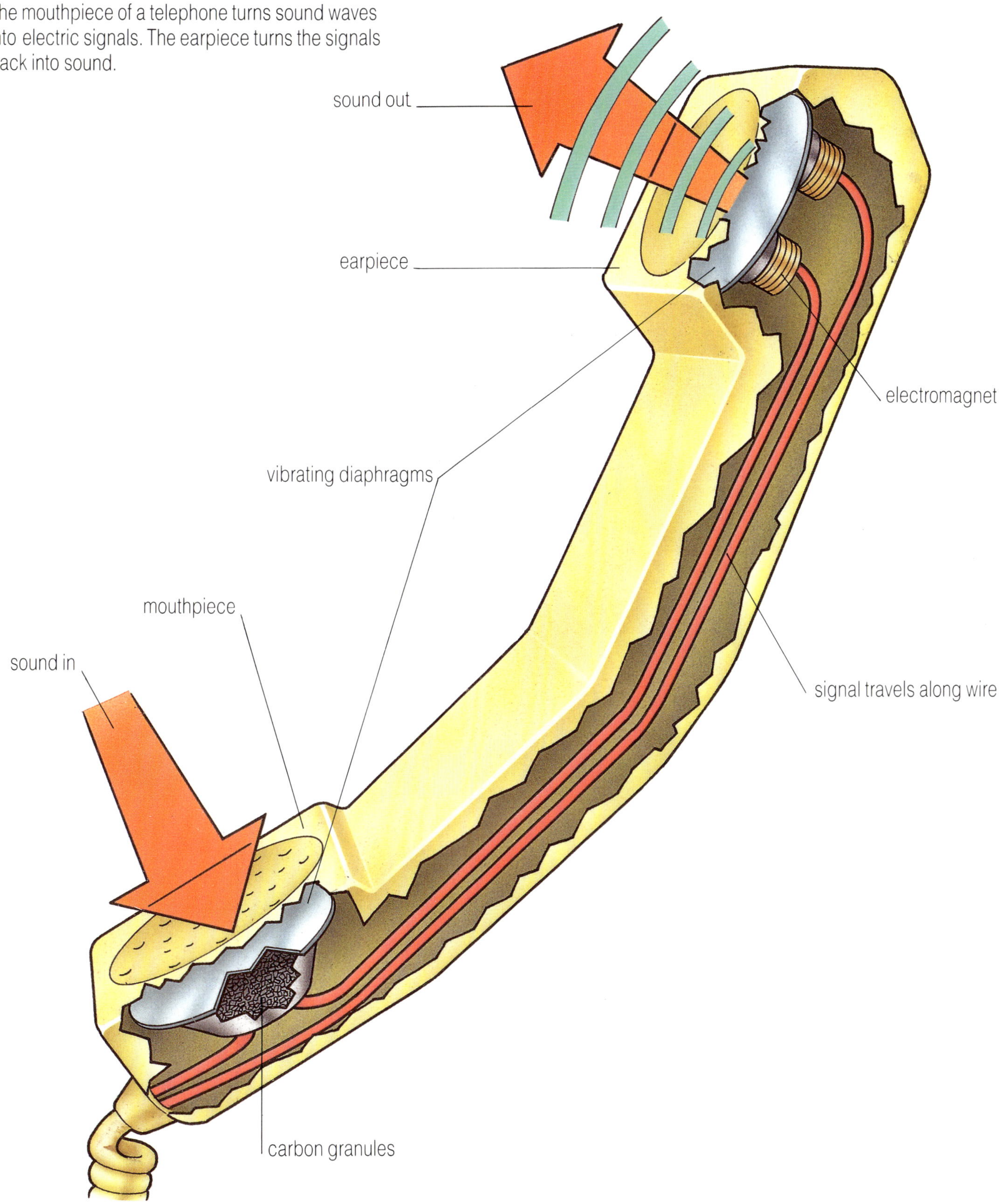

test *noun*
A test is a word which describes how something can be checked. An **experiment** is a kind of test. By doing tests, scientists can check the **properties** of things or how they behave. Tests also help people to find out if a **theory** is right or wrong.
She carried out a temperature test by putting her hand in the water.

test tube *noun*
A test tube is a kind of **apparatus**. It is a long, thin tube made of glass. A test tube has **parallel** sides and a round bottom. Scientists test **chemical reactions** in test tubes.
He poured the liquid into the test tube.

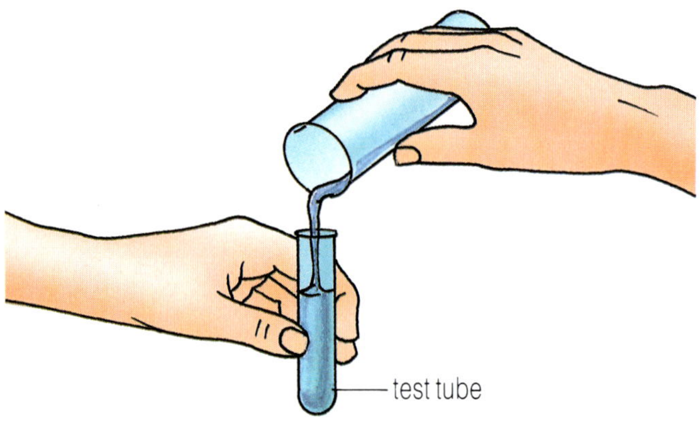

theory *noun*
A theory is an idea which explains the results of an **experiment**. Theories also explain why or how things happen. They include the theory of **evolution** and the theory of the **structure** of the atom.
Her theory tried to explain why all the dinosaurs died out.

thermal *adjective*
Thermal is a word which describes anything to do with **heat energy**. Thermal underwear keeps your body warm. A thermal imaging camera uses heat to take photographs. Thermal **conductivity** measures how well heat flows.
He put on his thermal socks to keep himself warm in the freezing weather.

thermal energy *noun*
Thermal energy is **heat energy**. When an object is hot, the **particles** in it move quickly. They have large amounts of **kinetic energy**. An object whose particles have high kinetic energy has high thermal energy.
Thermal energy flows from the hot end of a metal rod to the cold end.

thermometer *noun*
A thermometer is an instrument which measures **temperature**. Most thermometers are made up of a container for liquid which is attached to a thin, glass tube. When the liquid is warmed, it **expands** and rises up the tube.
She measured the temperature of the water with a thermometer.

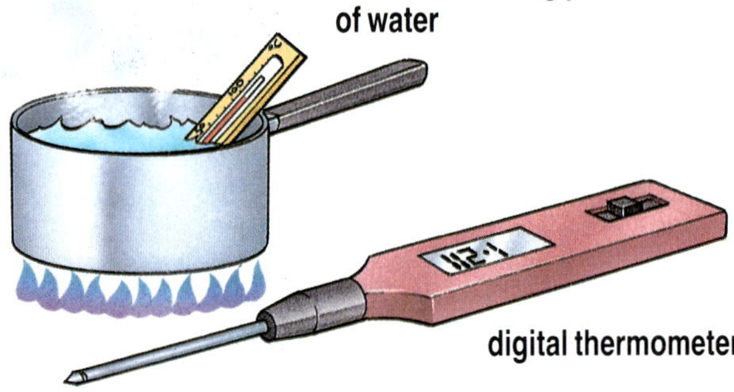

thermostat *noun*
A thermostat is a kind of **switch**. It turns a heater or a **boiler** on or off. Thermostats contain a strip made from two different metals. The metals are fastened side by side. As the strip heats up, it bends and works a switch.
The thermostat switched on the boiler when the temperature was too low.

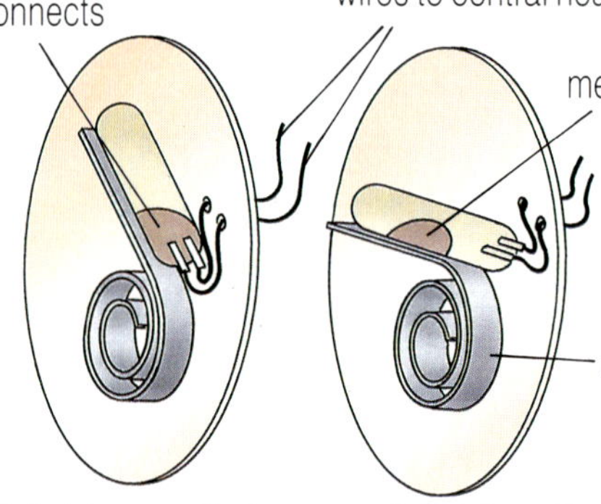

throttle *noun*
A throttle is a part of an **engine**. It is a **valve** which can open and close. When the throttle is open, more fuel flows into the engine which gives out more **power**.
The pilot opened the throttle and the aeroplane took off with a roar.

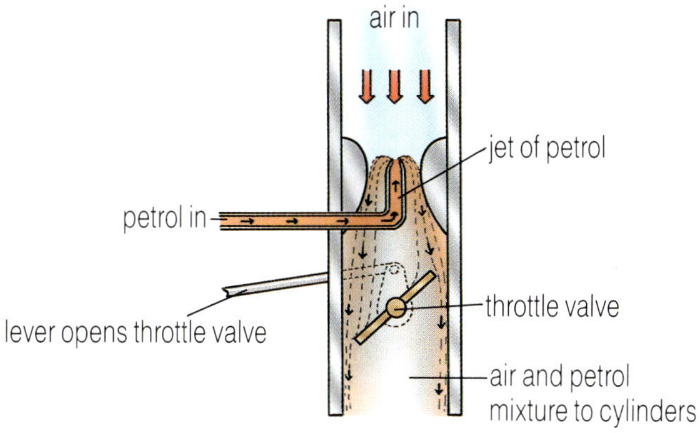

tidal power *verb*
Tidal power is a kind of **energy**. It is generated by the rise and fall of the sea's tides. Tidal power drives **turbines** in a tidal **power station** to generate electricity. The turbines are set in a **dam**, which is built across the mouth of a river at the coast.
There is a tidal power station in France, in Canada and in the Soviet Union.

tin *noun*
Tin is a chemical **element**. It is a soft, silvery **metal** which has a low melting point. Tin is used to make **solder**. Tin cans are made from steel which has a thin coat of tin. The tin coat stops the food inside from rusting the cans.
He was able to tear the sheet of tin with his fingers.

tissue *noun*
Tissue describes a group of plant or animal **cells** that have a similar **structure**. The group of cells that make up tissue all do the same work. Plants have leaf tissue and root tissue. Animals have skin tissue, muscle tissue and nerve tissue.
The bones of all animals are made up of bone tissue.

titanium *noun*
Titanium is a chemical **element**. It is a hard, white **metal** which does not **corrode** easily. **Alloys** which contain titanium help to make special parts in **turbines** and aircraft. Titanium **oxide** is the **pigment** in white paint.
Alloys which contain titanium are not affected by heat.

torque *noun*
Torque is a word which describes how much **effort** is used to twist a shaft. A vehicle uses torque from its engine to turn the wheels. When the torque is large, the vehicle **accelerates** quickly.
A large torque was needed to start the heavy train moving out of the station.

trace element *noun*
A trace element is a **metal** or **non-metal**. Trace elements are elements which are needed in very small amounts. They include zinc, copper, **iodine**, **cobalt** and **chromium**. Living things use trace elements to make **enzymes** and other, larger **molecules**.
All living things must take in tiny amounts of trace elements to stay healthy.

transformer *noun*
A transformer is an electric **device**. It can increase or decrease the **voltage** of an **alternating current**. Transformers are made up from two separate coils of wire which are wound on to an iron **core**.
The transformer decreased the voltage from the power station from 15,000 volts to 240 volts.

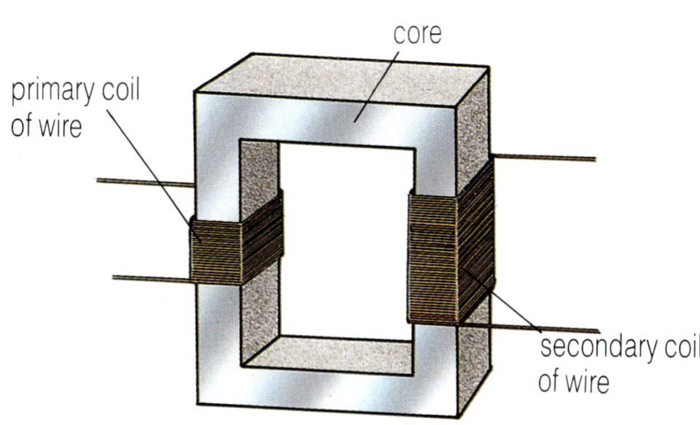

transistor *noun*
A transistor is an electronic **device**. It is made from a tiny piece of **silicon**. Three wires are attached to the silicon. Transistors can **amplify** electric **signals**. They are found in radios, televisions, computers and **video cassette recorders**.
The radio contained 12 transistors.

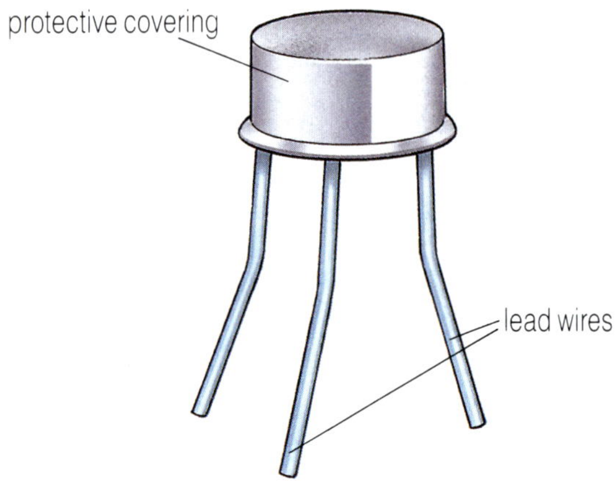

translucent *adjective*
Translucent describes a substance which allows some **light** to pass through it. Objects cannot be seen clearly through translucent substances. The opposite of translucent is **opaque**.
The translucent glass in the bathroom window was cloudy and it had a wrinkled surface.

transmit *verb*
Transmit is a word which means to send something out from a place. An **aerial** can transmit **radio waves**. A loudspeaker transmits **sound**.
She held up her flashlight and transmitted a message across the valley.

transmitter *noun*
A transmitter is an electronic **device**. It is connected to an **aerial** which **transmits** radio waves. These waves carry radio or television signals to **receivers** in other places.
A powerful transmitter can send a message from one continent to another.

transparent *adjective*
Transparent describes a substance which allows **light** to pass easily through it. Objects can be seen clearly through transparent substances.
Water and sheets of clear glass and plastic are transparent.

transpiration *noun*
Transpiration describes how plants lose **water vapour** through their leaves. Transpiration takes place mainly through tiny holes called stomata. Stomata are found on the undersides of plant leaves.
Transpiration made the dandelion leaves become floppy and wilt in the hot weather.

triangle *noun*
A triangle is a flat shape. It has three straight sides. The three **angles** inside a triangle always add up to 180 **degrees**.
He joined three straight sticks together to make a triangle.
triangular *adjective*

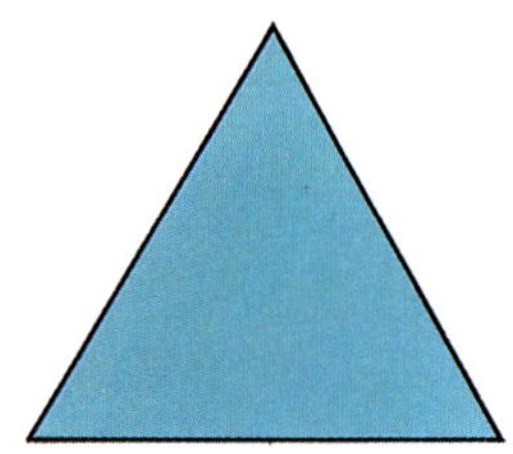

tune *verb*
Tune is a word which describes how a **receiver** is adjusted. A radio or television set is tuned to make it receive different stations. When the tuning control is adjusted, **radio waves** with different **frequencies** are selected.
He tuned the radio to receive the news programme.

tungsten *noun*
Tungsten is a chemical **element**. It is a grey **metal** which has a very high **melting point**. **Filaments** in electric light bulbs are made from tungsten. Steel tools for cutting are made from hard **alloys** which contain tungsten.
The tungsten did not melt when it was heated to over 3,000 degrees Celsius.

turbine *noun*
A turbine is a **machine**. It has a **shaft** which is joined to a set of blades. A gas or liquid flows past the blades and spins the shaft. The rotating shaft can do **work**. **Water turbines** and **gas turbines** are different kinds of turbine.
A steam turbine was used to drive the huge ship's engine.

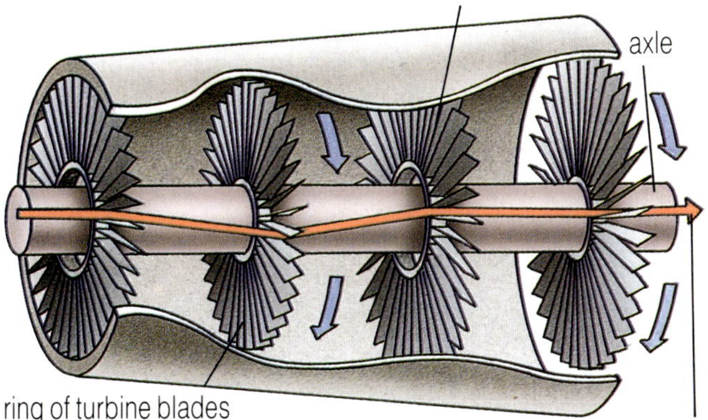

turbocharger *noun*
A turbocharger is a **device** which is fitted to some engines. It is a kind of **supercharger**. Exhaust gases from the engine drive a **turbine**. This runs another turbine which forces extra air into the engine.
They fitted a turbocharger to the motor car's engine to make it more powerful.

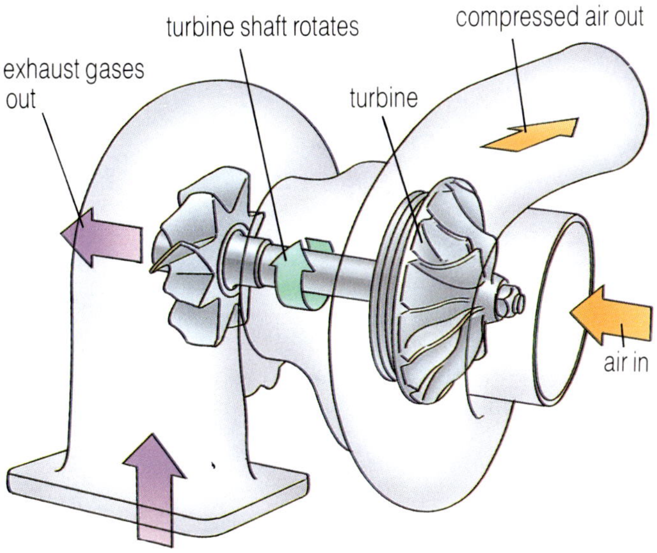

turbojet *noun*
A turbojet is a kind of **engine**. It is a **gas turbine** engine which is found in some aeroplanes. Fuel burns inside the engine, and a jet of hot gases comes out from the rear of the engine. This makes a thrust which pushes the engine forward.
A turbojet powers the aeroplane as it flies 10,000 metres above the ground.

turbulent *adjective*
Turbulent is a word which describes how some **fluids** move. Water or air flows smoothly around a **streamlined** shape. When a shape is not streamlined, the flow around it is turbulent. This results in **drag**.
The water suddenly became turbulent as it flowed around the rocks.
turbulence *noun*

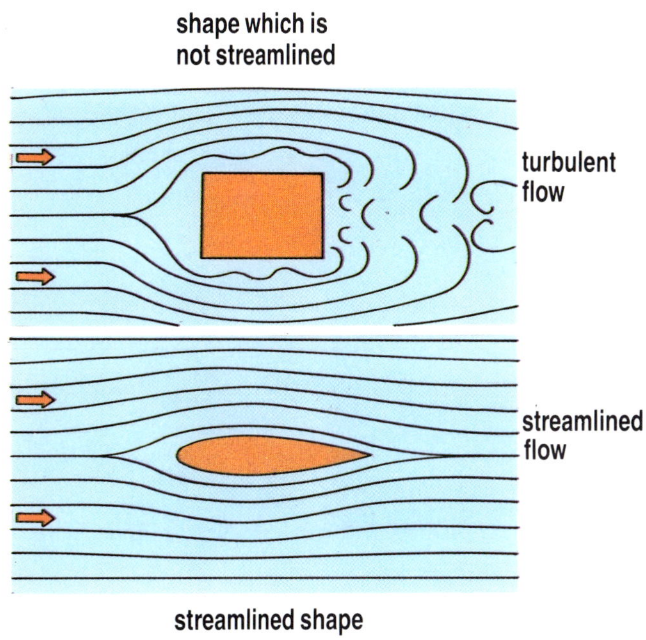

turntable *noun*
A turntable is a kind of **machine**. It is made up of a motor which turns a flat **disc.** The disc **rotates** an object placed on top of it.
A record-player has a small turntable which spins a record. A large turntable turns a railway engine around on its track.
The turntable on the record-player spins 33⅓ times each minute.

two-stroke engine *noun*
A two-stroke engine is a kind of **internal combustion engine**. Each stroke is a movement of a **piston** up or down inside the engine. A two-stroke engine is like a **four-stroke engine**, but it uses only two strokes of a piston to make **power**.
His motorbike was powered by a two-stroke engine.

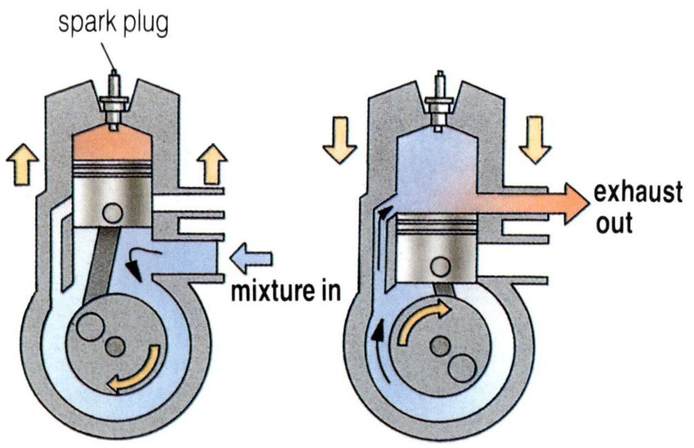

piston moves up   piston moves down

U

UHF *noun*
UHF stands for ultra-high **frequency**. It describes **radio waves** which have frequencies between 300 million **hertz** and 3,000 million hertz. UHF radio waves carry telephone and television signals between **satellites** and the Earth.
A UHF television set must be fitted with the right kind of aerial.

ultrasonics *noun*
Ultrasonics is a **scientific** subject. It is the study of **ultrasound**. Doctors use ultrasonics to help them to see inside a patient's body. Ultrasonics also helps to clean **surfaces**.
Ultrasonics made it possible for the engineer to find the crack in the metal pipe where it lay underground.

ultrasound *noun*
Ultrasound is a kind of **vibration**. Ultrasound is made up of **sound** waves which have a **frequency** above 20,000 **hertz**. Humans cannot hear ultrasound. Bats and some other animals use ultrasound to communicate with each other and to find their prey.
Bats give out short bursts of ultrasound and listen for the echoes.

ultraviolet ray *noun*
An ultraviolet ray is a kind of **electromagnetic radiation**. The Sun gives off ultraviolet rays, as well as **infra-red rays** and light. Animals cannot see these rays. Ultraviolet rays have **frequencies** which are higher than those in the **visible spectrum** of light.
Ultraviolet rays turn fair skin darker.

umbra *noun*
The umbra is a part of a shadow. It is the darkest part of the shadow, where the light is completely cut off.
If the source of light is large, then the shadow has a pale edge around the umbra.

unit *noun*
1. A unit is a kind of measurement which people have agreed to use. The unit of length is one **metre**, the unit of time is one **second** and the unit of **mass** is one **kilogram**. Scientists use the **metric system** of **SI units**.
We buy our petrol in units called litres.
2. Unit is another word for one. The number 4 contains four units. A unit **mass** can weigh 1 gram, 1 kilogram or 1 tonne.
She drew a square with sides one unit long.
3. A unit is an electrical measurement. It measures how much **energy** an appliance has used. When 1 **kilowatt** of **power** works for 1 hour, 1 unit of electrical energy is used.
The electric heater used 3 units of electricity in 1 hour.

upthrust *noun*
Upthrust is a kind of **force**. It pushes upwards on an object which is surrounded by a **fluid**. The strength of the upthrust is equal to the weight of fluid that the object pushes out of the way. **Archimedes' principle** explains how upthrust makes ships and **helium** balloons float.
Upthrust made the rock in his hand feel lighter in water then it felt on land.

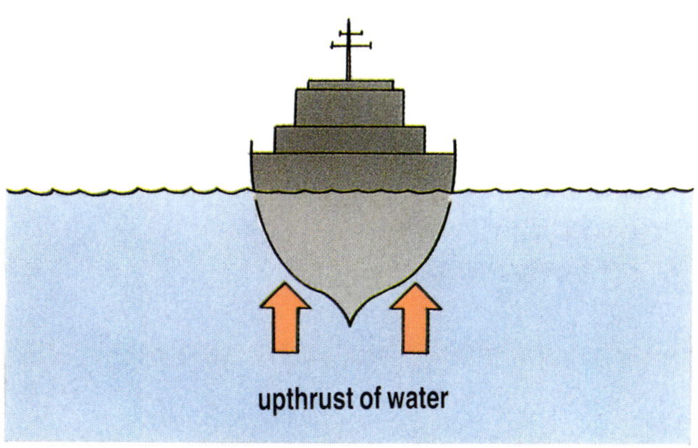

uranium *noun*
Uranium is a **radioactive element**. It is a very heavy, white **metal**. Uranium makes the energy on which **nuclear power stations** run.
A cube of uranium weighs twice as much as a cube of iron of the same size.

urea *noun*
Urea is a **substance** which is found in the urine of animals. It is a waste **product**. Urea contains **nitrogen** and is made when **protein** is broken down in the liver. It is carried by the **blood** from the liver to the kidneys where urine is produced. The urine then passes into the bladder.
Urea passes out of an animal's body in the urine.

V

vacuum *noun*
A vacuum is a **space** which contains no **particles**. When as much air as possible is pumped out of a space, a high vacuum is made. When only some of the air is pumped out, a low or partial vacuum is made. The **pressure** of a perfect vacuum is **zero**.
There is an almost perfect vacuum on the Moon.

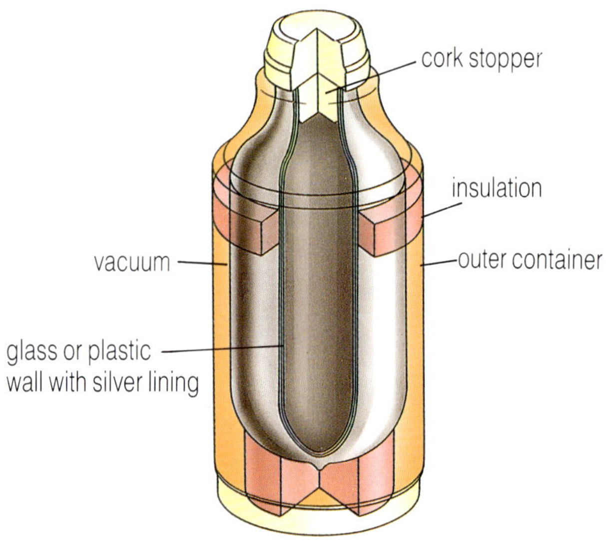

valve *noun*
A valve is an **electronic** device. It contains a hot **filament** which gives off a stream of **electrons**. These electrons help to **amplify** signals as they move through a **vacuum** inside the valve. **Transistors** have now replaced valves.
The valves in an old radio set look like small electric light bulbs.

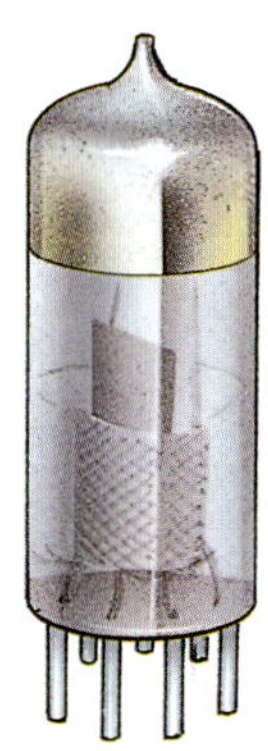

valve *noun*
A valve is a **device** which is found in a pipe or an opening. Valves control the amount of fluid that can flow through the pipe or opening. Some valves allow the fluid to flow in one direction only.
She turned the handle on the valve and water came out of the pipe.

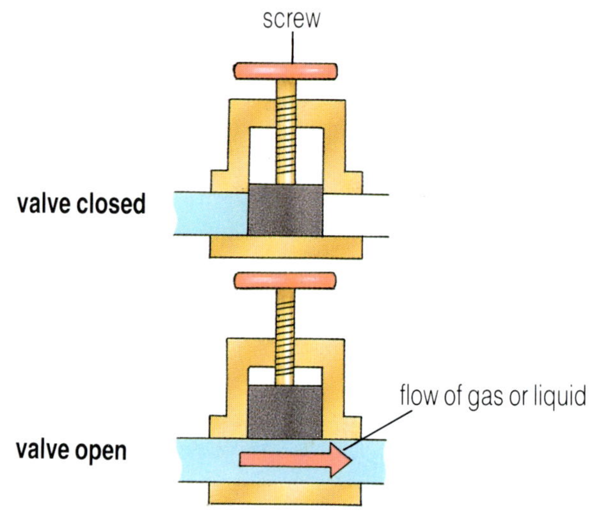

vapour *noun*
A vapour is a kind of **gas**. Liquids give off vapour, even when they are not boiling. Petrol vapour **evaporates** easily from liquid petrol. Wet clothes become dry because they give off water vapour. Plants give off water vapour during **transpiration**.
He opened the bottle of scent and smelled the vapour coming from it.

variable *noun*
Variable is a word which describes a **quantity** that can change. **Algebra** uses variables in **equations** to solve problems. The equation $A = L \times B$ tells us the area (A) of any rectangle. L and B are the variables which stand for length and breadth. The opposite of a variable is a **constant**.
She multiplied the two variables to work out the area of her garden.

VCR ► video cassette recorder

VDU ► visual display unit

velocity *noun*
Velocity is a kind of **speed**. It measures a speed in a particular direction. Two bicycles can have the same speed, but if one is travelling to the north and the other is travelling to the west, then they have different velocities.
He threw the ball with a tremendous velocity.

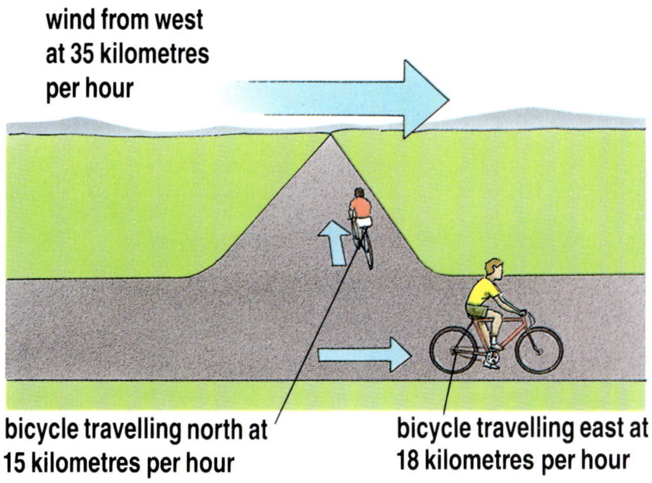

vertical *adjective*
Vertical is a word which describes a direction. A vertical direction goes straight up. Vertical describes flat surfaces, such as walls, or lines, such as the upward path of a rocket.
He climbed up the vertical rope.

VHF *noun*
VHF stands for very high **frequency**. It describes **radio waves** which have frequencies between 30 million **hertz** and 300 million hertz. VHF radio waves carry radio and television signals from **transmitters** to **receivers**.
The taxi drivers talked to each other on their VHF radios.

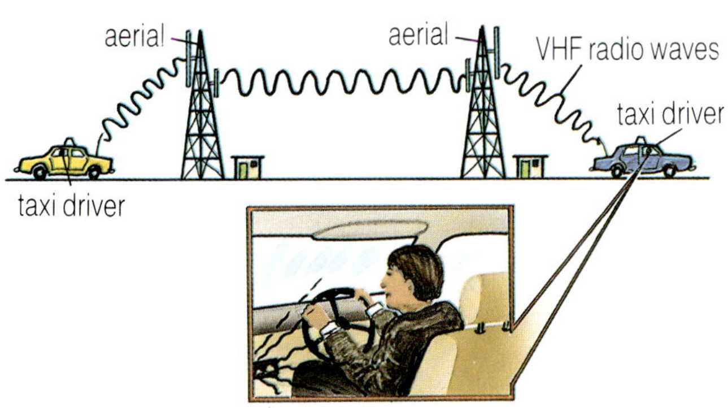

vibrate *verb*
Vibrate is a word which describes how some things move quickly backward and forward. **Frequency** measures the **rate** of this movement.
A sheet of metal vibrates when you hit it with a hammer.

vibration *noun*
A vibration is a shaking movement. It happens when something **vibrates**. You can feel vibrations in the ground when a heavy truck drives past. Vibrations in the air carry sound from one place to another place.
She felt the vibrations from his voice when she placed her hand against his throat.

video cassette recorder ► page 150

viewdata *noun*
Viewdata is a **system** which is made up from computers that are connected together. It helps people to exchange information. **Teletext** allows information to flow in one direction only. Viewdata allows it to flow in all directions.
Viewdata helped the travel agent to book the aeroplane flights for his customers.

virus *noun*
A virus is a kind of **micro-organism**. It causes diseases in animals and plants. Viruses invade healthy **cells** and force them to make more viruses. This causes the cells to burst and die. More cells are then invaded.
The common cold is caused by viruses which attack the inside of your nose.

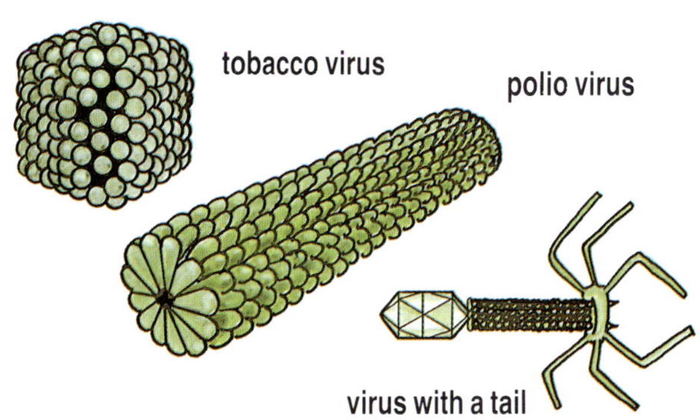

video cassette recorder *noun*
A video cassette recorder, or VCR for short, is a **machine** which records and plays back moving pictures and sound. A video camera changes light into electric **signals**. The signals are stored on **magnetic tape.** The video cassette recorder passes the stored signals from the video tape to a television screen.
She recorded her favourite television programme on the video cassette recorder so that she could watch it later.

video camera

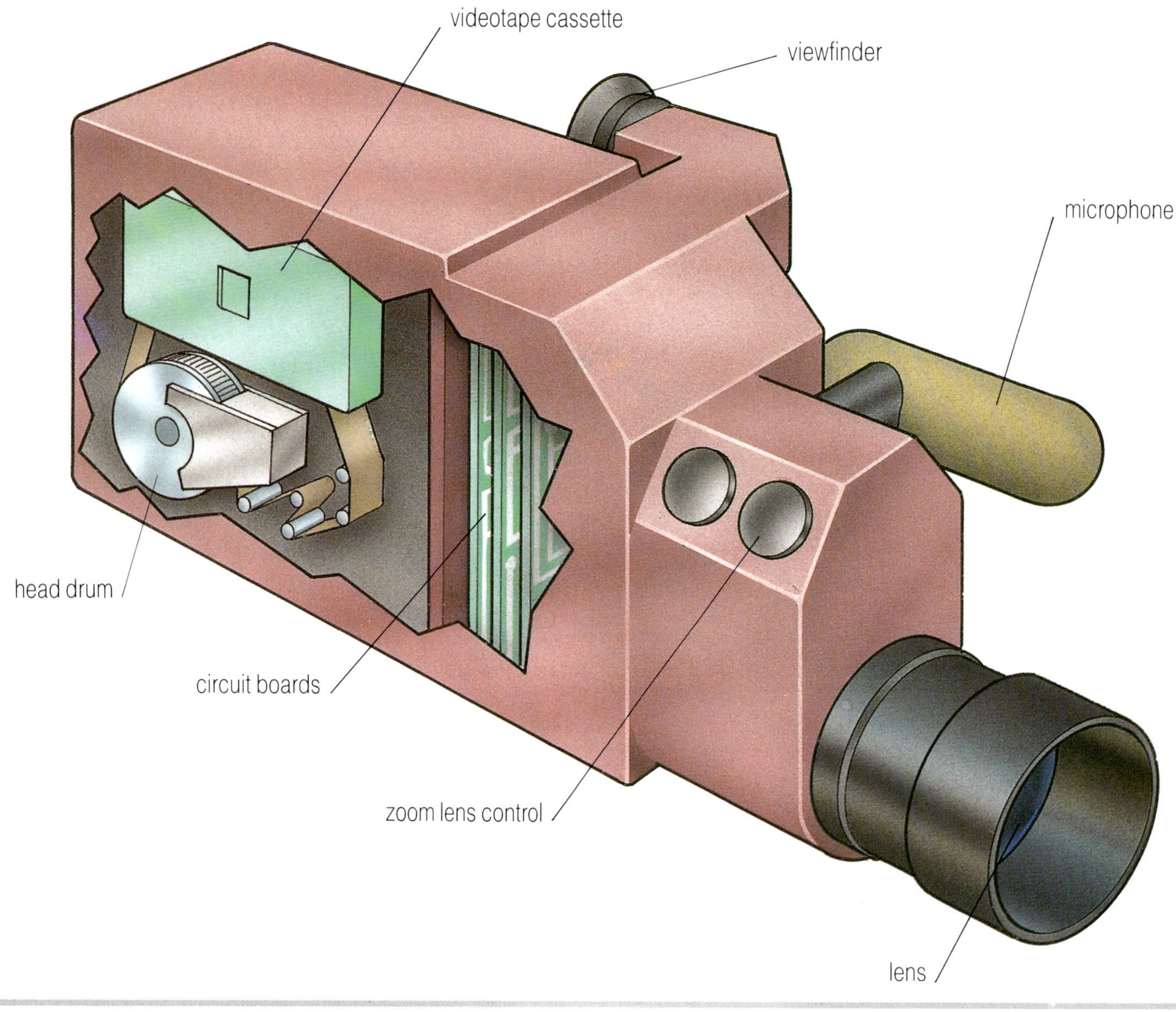

video cassette recorder

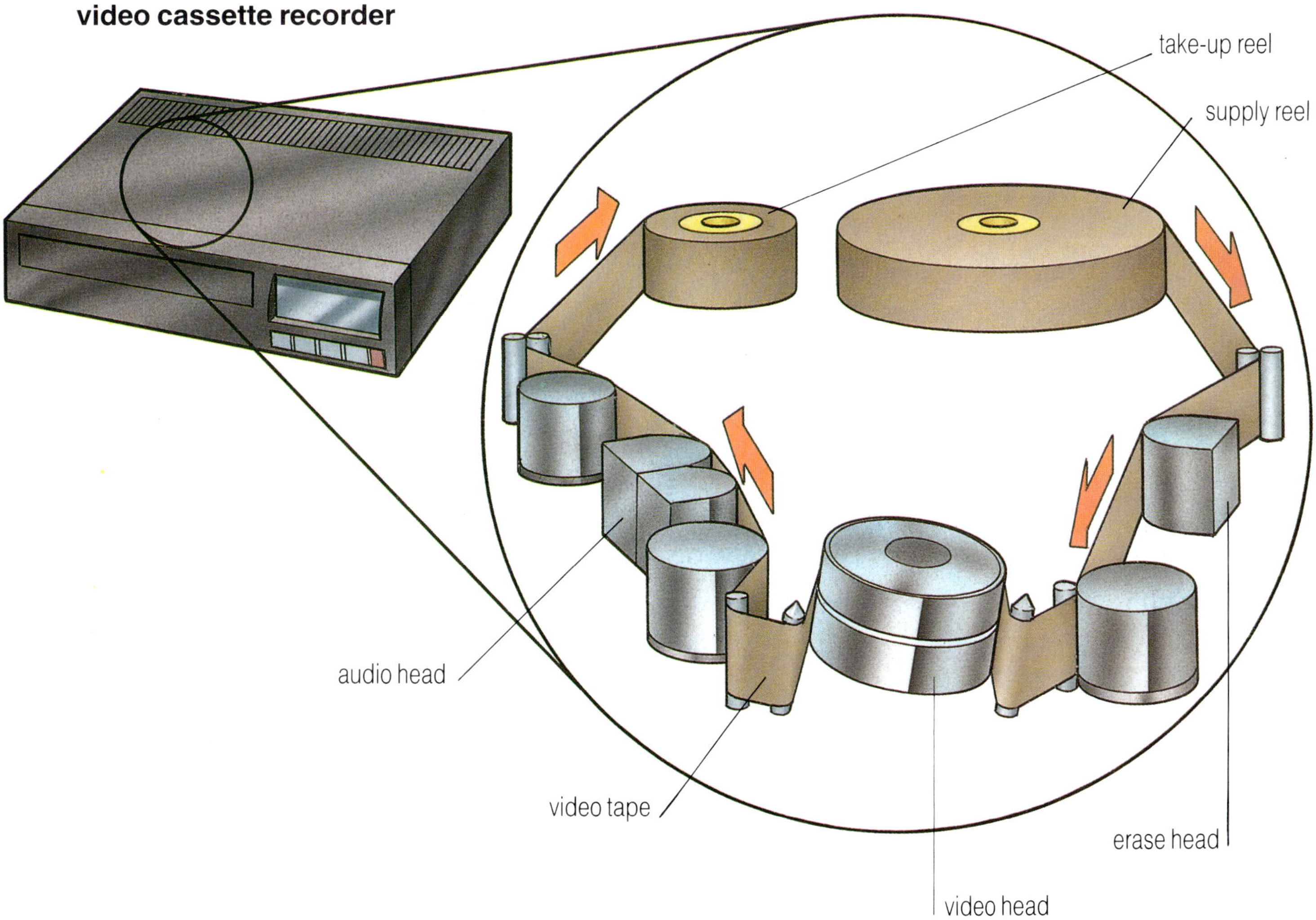

making a video

person

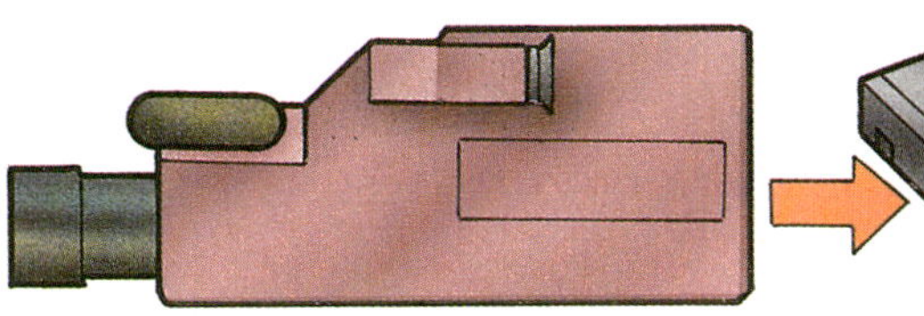

video camera takes pictures of person and records them onto videotape cassette

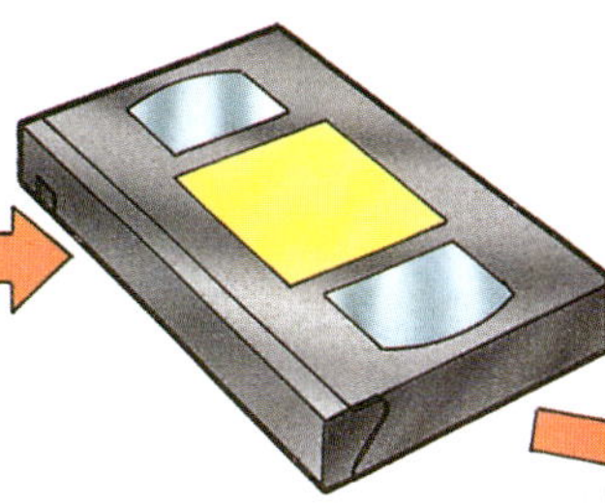

videotape cassette is put into video cassette recorder

image appears on TV screen

viscous *adjective*
Viscous is a word which describes the stickiness of a **liquid**. Oil is more viscous than water. Hot oil is less viscous than cold oil.
A metal ball sinks slowly through a viscous liquid.
viscosity *noun*

visible spectrum *noun*
The visible spectrum is a part of the **electromagnetic spectrum**. It is a **spectrum** which is made up of all the colours of light that we can see. The main colours of the visible spectrum are red, orange, yellow, green, blue and violet.
The edge of the mirror broke the sunlight into the colours of the visible spectrum.

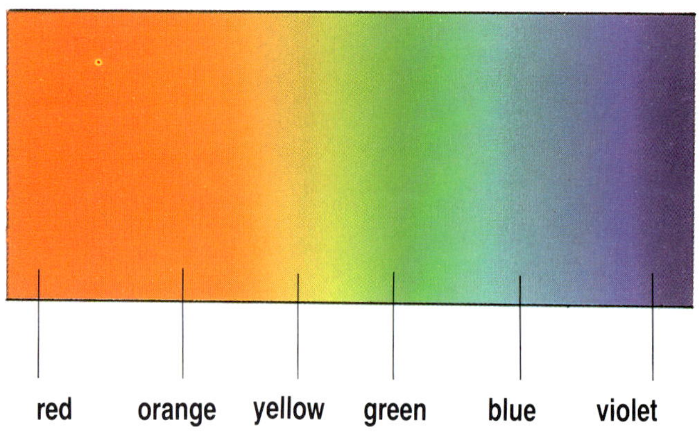

visual display unit *noun*
A visual display unit, or VDU, is a part of a **computer**. It has a **screen** and looks like a television set. The screen shows information which is typed on the keyboard. The visual display unit also shows the results from the computer's **programs**.
Words, numbers and pictures appeared on the visual display unit.

volatile *adjective*
Volatile describes some **liquids**. A volatile liquid changes easily into a **vapour**. Petrol is more volatile than water because petrol **evaporates** more quickly than water.
When a liquid is heated, it becomes more volatile.

volt *noun*
A volt, or V for short, is a **unit** of measurement. Volts measure the strength of the **force** which pushes an **electric current** around an electric circuit. When the number of volts is doubled, the electric current in a simple circuit is also doubled.
She placed a new 6-volt battery inside her flashlight.

voltage *noun*
Voltage is a word which describes the number of **volts** that are measured in an **electric circuit**. Batteries usually have a voltage between 1.5 and 12 volts. Voltage is measured with a **voltmeter**.
The voltage of the electricity supplied to most homes is about 110 volts or about 230 volts.

voltmeter *noun*
A voltmeter is an electrical instrument. It measures **voltage**. Voltmeters are either **analogue** or **digital** meters, and they have two connections. Wires join these connections to the electric circuit which is being measured.
The voltmeter helped him to find out why the radio was not working.

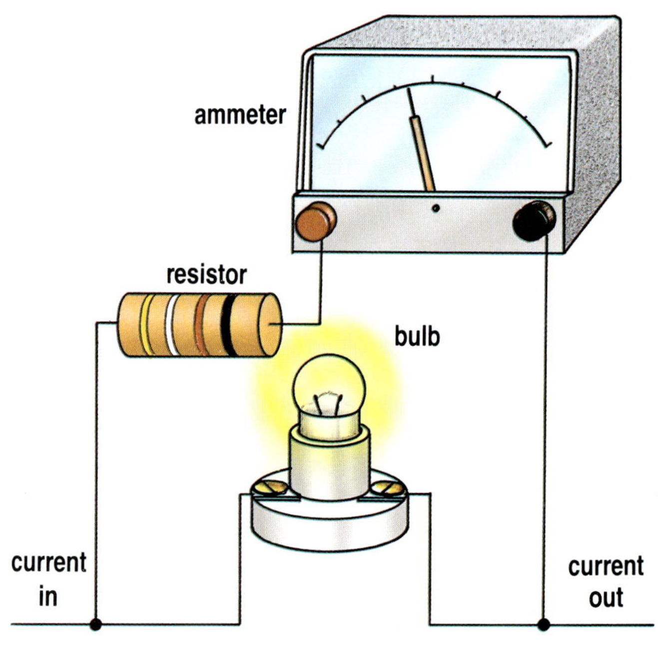

circuit inside voltmeter

volume *noun*
1. Volume is the amount of **space** inside something. The **units** for measuring volume are cubic metres and cubic centimetres. **Fluids** are measured in litres.
The volume of the box was 1,500 cubic centimetres.
2. Volume is the loudness of a **sound**. The **unit** of loudness is the **decibel**. The volume control on a radio or television alters the loudness of the sound.
Her neighbours complained because the volume of her radio was too loud.

W

washer *noun*
A washer is a flat **disc** which has a hole through its middle. A **bolt** passes through the hole in a washer, and a **nut** holds it tight. Washers help to keep the nut tight on the bolt.
A bolt, a washer and a nut held together the two sheets of metal.

water-cooled *adjective*
Water-cooled describes a **machine** that has cold water flowing around it to stop it becoming too hot. A series of pipes carries the water around a water-cooled machine. Some of the huge machines in factories are water-cooled. Boat engines are water-cooled.
He filled the motor car's radiator with water to stop the water-cooled engine overheating.

water cycle ► page 154

waterproof *adjective*
Waterproof is a word which describes something that does not allow water or **water vapour** to pass through it. Plastic-coated **materials** and rubber are waterproof. Glass, metal and some kinds of stone are waterproof.
The children splashed through the puddles in waterproof boots.

water turbine *noun*
A water turbine is a kind of **machine**. It is a **turbine** which has a set of blades and a **shaft**. Water rushes past the blades which spin the shaft. **Hydro-electric power** is generated with the help of water turbines.
A lake high up in the mountains supplied water to the water turbine.

water cycle *noun*
Water cycle is a term which describes how water moves around between the **atmosphere**, the land and rivers, lakes and seas. Water **evaporates** from the sea to form clouds which drop rain on to the land. The rain falls into rivers and flows back to the sea.
Plants and animals are part of the water cycle because they take in and give out water.

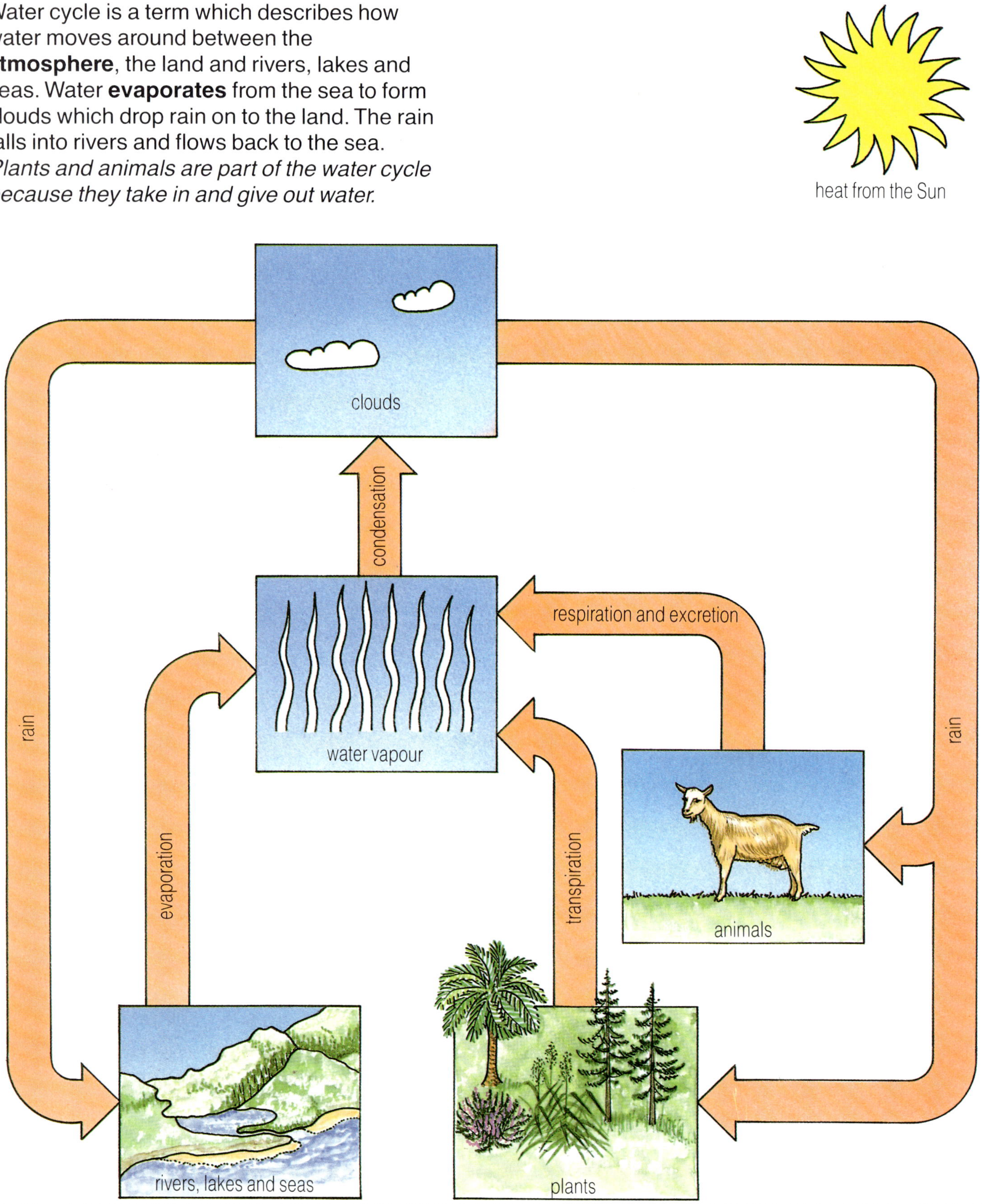

water vapour *noun*
Water vapour is a **gas**. It **evaporates** from liquid water. Water vapour rises from the sea to form clouds. Wet clothes give off water vapour as they dry.
Mist and fog contain tiny drops of water which form when water vapour cools.

watt *noun*
A watt, or W for short, is a **unit** which measures **power**. A power of 1 watt results when 1 **joule** of work is done in 1 second. Watts measure the power given out or used by **machines** and electric **devices**.
A 200-watt light bulb shines very brightly.

wave *noun*
A wave is a word which describes how some kinds of **energy** move along. The energy in a wave **oscillates** as it moves. **Electromagnetic radiation** and sound waves are different kinds of wave. **Frequency** and **wavelength** measure different waves.
Sound waves can travel through the air or through water.

waveband *noun*
A waveband is a group of **radio waves**. The radio waves in each waveband have similar **frequencies** or **wavelengths**. Wavebands include the long waveband, the medium waveband and the short waveband.
He switched his radio to the medium waveband.

wavelength *noun*
Wavelength is a word which describes a **wave**. It is the distance between the peak of one wave and the peak of the following wave. Parts of a wave may become stronger and weaker as the wave travels along.
The wavelength of the sound was 300 centimetres.

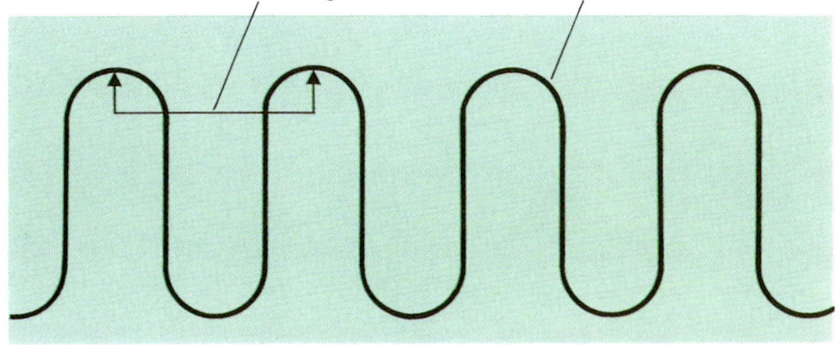

weight *noun*
Weight is a word which describes what happens when **gravity** pulls on the **mass** of an object. A 6-kilogram mass has a weight of 6 kilograms on Earth. It has a weight of 1 kilogram on the Moon. In space, a mass has no weight because there is no gravity.
The weight of an object is the same anywhere on Earth.
weigh *verb*

weld *verb*
Weld is a word which describes how two pieces of **metal** are joined together. A very hot flame or an electric **arc** melts a part of each piece of metal. The two **molten** parts flow together and become solid when the metal cools.
They welded together the steel plates to make the huge ship.

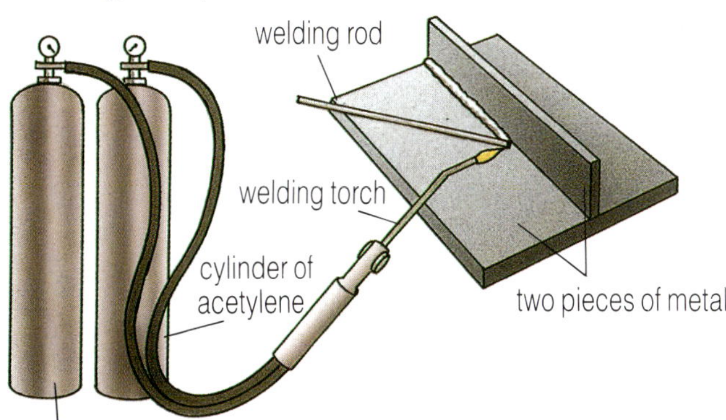

oxyacetylene welding

wind power *noun*
Wind power is a term which describes **machines** that the wind moves. Wind turns a **propeller** which can drive a water pump, a corn grinder or an electric **generator**.
Wind power grinds the corn on the farm.

traditional windmills

These windmills have been used for hundreds of years to grind corn.

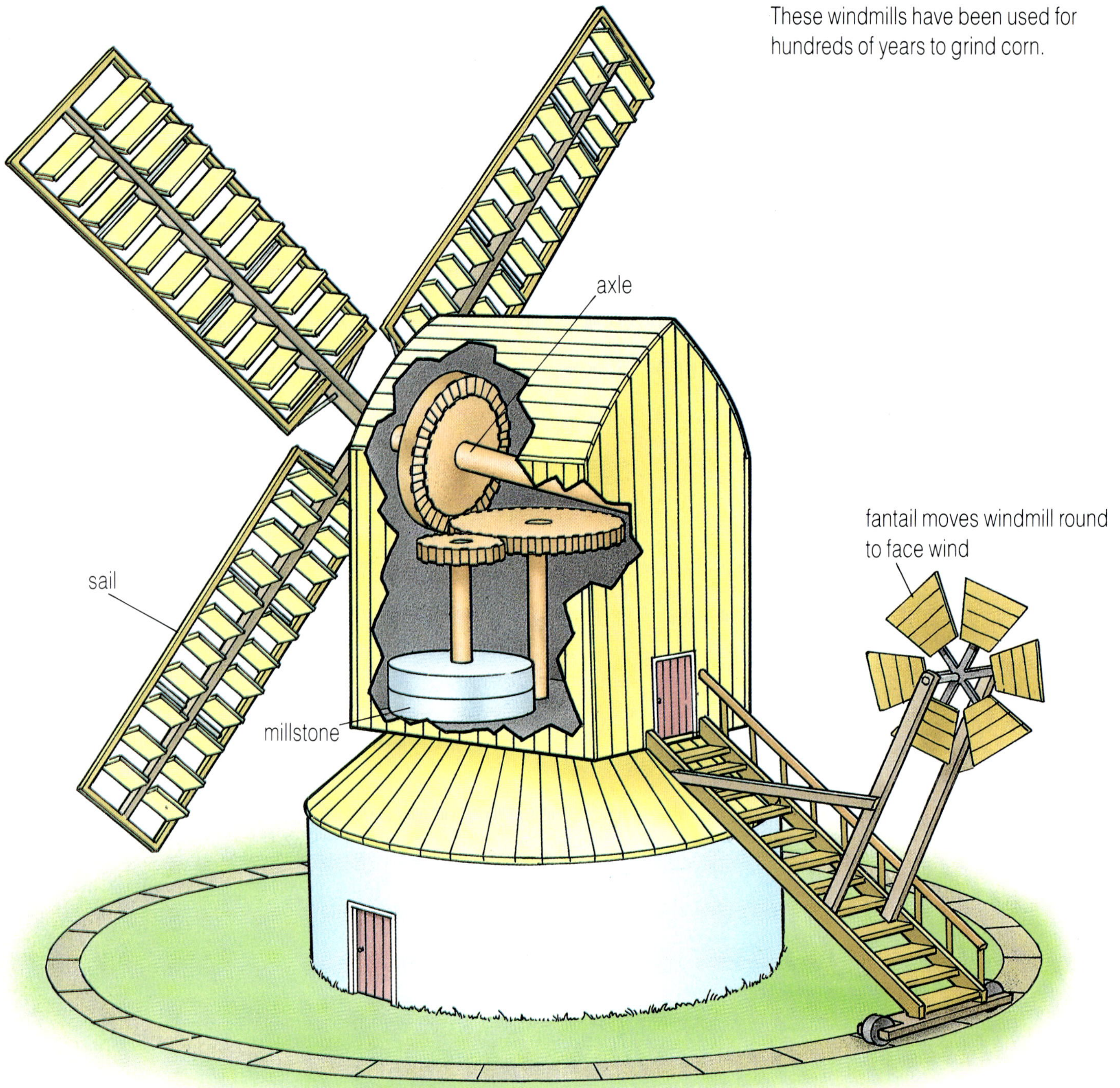

Modern wind generators provide electricity even in a moderate wind.

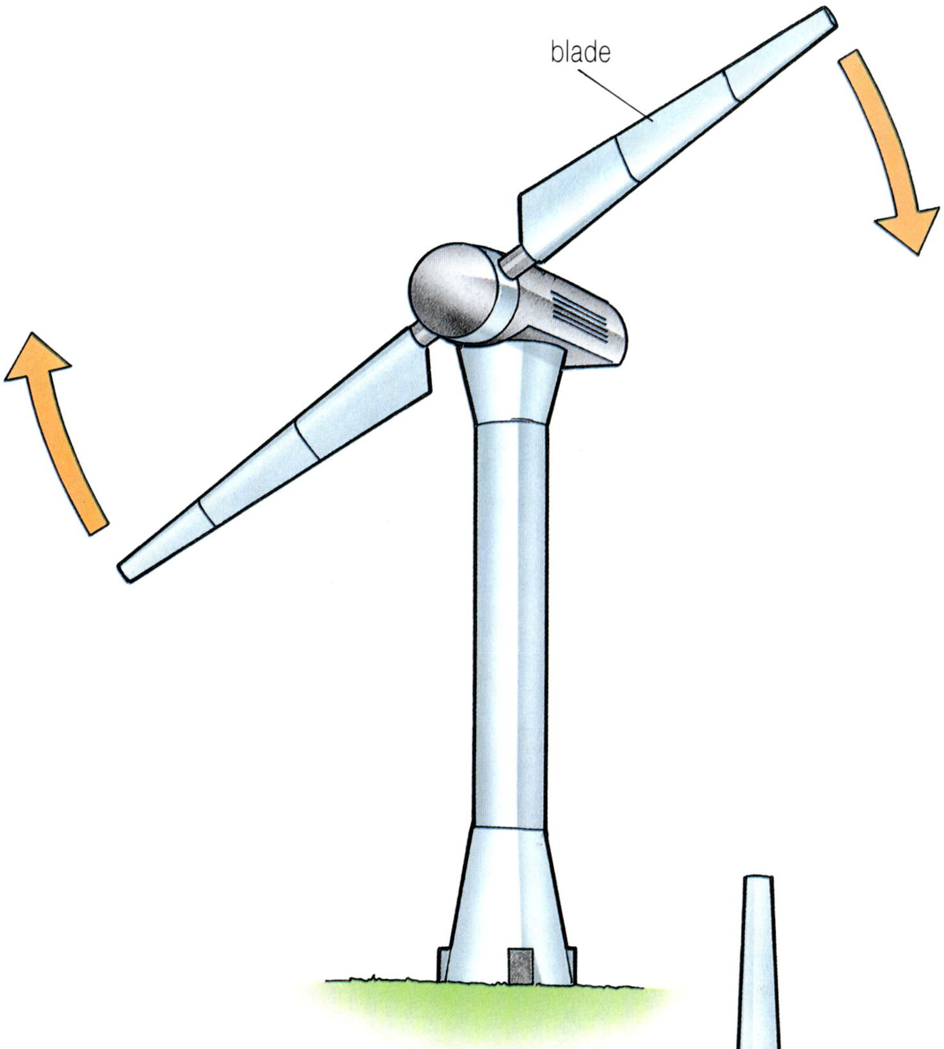

wind generator with a horizontal axis

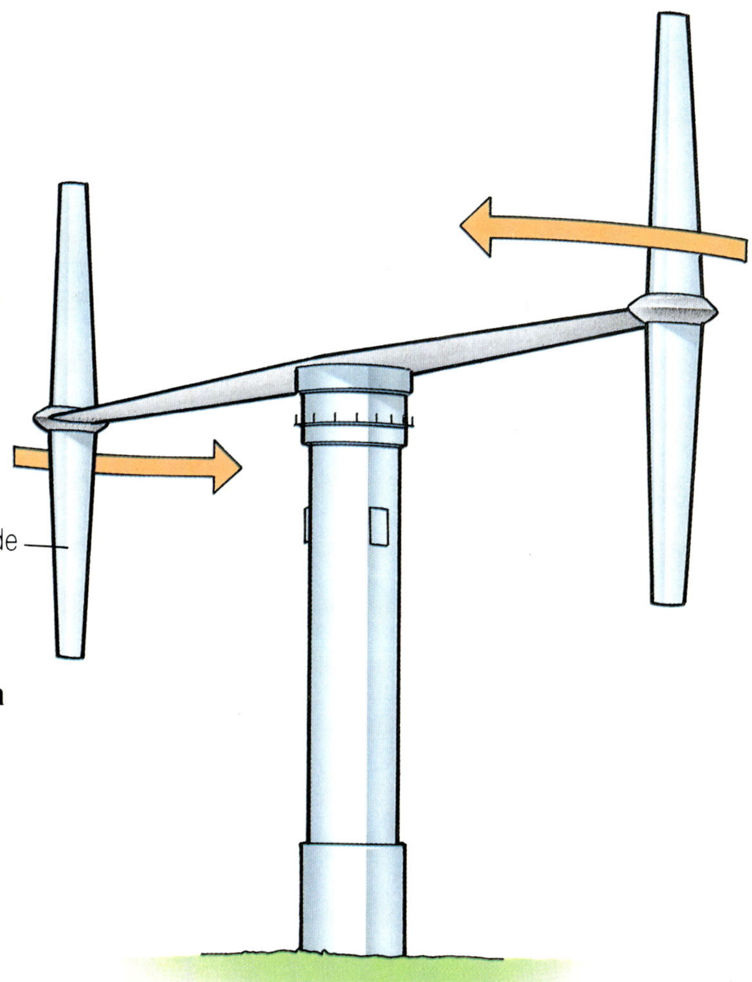

wind generator with a vertical axis

wheel *noun*
A wheel is usually a round **disc**. It **rotates** around an **axle** which is fixed through its **axis**. Bicycles, cars and trucks travel on wheels which are fitted with rubber tyres. **Gears** are wheels with **cogs**. Bicycle chains fit on wheels with **sprockets. Cams** are wheels that are not round.
The bicycle wheels turned so quickly that he could not see the spokes.

white light *noun*
White light is a kind of **electromagnetic radiation**. We see white light when all the colours in the **visible spectrum** mix together. A **prism** can split white light into different colours. A rainbow is formed when raindrops split white light from the Sun into colours.
The electric lamp gave out white light.

wind power ► page 156

wire *noun*
Wire is a thin piece of **metal**. Electric wires are made from copper and have a plastic coat. This coat **insulates** the wire and makes it safe to use. Bundles of wires are called **cables**.
He connected the wire to the electric plug.

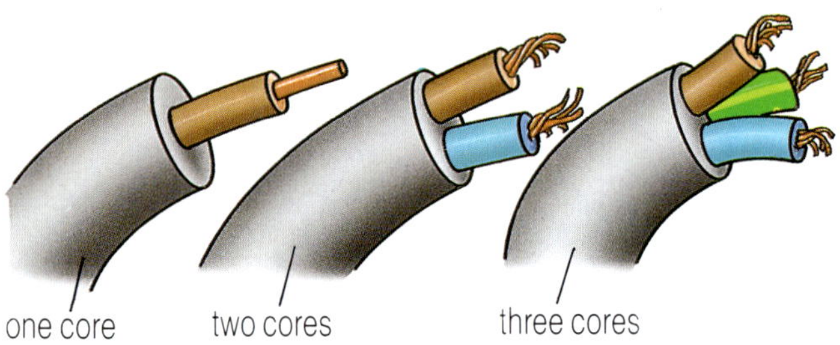

wireless *noun*
Wireless is another word for **radio**. Radio was called wireless telegraphy when it was invented more than 90 years ago. This name was chosen because **radio waves** do not need wires to travel. Long wires were used for the **telegraph**.
The wireless brought news to people faster than the newspapers.

wordprocessor *noun*
A wordprocessor is a **computer** which uses a special kind of **program**. Words are typed on a **keyboard** and they appear on the screen of a **visual display unit**. It is easy to change words and move them about on a wordprocessor.
He wrote the whole book on a wordprocessor.

work *noun*
Work is a word which describes what is done when a **force** moves an object. It is measured in **units** called **joules**. Work is done when **energy** is used up.
She did twice as much work as him because she pushed the wheelbarrow twice as far.

X

x-axis *noun*
The x-axis is a part of a **graph**. It is the **horizontal** line along which one set of numbers is written. The other set of numbers is written along the **y-axis**.
He drew a graph with the time in hours and minutes shown on the x-axis.

X-ray *noun*
An X-ray is a kind of **electromagnetic radiation**. X-rays are made when powerful beams of **electrons** hit a metal target. **Radiography** uses X-rays to take pictures that show the insides of our bodies.
They took an X-ray photograph of his leg to see where the bone was broken.

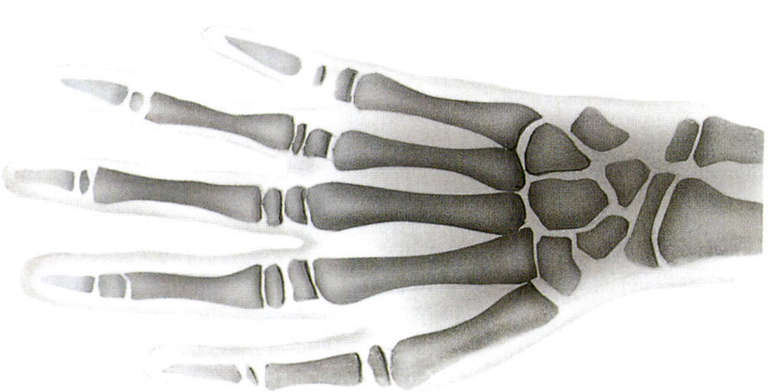

X-ray of a hand

xenon *noun*
Xenon is an **inert element**. It is a colourless **gas**. Xenon is used in powerful electric lamps and in **electronic** flash guns for cameras.
Very small amounts of xenon are found in the atmosphere.

Y

yard *noun*
A yard is a unit of measurement. It measures length or distance. One yard is equal to 0.9144 metres.
The electrician ordered 10 yards of insulated wire.

yaw *verb*
Yaw is a word which describes the way in which a ship or an aeroplane moves unsteadily from side to side.
The rough sea made the ship yaw.

y-axis *noun*
The y-axis is a part of a **graph**. It is the **vertical** line along which one set of numbers is written. The other set of numbers is written along the **x-axis**.
He drew a graph with the temperature in degrees Celsius shown on the y-axis.

yolk *noun*
Yolk is a part of an **egg**. It is a **substance** which surrounds the egg **cell**. Yolk is made up mainly of fat and protein. It also contains very small amounts of vitamins and **minerals**. It is a rich source of food for the **embryo** when it is growing inside the egg.
Chicken's eggs have dark yellow yolks which can be used in cooking.

Z

zero *noun*
Zero, also written 0, is another name for nought or nothing. When you add zero to a number, the number does not change. When you subtract zero from a number, the number does not change. Most **scales** of measurement begin at zero.
His score was zero at the end of the game.

zinc *noun*
Zinc is an **element**. It is a grey **metal** which is quite soft. Zinc is used to coat **galvanized** steel and to make **batteries**. Brass is an **alloy** which contains zinc and copper.
The outside case of many batteries is made from zinc.

zoology *noun*
Zoology is a **scientific** subject. It is the study of all the different kinds of animal, from the smallest **micro-organism** to the largest **mammal**. A zoologist is a person who studies zoology. Zoologists study everything about animals, such as the way they are made, the way they grow and the way they reproduce.

zoom *adjective*
Zoom describes a kind of **lens**. A zoom lens can be fitted to single-lens reflex cameras or to movie **cameras**. Photographers or cameramen can then zoom in on the subject of their picture. Without moving forward, they can take close-up views or wide-angle views of the subject.
Using a zoom lens, the cameraman filmed a bird's nest high on the cliff.